C0-AKD-152

BERLIN

Berlin's Transportation Links to West Germany

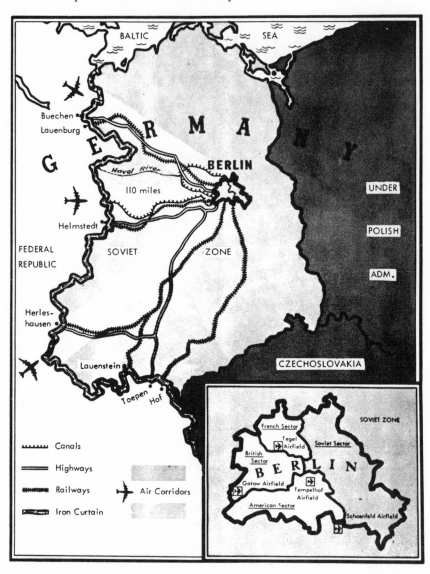

Source: German Information Center, New York.

BERLIN

From Symbol of Confrontation
to
Keystone of Stability

James S. Sutterlin and David Klein

PRAEGER

New York
Westport, Connecticut
London

DD
881
S88
1989

ROBERT MANNING
STROZIER LIBRARY

MAR 12 1990

Tallahassee, Florida

The appendix of this book is reprinted from *Documentation Relating to the Federal Government's Policy of Détente* (public document). Press and Information Office of the Government of the Federal Republic of Germany, Bonn, 1978. pp. 87–110.

Library of Congress Cataloging-in-Publication Data

Sutterlin, James S.
  Berlin : from symbol of confrontation to keystone of stability /
James S. Sutterlin and David Klein.
    p.   cm.
  Bibliography: p.
  Includes index.
  ISBN 0–275–93259–1 (alk. paper)
    1. Berlin (Germany)—History.   I. Klein, David, 1919–
II. Title.
  DD881.S88   1989
  943.1'55–dc20   89–33974

Copyright © 1989 by James S. Sutterlin and David Klein

All rights reserved. No portion of this book may be
reproduced, by any process or technique, without the
express written consent of the publisher.

Library of Congress Catalog Card Number: 89–33974
ISBN: 0–275–93259–1

First published in 1989

Praeger Publishers, One Madison Avenue, New York, NY 10010
A division of Greenwood Press, Inc.

Printed in the United States of America

The paper used in this book complies with the Permanent
Paper Standard issued by the National Information Standards
Organization (Z39.48–1984).

10 9 8 7 6 5 4 3 2 1

For Betty and Anne

Contents

Preface

The initial contacts in Berlin between the Western occupying powers—Britain, the United States, and France—and the Soviet Union after the capitulation of the German Reich were the work of the respective military commanders. They were essentially friendly, colored by the spirit of mutual victory, but from the very beginning they were marked by a degree of suspicion. The Soviet commander was unwilling to authorize the entry of the Western forces until the U.S. Army withdrew from the forward positions it had occupied in what had previously been designated as the Soviet area of occupation in Germany. Thus began the Soviet contention that the Western powers were in Berlin only with the permission of the Soviet Union, whose army had captured the city.

The initial harmony, such as it was, did not last long. Berlin became the central stage for the struggle between Western and Soviet ideology and influence in Europe. It reflected, as a microcosm, a basic change in the international situation resulting from the war: the division of Europe into two hostile camps facing each other across a line that bisected Germany. U.S. and Soviet forces met head-on. The tension between East and West in Berlin was prolonged, heightened by repeated crises. All aspects of relations between Moscow and Washington were influenced negatively for fifteen years, at least, by their differences with regard to the city. President Kennedy referred to the Berlin problem as a millstone around his neck, while Nikita Khrushchev, apparently frustrated over his inability to resolve the problem in accordance with Soviet designs, is said to have likened Berlin to "a bone in his throat." As long as Berlin remained a source of tension and confrontation between East and West, stabilization of the broader East–West relationship in Europe was compromised. The negotiations of the Four Powers that culminated in the Quadripartite Agreement of September 3, 1971, were an effort to eliminate Berlin as a continuing burden on the relationship between Moscow and the Western powers, especially the United States and the Federal Republic of Germany. To a remarkable extent the effort succeeded.

Stabilization of relations in Berlin was achieved not by defining a new status for the city or by altering the legal position of either side. On the contrary, a basic principle of the Quadripartite Agreement as drafted is that previous agreements and decisions of the Four Powers are not affected. Their rights and responsibilities—as interpreted by each side—remain unchanged. Thus, the modus vivendi that has been achieved in Berlin rests on the whole history of the relationship between the Americans and the British, and later the French, on the one side, and the Russians, on the other, with regard to the city.

The purpose of this book is to trace that history and to examine in some detail how the Quadripartite Agreement was formulated and negotiated in order to bring about a notably improved situation *without* changing the longstanding positions of principle on either side. The unmodified word "Berlin" itself is never used, since to have acknowledged in the text that the agreement was about all of Berlin, rather than only the Western sectors, would have contradicted the firmly held position of the Soviet Union on the status of the city. The Quadripartite Agreement may, indeed, be the only important international instrument in which the subject is never defined.

The interpretation and implementation of the Quadripartite Agreement by the powers directly concerned, including most particularly the West and East Germans, is a continuing process that is bound both to influence and reflect the state of the broader East–West relationship in Europe. The Quadripartite Agreement will need to be understood in the context of the earlier wartime and postwar agreements that it incorporates as well as the negotiating process through which it was achieved. The present book is intended to help meet this need. Where not otherwise indicated, information regarding the Four Power negotiations derives from the recollections and personal notes and correspondence of the authors, both of whom were directly involved, one in Washington and one in Berlin.

This examination of the quadripartite relationship with regard to Berlin has been written with the assistance of a generous grant from the Volkswagen Foundation of Germany. The Institution for Social and Policy Studies at Yale University, where James Sutterlin enjoyed a fellowship, provided an encouraging environment for preparation of the final manuscript. The Aspen Institute Berlin and the American Institute for Contemporary German Studies of Johns Hopkins University held useful meetings at which portions of the manuscript could be discussed among persons having special knowledge and experience with regard to the subject matter.

The authors wish particularly to acknowledge the assistance of Dr. Manfred Goertemaker, professor at the Free University of Berlin, who is largely responsible for the chapters on the development of the local city government in Berlin and on the agreements between the Federal Republic of Germany and the Berlin Senate and the German Democratic Republic that were incorporated into the

Quadripartite Agreement. The authors are also grateful to Dr. Manfred Ernst, who spent long hours exploring the archives of the Department of State, the Department of the Army, and the Truman and Eisenhower presidential libraries, and who also systematically assembled information incorporated in the early chapters of the book.

A number of talented and helpful individuals undertook the difficult work of transcribing the illegible script of the two authors. It would be impossible to name them all, but particular gratitude is expressed to Mr. V. Subramanian and Ms. Jill Dale, who began the work, offering many useful suggestions to the authors, and to Ms. Betty Faison, who undertook the onerous task of preparing the final manuscript.

BERLIN

1

The Enduring Fruits of Confusion

On April 11, 1942, the Political Subcommittee of the Advisory Committee on Postwar Foreign Policy held its initial meeting in the Department of State under the chairmanship of Under Secretary of State Sumner Welles. In the course of the discussion, which centered largely on whether Germany should be partitioned or remain a united nation and on what its future boundaries should be, the possibility of a communist revolution in postwar Germany was raised. Within this context, the under secretary suggested that Berlin and East Prussia should be "handled differently" from the rest of Germany, "since they must be subjected to military occupation." An efficient occupation of these two areas—he apparently was thinking of a Western occupation—would save all of Germany from such a possibility. Two weeks later on April 25, 1942, after the committee had devoted a good bit of time to the future of East Prussia, Mr. Welles returned to the subject of Berlin and proposed that the city should cease to be Germany's capital after the war, and should serve as the capital only of Prussia. The committee concurred in this proposal.

These exchanges in the Political Subcommittee appear to represent the first official consideration given in Washington to the postwar fate of Berlin. Mr. Welles was prescient in suggesting that Berlin should be "handled differently" since it became, and remains, an area apart from the rest of Germany, and in foreseeing the military occupation of the city, something that endures today, almost half a century after the end of World War II. While he presumably had in mind quite a different kind of "revolution," on the order of the short-lived Spartakus "November revolution" in Berlin at the end of World War I, the under secretary's concern about a communist regime in Berlin (and in East Prussia, too, for that matter) was justified by the events of the postwar years, which brought to power in part of the city a communist administration.

In truth, however, Mr. Welles' prescience was largely fortuitous, the result of insights having little connection with the realities that would soon become apparent in the closing phase of the war in Europe. Moreover, his suggestion that Berlin should be "handled differently" was not followed up within the Washington planning apparatus. The city's unique status was to develop more from British and Soviet initiatives than from American thinking. The reason for this lay not in the absence of U.S. postwar planning but rather in the focus of this planning and, ultimately, in the disjunction between the planners and major participants in the decision-making process, especially the president.

U.S. postwar planning was centered in the Department of State, where in early 1941—before the United States entered the war—Secretary Cordell Hull created a Division of Special Research to study postwar problems. Subsequently the secretary established the Advisory Committee on Postwar Foreign Policy, the purpose of which was to engage influential figures outside the government in the planning process and ensure broad support for the policies that the government would eventually adopt. These two structures, which involved various subcommittees (including the one chaired by Sumner Welles) and went through a bewildering series of transformations, gave detailed consideration to Germany. Indeed, by 1943 there was a Departmental Committee on Germany. Secretary Hull, in his memoirs, recalls that in March of that year he had a long discussion with President Roosevelt on the postwar treatment of Germany, and they agreed that "it was not too soon to begin a serious study of the question." On March 23, the president sent a follow-up note to Secretary Hull that stated,

Apropos of our conversation the other afternoon, I wish you would explore, with the British, the question of what our plan is to be in Germany and Italy during the first few months after Germany's collapse. I think you had better confer with Stimson[1] about it, too. My thought is, if we get a substantial meeting of the minds with the British, that we should then take it up with the Russians.

The study of the future status of Germany, which by then was well advanced in the Department of State, was now given higher priority. Secretary Hull records that "in the following months we discussed the subject intensively at the State Department, with the British, and with Secretary Stimson until we perfected the project I now presented at Moscow." This "project" was a proposal for the postwar treatment of Germany that Hull handed to Soviet Foreign Minister Molotov at the Conference of the Soviet, British, and U.S. foreign ministers, held in Moscow in October 1943.[2] The proposal called for the unconditional surrender of Germany, an "Inter-Allied Control Commission" to carry out the terms of surrender, occupation by British, Soviet, and U.S. forces, reparations, demilitarization, and denazification. On the central question of Germany's future political status the proposal was circumspect. It noted that there was as yet no indication whether the reaction to defeat would be a strengthening of the trend toward political unity within Germany or the emergence of a spontaneous movement for the creation of several separate states. The secretary of state, in an exchange with Molotov, remarked that there had been a general disposition "in higher quarters in the United States" in favor of dismemberment of Germany when the study of this problem had begun, but there was now an increasing disposition to develop an open mind on this point—although dismemberment was still in favor. The secretary added that he himself had been opposed to dismemberment from the beginning.

Mr. Hull was more hopeful than accurate in describing an increasing disposition in high quarters to keep an open mind on the subject of dismemberment. It would be evident when the three heads of government met subsequently in Teheran that President Roosevelt was still enthusiastic about dividing Germany into three or five states, an idea he never abandoned. In stating his own rejection of dismemberment, however, Secretary Hull accurately reflected the conclusions of his department, which had devoted extensive analysis to the subject.[3]

The Department of State's rejection of partition was a major reason why Berlin did not figure prominently in its postwar thinking. Berlin was simply one of a number of major cities designated for military occupation. Sumner Welles' early thought that it should be replaced as the capital of the new Germany was retained in a number of papers. The proposal for Germany put forward by Secretary Hull in Moscow in October 1943 made no mention of Berlin. While the proposal foresaw tripartite occupation, there was no mention of zones, which might have raised the question of Berlin. It was only when the zone concept was put forward that the question of the status of the *Reichshauptstadt* would be posed, and this would be done first by the British.

In 1943 British military and civilian officials were giving thought to the shape of the military occupation of Germany in two different forums. First, the largely British staff of the chief of staff, Supreme Allied Command (COSSAC), developed a plan under the code name of RANKIN for the contingency that Germany would collapse militarily before the Allied forces crossed the German borders. This plan, which was presented to the combined chiefs of staff at the first Quebec Conference in August 1943, included the idea of a zonal division of Germany. It assigned northwest Germany, including the Ruhr, to British forces and the Rhine Valley, from the Swiss border to Dusseldorf, to the Americans. No effort was made to define the eastern limits of these zones since it could not then be militarily foreseen how deeply Soviet forces might penetrate into Germany. In the same time frame, a politically far more significant British report on the future occupation of Germany was developed in the high-level Armistice and Postwar Committee, of which the deputy prime minister, Clement Attlee, was chairman, and the foreign secretary and the secretary of war were members. This report proposed the division of Germany into three zones of occupation, the northwestern zone going to the British, the southwestern to the Americans, and the Eastern zone to the Soviets. The borders of the zones were essentially those eventually adopted by the three powers. Berlin was to be an area of tripartite administration surrounded by the Soviet zone. The problem of access was not dealt with in the report. In essence, the postwar quadripartite history of Berlin with which this book is concerned begins with this British report.

On October 14, 1943, a British embassy representative in Washington discussed this plan with Dr. Harley Notter, who at that time was deputy director of the division of special research in the State Department. On the next day the embassy sent him a copy of the map that illustrated the proposed division of Germany.[4] There is no indication that the proposal, significant though it would be, was noted at the time by the policy level in the State Department, possibly because the British embassy had cautioned that it had been developed at the planning staff level and "should not therefore be considered in any way to be authoritative British views."[5] When the British tabled it on January 15, 1944, at the European Advisory Committee in London, the American representative appears to have had no forewarning and no instructions.

The same British proposal was also communicated to the War Department in Washington by General Morgan, chief of staff of the Supreme Allied Commander (who had not yet been named), as a revision of the COSSAC plan that had been presented to the combined chiefs of staff in Quebec. Far from allowing the proposal to remain at the planning level, as the State Department apparently did, the joint chiefs' staff planners viewed the plan as likely official British policy and recommended that it be brought to the attention of President Roosevelt. The president considered the question with the joint chiefs on 19 November 1943 on board the battleship *Iowa,* en route to the conferences at Cairo and Teheran. No State Department representative was present at this meeting nor was the department informed of what occurred. The president, having in mind, as always, the partition of Germany into three or five states, accepted the concept of separate zones, but his idea of how the zones should be constituted was quite different from that of the British. He considered it essential for the United States rather than the British to occupy the northern zone with its major ports, since he wished to be able to repatriate U.S. forces from Germany quickly once victory in Europe was achieved and was convinced this would be far more difficult from southwest Germany. He feared that French ports might not be available because of a communist revolution in France. Thus began a dispute that was to dominate U.S. concerns for the next year relative to the occupation of Germany. As part of his concept, the president declared that "Berlin should be American," and being given a National Geographic map of Germany, he drew on it a zonal division which extended the northern "American" zone to Berlin. It is not clear whether President Roosevelt had in mind the problem of access when he drew his bold and quixotic line, which appears to go through the city.[6] It seems more likely that it struck him as historically appropriate for the United States, which would clearly emerge from the war as the strongest of the Allies, to occupy the capital of the defeated enemy. It became evident later that while he attributed great importance to the U.S. occupation of the northern zone that the British had designated for themselves, he was much more relaxed about Berlin. But in the meantime the president's personal concern about the future of the German capital caused confusion within the U.S. government, which was already encountering severe difficulty in achieving a coordinated policy on the occupation of Germany.

At the Moscow foreign ministers conference of October 1943 it was decided to establish the European Advisory Commission (EAC), with its seat in London, to work continuously on tripartite postwar policy in Europe. According to its terms of reference, this new body was to "study and make recommendations to the three Governments upon European questions connected with the termination of hostilities which the three Governments may consider appropriate to refer to it." As has already been noted, when it first met on January 14, 1944, the British representative tabled a plan for the future occupation of Germany. Just over a month later on February 16, 1944, the Soviet representative—to the surprise of Washington, which had been preoccupied with the president's determination to obtain the northwest occupation zone for the United States—presented draft surrender terms that included a zonal division of Germany almost identical to that contained in the British plan. Greater Berlin was designated as a separate area of joint Allied occupation. It is highly significant that Berlin was not claimed as part of the Soviet zone of occupation. The wording in the Soviet text is unequivocal: "(d) There shall be established around Berlin a 10/15 kilometer zone which shall be occupied jointly by the armed forces of the Union of Soviet Socialist Republics, the United Kingdom and the United States of America."[7] In the treatment of Berlin, as with the zonal boundaries, the Soviet Union followed the British plan. One can speculate that the British informed Moscow of their thinking at the same time that they informed Washington, in October 1943. This would explain how the Soviet side was able to put forward its own similar plan with relative alacrity in a body that was to be characterized by the glacial pace of its progress. There is, however, no documentary evidence yet of Soviet knowledge of the British plan before it was tabled on January 14, 1944.

Washington at this point had not sent any instructions to the U.S. representative in the EAC, Ambassador John E. Winant, beyond the insistence on occupying northwestern Germany and an indication that the joint chiefs of staff considered a zonal system to be "the most practical solution."[8] There was no word about Berlin. In fact, there could not have been, since Washington was "staffing out" President Roosevelt's proposal to include the city, or part of it, in the U.S. zone of occupation.

Toward the end of 1943, shortly after the decision was taken by the three foreign ministers in Moscow to establish the EAC, an interdepartmental committee, consisting of representatives from the Departments of State, War, and the Navy, was set up in Washington to coordinate the views of the three departments on subjects to be dealt with in the EAC and to draft instructions to the U.S. representative. The committee was designated the Working Security Committee (WSC). It proved to be a remarkably ineffective organization, repeatedly immobilized by the strongly held view of the Civil Affairs Division of the War Department and of the JCS that the EAC should not deal with "military concerns," which, they felt, encompassed all aspects of the occupation of Germany. Throughout January 1944 the WSC was engaged in extensive consideration of the form that the military government of Germany by the Three Powers should take. An early paper shows the State Department as reluctant to endorse separate zonal administrations with a tripartite board to formulate recommendations for concerted policy on the part of the separate administrations, since such a board could not "obviate the difficulties inherent in attempting to maintain two or three separate administrations of a wide gamut of activities whose effectiveness is dependent upon continuing their existing integration."[9] By the end of the month, however, the Civil Affairs Division (CAD) of the War Department had prepared a paper proposing that Germany be divided into three zones. Each zone would be administered separately, the only exception being

the Berlin area where direct local administration would be in the hands of a combined administrative authority. The combined administrative authority or Control Council, would, in addition to exercising direct local administration over the Berlin area, supervise those governmental and economic activities which the Occupation authorities may determine should continue to function on a national basis in the interest of a stable and orderly life in Germany.[10]

Thus, before the Soviet draft text on the terms of surrender was submitted in London, the WSC was not only thinking along the lines of the British plan but had also expanded it by describing a Control Council and its relation to Berlin very much in terms of the organization that eventually emerged. (The CAD was careful to stipulate that all instructions to the Control Council should emanate from the chiefs of staff of the respective governments.)

On February 25, 1944, the State Department prepared a draft instruction to Ambassador Winant, informing him that the U.S. government had approved the plan for military government described in the paper drafted by the CAD (WS–15C) and indicating that if this plan were adopted "there would be no objection to establishing the boundaries of the zones as proposed by the Governments of the United Kingdom and of the Soviet Union," it being understood that the northwestern zone would be assigned to the United States.[11] But the instruction was not sent. Suddenly at the end of February, to the shock and dismay of the State Department, which only now was informed somewhat sketchily of President Roosevelt's discussions of the future zones in Germany on board the *Iowa*, the War Department representatives introduced a new proposal into the WSC on the delimitation of the proposed zones in Germany. They insisted that it be forwarded to Ambassador Winant for presentation in the EAC. This proposal consisted of a roughly drawn map in which a greatly expanded "American" northwestern zone would extend to Berlin, as would the southern "British zone". The city was left in the Soviet zone (unlike the president's idea), but the demarcation line was placed as far east as Cottbus, south of Berlin, to take in the Leipzig–

Cottbus railway line and three connecting lines to Berlin. Since Leipzig was also in the proposed American zone, any problem of access to Berlin would have been eliminated. But the plan had no chance of success. Unaware of the extent of President Roosevelt's direct involvement, the State Department attributed authorship of the plan to the JCS and in an analytical assessment[12] noted that since there was no indication "as to how the eastern extent of this territory (i.e., the Soviet zone) was established," the comments offered "must, consequently, leave military considerations in abeyance." The State Department analysts suggested that if the objective was to reduce Soviet influence, two methods might be attempted: (1) limitation of Soviet occupation forces to as small a part of Eastern Germany as possible; or (2) concentration of power in a tripartite control mechanism for Germany, with the zonal commanders empowered only to enforce joint decisions. If this second method were chosen, "from a political point of view the exact location of the lines between the zones would have no great significance." The State Department analysis pointed out, with admirable restraint, that an attempt to push the Russians back east of the line they had indicated would face "serious difficulties," especially "since the British show no interest in having their zone contiguous to that of Berlin." The State Department presumably thought of access as a military matter or they did not think of it at all, since they only dealt with the "JCS plan" within the context of limiting Soviet influence in Germany and not from the point of view of access to Berlin.

The State Department forwarded the new plan to Ambassador Winant in London "for your consideration and for your recommendations,"[13] without any instructions to table it in the EAC. The ambassador, who one suspects may have received by informal communication an indication of the White House role in the plan, was so disturbed that he promptly sent the counselor of the U.S. delegation to the European Advisory Commission, George Kennan, to Washington to speak with the president. On April 3, 1944, Kennan saw Roosevelt and communicated Winant's belief that if the JCS plan were tabled, which reduced by 50 percent the area that both the British and the Russians had proposed for the Soviet zone, "this would cause them (the Russians) to be highly suspicious of our motives," and the ambassador was not in a position to give an adequate explanation. Similarly, the other members of the EAC would wish to know why the Russians were being deprived of the important railway junction at Cottbus and why the boundaries proposed by the Americans did not coincide with any German administrative boundaries. Finally, the ambassador would certainly be asked if the U.S. government had given any attention to the previous British and Soviet proposals on zonal boundaries and, if so, what were the U.S. objections.

The president, who, according to Kennan, did most of the talking,[14] agreed without further argument to the boundaries of the Soviet zone as proposed by the British and the Russians. Almost a month later, on May 1, 1944, the secretary of state sent an instruction to Winant authorizing him to concur in the boundaries of the Soviet occupation zone as proposed by the Soviet delegation and in the boundary between the northwestern zone and the southern zone as proposed by the British delegation. The one thing that Washington did not agree to was that the northwestern zone should go to the British. Winant then informed his British and Soviet colleagues orally of the U.S. position, but he delayed circulating this position in writing until June 12 in the unwarranted expectation, according to Philip Mosely, the political adviser to Ambassador Winant, that additional instructions would be forthcoming from Washington concerning Allied access to Berlin.

Thus ended this early but short-lived U.S. effort to make the western zones contiguous to Berlin. Had it succeeded there could never have been a Berlin blockade and the course of events in Germany would have been vastly different. But coming when it did, with glaringly unequal treatment of the Soviet Union, it stood no chance of acceptance. In this Ambassador Winant and the State Department were surely right. Had there been a strong argument on the grounds of access and a willingness to compromise in terms of territory, a different solution than the one accepted might have been developed. The swiftness with which the plan was dropped, in contrast to the long-held U.S. insistence on gaining the northwestern zone, suggests that the plan was only intended to meet a fleeting idea of the president. The JCS planners, in extending the U.S. zone to include Cottbus and Leipzig, must have had the railway links in mind. But the desirability of safe access to Berlin does not appear in any official correspondence now available as a justification for pursuing the plan. It was a U.S. diversion, poignant in its unreality and its unconscious foresight.

Berlin's status as an area of tripartite administration surrounded by the Soviet zone of occupation was thus settled. The next question to be dealt with was the form that this administration should take. This time it was the Soviet Union that first put forward a detailed plan, a plan which, with minor modifications, was to determine how Berlin would be governed. On July 1, 1944, the Soviet representative introduced in the ECA an amended text of the proposed protocol on the delimitations of the zones in Germany, which added a delimitation of "the three zones of occupation within Greater Berlin" and an outline regarding the joint administration of the city. The text of this proposal reads as follows:

The Berlin area, by which expression is understood the territory of "Greater Berlin" as defined by the law of the 27 April 1920, will be occupied by the armed forces of the USSR, UK and USA. For the purpose the territory of "Greater Berlin" will be divided into three zones:

Northeastern part of the city (districts of Pankow, Prenzlauerberg, Mitte, Weissensee, Friedrichshagen, Lichtenberg, Treptow, Koepenick) will be occupied by the forces of the USSR;

Northwestern part of the city (districts of Reinickendorf, Wedding, Tiergarten, Charlottenburg, Spandau, Wilmersdorf) will be occupied by the forces of blank;

Southern part of the city (districts of Zehlendorf, Steglitz, Kreuzberg, Tempelhof, Neukoelln) will be occupied by the forces of blank.

The central aerodrome of Berlin, Tempelhof, will be used by the USSR, UK and USA on equal terms.

(a) An inter-Allied governing authority [*Komendatura*][15] will be established to administer "Greater Berlin" consisting of three commandants—one from each of the Allied powers. The head of the inter-Allied governing authority will be the Chief Commandant, whose duties will be carried out in rotation by each of the three commandants. Each of the three commandants shall hold office of Chief Commandant for a period not exceeding 15 to 20 days.

(b) The necessary technical machinery, staffed by personnel of the three Allied powers, will be set up at the offices of the inter-Allied governing authority, and its form will, in general, correspond to the structure of the municipal organizations of Greater Berlin. The inter-Allied governing authority will communicate directly or through this machinery with the municipal organizations of Berlin.

(c) The inter-Allied governing authority for the administration of "Greater Berlin," parallel with its functions of administering the city, will also exercise day-to-day supervision over the activities of the municipal organizations of Berlin controlling the various departments of the city's daily life.

(d) The Allied forces stationed in the territory of "Greater Berlin" will also be responsible for the maintenance of public order in the respective zones of "Greater Berlin" and for the protection both of the inter-Allied governing authority administering "Greater Berlin" and of all other agencies that may be set up by the Allies in the city.[16]

The concept of a joint administration of Greater Berlin had previously been accepted. Nonetheless, the detailed Soviet plan took both the British and the Americans by surprise. Washington, on examining the plan, had two major concerns. First, and most tenaciously, it feared that demarcation lines established in an irrevocable fashion in advance might prove unrealistic given the state of destruction that might prevail at the time of actual occupation. It wanted sufficient flexibility to ensure that the U.S. "zone" could accomodate the American occupation contingent. Second, the United States did not want the tripartite division of Berlin to alter the tripartite administration of the city as a whole. The U.S. side felt also that not just Tempelhof airport, but all major facilities in Berlin should be equally available for the use of the occupying powers. On July 6, 1944, only five days after receipt of the Soviet plan, the secretary of state cabled to Ambassador Winant that "The Soviet proposal to divide Berlin into zones is acceptable in principle on the assumption that the actual administration of the city is a combined function and that the zones are for billeting and police purposes only."[17] On the other hand, "An agreement on specific delimitation of the zones at this time seems premature, since due to destruction, facilities in zones delimited now may be inadequate at the time of occupation."[18] Ambassador Winant presented this response in an informal meeting with his Soviet and British colleagues and then, through his military advisor, consulted with Supreme Headquarters Allied Forces in Europe (SHAEF) as to whether the U.S. military authorities could function from an operational point of view if the Soviets remained adamant. The U.S. military answer was, in effect, that they could live with it.[19] And live with it the Americans and British did. The Soviet Union insisted on the demarcation lines and it resisted the idea of equal access to all major facilities in Berlin.

The Soviets did not quarrel, however, with the U.S. insistence that Berlin was to be jointly administered, and at U.S. suggestion, the word "zone" was dropped in describing the divisions in Berlin to avoid analogy with the separately administered zones of occupation. Signature of the Protocol on the Zones of Occupation in Germany and the Administration of Berlin by the U.S., British, and Soviet representatives took place in the EAC on September 12, 1944, having been delayed primarily by the continuing disagreement between the Americans and the British on their respective zones of occupation. In the protocol, demarcation of the three "parts" (instead of zones) of Berlin remained exactly as proposed by the Soviet Union. Provision for joint use of Tempelhof was also dropped and no mention was made of the joint availability of any of Berlin's facilities. The organization of the *Komendatura* as proposed by the Soviets was also adopted in its essentials, as was the relationship between the *Komendatura* and the city government, although the latter was considerably simplified from the original Soviet draft.

It would be easy to conclude that by being the first to table a detailed proposal on the division of Berlin and holding to it tenaciously the Soviet Union was able to prevail over the Americans and the British. This would be somewhat misleading, since while the Americans had not gotten around to tabling a proposal, they were thinking in much the same terms as the Soviets. On June 28, 1944— that is, before the Soviet draft was tabled—the U.S. embassy in London forwarded to the Department of State an extensive staff study prepared by the SHAEF planning staff on the "Command, Organization and Administration of the International Zone, Berlin." This study foresaw that Berlin should have a central "denationalized sector" where the tripartite administrative offices would be located, and three national sectors of approximately equal size, with the Soviet Union to have the eastern sector and the British and the Americans to have the northwest and southwest sectors, depending on the final decision on the British and U.S. occupation zones. The idea of a tripartite administrative body made up of the three commandants subordinate to the Control Council was also included. There was in this paper a further thought that did not figure in the ultimate decisions or in the instructions sent to Ambassador Winant by Washington. Under the heading "Access into the Zone" the following appears:

It must be recalled that Berlin lies some 100 miles from the North-West zone and 150 miles from the South-West zone. Movement into the Berlin zone by road, rail and air of all personnel and supplies must therefore necessarily be through the RUSSIAN zone. Agreement with the RUSSIANS as to how this is to be effected is consequently a first essential. There would appear to be three alternative methods of arrangement:

(a) The establishment of road and rail corridors either to each of the Western zones or solely to the North-Western zone.

(b) The allotment of selected routes.

(c) The principle of free access.

26. It must be borne in mind that the transportation problems during the post-hostilities period will be so heavy as to require the minimum interference or restrictions on movement. Apart from the requirements of the occupying forces there will be very considerable inter-zonal movement related to prisoners of war, displaced persons and disposal of German forces. It is to be assumed that movement control will be on a tripartite basis at the centre.

27. It is thought, therefore, that the establishment of corridors, or the permanent allotment of selected routes between the international and the Western zones is likely to prove uneconomic of transport facilities and consequently to be undesirable.

The alternative of the principle of free access, implying the use of any convenient road or railway which is determined by the tripartite movement control organization, would appear to be the most favorable solution and is recommended.[20]

The historically determinative fact is that Washington never sent any instructions to its representative in the EAC to seek an agreement or understanding on access to Berlin. As evidenced by the SHAEF study this was not because no one thought of it. Philip Mosely, who has left the most valuable recollections on this subject, recalls that already in December 1943—that is within two months of the presentation of the "unofficial" British plan, which placed Berlin in the middle of the Soviet zone—the Interdivisional Committee on Germany in the Department of State had completed a draft plan on zones of occupation in Germany for submission to the WSC, which appears to have been based on the assumption that Berlin would be the center of Allied administration in Germany and that Berlin would be within the Soviet zone. Mr. Mosely states that the plan included a proposal, for which he was responsible, for a corridor connecting the prospective western areas of occupation with Berlin "this to be accomplished by joining certain intervening districts of Saxony-Anhalt and Brandenburg to the western zones."[21] This plan was never acted on in the WSC because the Civil Affairs Division of the War Department, which was reluctant to participate in the WSC at all, took the position that the determination of future zones of occupation in Germany was a military matter and not something to be dealt with in the WSC or the EAC.[22] The CAD argued that zones of occupation would be determined by the location of troops at the time of Germany's surrender or collapse. The State Department considered this a risky approach and one that was certain to generate suspicion among the Allies.

In May Ambassador Winant visited Washington and, according to Mr. Mosely, specifically proposed, during discussions with the Civil Affairs Division, detailed provisions "safeguarding American access by highway, railroad and air." Winant was confident that concrete provisions could be negotiated in the EAC without great difficulty since the Soviet representative had repeatedly indicated that there would be no difficulty in arranging for transit through the Soviet zone to Berlin and that the presence of U.S. and British forces in Berlin, "of course," carried with it all necessary facilities of access. Ambassador Winant spoke only of U.S. access and not German access since planning was proceeding on the assumption that Germany would be treated as a political and economic unit. The Civil Affairs

Division, however, felt it was impossible to foresee in advance what railroads and highways would be needed and it therefore opposed the insertion of specific provisions in the Protocol on Zones of Occupation concerning access to Berlin.[23]

During the ensuing months, President Roosevelt and Prime Minister Churchill continued to argue as to which country should have the northern zone, and even after Roosevelt finally conceded in September there followed lengthy U.S.–British negotiations over transit between the ports of Bremen and Bremerhaven in the north, which were assigned to the Americans, and the U.S. zone in the south. At a meeting of the EAC on November 6, 1944, the Soviet representative strongly urged the immediate insertion "of a general provision regarding the United States control of port and transit facilities within the United Kingdom zone, leaving detailed arrangements to later agreement between either the Governments or the Commanders concerned or to the Tripartite Control Council." He then stressed what the U.S. reporting cable termed the "cogent point," that "similar arrangements for transit facilities will be made, providing United States and United Kingdom forces and control personnel full access to the Berlin zone across Soviet-occupied territory."[24]

Under this prodding the United States reluctantly accepted the following wording, on which the British had insisted, concerning transit in the Agreement Amending the Protocol on Zones of Occupation signed by the Three Powers on November 14, 1944:

For the purposes of facilitating communicationss between the South-Western Zone and the sea, the Commander-in-Chief of the United States forces in the South-Western Zone will . . .

(b) enjoy such transit facilities through the North-Western Zone as may be agreed hereafter by the United Kingdom and United States military authorities to meet his requirements.[25]

Thus the U.S. transit rights were made subject to agreement with British military authorities. The United States did not obtain free transit as the War Department had wanted. The significance of this formulation was presumably not lost on the Soviet side, which had said "similar arrangements" would be made for transit to Berlin.

The question of access to Berlin appears to have been discussed between U.S. and British military representatives at the Yalta Conference, and as a result the United States in February 1945 made its first formal proposal to Soviet authorities on the subject. The proposal took the form of identical memoranda transmitted by the U.S. chiefs of staff to the British chiefs of staff and the Soviet general staff, in which it was suggested "that the general principle of freedom of transit across zones of occupation and zones of tripartite occupation be accepted." The Soviet general staff did not reply.

Until the Yalta Conference the United States did not take the necessary action to give legal effect to the Agreement on the Zones of Occupation, which had been signed in London. At the urging of Ambassador Winant this was finally forthcoming on February 2, and the Soviet approval followed on February 6. With this the Three Power Agreement on the Zones of Occupation came into force. It was thought that the control authority for Germany provided for in the Agreement on Control Machinery in Germany would now begin to function in embryo form in London to prepare detailed plans for the occupation. There was a clear expectation on the U.S. side at the working level in the Department of State and in London that Allied access to Berlin would be dealt with in this forum. But the Soviet government never sent a representative to London to participate in the new body. Quite apart from the attitude of the Soviets—which was still largely untested—the War Department held to its position that the EAC was not authorized to deal with occupation questions. It was strengthened in this position by President Roosevelt's inclination to look to Secretary of War Stimson for advice on Germany as a military matter and by his reluctance to agree to specific plans for the occupation at this point. In a memorandum to Secretary Hull on October 20, 1944, Roosevelt had said, ''I dislike making detailed plans for a country which we do not yet occupy.''[26]

As it turned out, the lack of advance planning and agreement was compensated to an important degree by the military progress of the U.S. forces in Germany. Moving more rapidly than had been anticipated, they had advanced by VE Day well into territory designated in the London agreements for Soviet occupation, as had the British to a lesser extent. Churchill was convinced that the U.S. and British forces should stay where they were until satisfactory solutions were worked out with the Soviets on Poland and other outstanding problems. Churchill cabled the new U.S. president to this effect on May 11, 1945. On May 24, 1945, the British embassy in Washington sent an *aide-mémoire* to the Department of State concerning the draft of the declaration to be made on the defeat of Germany, which contained the following sentence: ''His Majesty's Government would be glad to know . . . whether the United States Government agrees that the British and American armies should continue to stand firm on the present tactical boundary line after the issue of the Declaration.'' The State Department, which may not have been aware of Churchill's earlier cable to Truman, promptly inquired just what the British had in mind. On May 28, the following explanation was provided by the embassy:

The Foreign Office now states that by this passage they meant that British and American forces should not withdraw to their respective permanent zones of occupation in Germany until the whole question of the future relations of the two Governments with the Soviet Government in Europe generally had been discussed and settled at the projected meeting of the President of the United States, the Prime Minister and Marshal Stalin.

The Department of State told the British ambassador that the United States ''could not go along with the British side on this.'' A week later, on June 4, 1945, Prime Minister Churchill sent the frequently quoted personal message to President Truman stating:

... I view with profound misgivings the retreat of the American army to our line of occupation in the Central Sector, thus bringing Soviet power into the heart of Western Europe and the descent of an iron curtain between us and everything eastward.

I hoped that this retreat, if it has to be made, would be accompanied by the settlement of many great things which would be the true foundation of world peace. Nothing really important has been settled yet and you and I will have to bear great responsibility for the future.[27]

Truman did not agree with Churchill, although he shared Churchill's concern over Soviet intentions. "My aim," he wrote in his memoirs, "was always to carry out to the letter all agreements entered into by Roosevelt with our allies."[28] He told Churchill that the United States had no intention of extending itself beyond the agreed zones. Meanwhile, when the four Allied commanders signed the Declaration Regarding the Defeat of Germany on June 5, 1945, in Berlin, the Soviet commandant, Marshal Zhukov, made clear that the control machinery for Germany could not begin to function until the U.S. and British forces had withdrawn to the agreed zones of occupation. This situation set the stage for the single most important step taken with regard to Allied access to Berlin. Harry L. Hopkins, President Roosevelt's closest confidant, who was functioning as special assistant to President Truman, after talking with General Eisenhower in Frankfurt, cabled Truman on June 8, 1945, advising that the Allied troops be withdrawn to the agreed zonal boundaries. He suggested that

As a concurrent condition to our withdrawal we should specify a simultaneous movement of our troops to Berlin under an agreement between the respective commanders which would provide us unrestricted access to our Berlin area from Bremen and Frankfurt by air, rail, and highway on agreed routes."[29]

(This concept may have originated with Philip Mosely in London, since he reports that he had had an extensive conversation on the subject with a visiting SHAEF representative to whom he gave a copy of a detailed plan he had developed.) Three days later, on June 11, 1945, Truman sent to Churchill the text of a message that he proposed to cable to Stalin, which stated that he was

ready to have instructions issued to all American troops to begin withdrawal in their own zone on 21 June in accordance with arrangements between the respective commanders, including in these arrangements simultaneous movement of the national garrisons into Greater Berlin *and provision of free access by air, road and rail from Frankfurt and Bremen to Berlin for U.S. forces.* [Italics added]

Churchill's unhappiness was evident in the opening sentence of his response: "Obviously we are obliged to conform to your decision, and necessary instructions will be issued." But he concurred in the wording, and on June 14 Truman sent the message to Stalin. Churchill followed with a message on June 15 proposing the same procedure with regard to British troops, although he used an elliptical wording that omits specific mention of free access as contained in the Truman cable.[30] In his reply on June 16, 1945, Stalin suggested that the movement of troops be delayed until July 1 and said that "all necessary measures" would be taken by Soviet authorities "in accordance with the above-stated plan."[31] He neither confirmed nor denied Truman's claim to free access for U.S. forces. An effort was accordingly made to clarify this point through military channels. On June 25 General Marshall cabled to General Eisenhower and to the head of the U.S. military mission in Moscow, General Deane:

It will be noted that the proposed . . . directive (on the administration of Germany and Austria) . . . contains no action to obtain transit rights to Berlin and Vienna on a combined basis. In accordance with the President's message to Stalin . . . these should be arranged with Russian commanders concerned. . . . It is assumed that appropriate Russian commanders have been instructed accordingly . . . it is desired that Deane confirm this with the Soviet staff.

Deane was unable to obtain confirmation of this but expressed the opinion that "when our representatives meet with Zhukov there will be little difficulty in arranging for free access for our troops to Berlin."[32]

The meeting with Marshal Zhukov took place at his headquarters in Berlin on June 29, 1945. The senior American participant was General Lucius D. Clay, who had been named deputy military governor and had joined General Eisenhower's staff in April. He had not visited the Department of State or talked to its officials prior to leaving Washington, an omission that Clay in the retrospect of his memoirs considered amazing. He was accompanied to the June 29 meeting by Robert Murphy, the political advisor to the military governor, and Major General Floyd Parks, who had been designated to command the U.S. troops in Berlin. The senior British representative was Lieutenant General Sir Robert Weeks. Although French participation in the occupation had already been agreed, there was no French representative at this meeting.

After reaching agreement rather easily with Marshal Zhukov on the details of the withdrawal of U.S. and British forces to the agreed zonal boundaries, the movement of Allied forces to Berlin was raised. Marshal Zhukov noted that he had received requests for three rail lines, two highways, and two air routes, one from Bremen and one from Frankfurt. He thought that one railway and one highway should be sufficient to meet the needs of a "small garrison" of 50,000 troops that the Americans and the British together would be bringing to Berlin.[33] Moreover, he could not agree to two air lanes and suggested instead a route to Berlin through Magdeburg and Goslar. General Clay records that he and General Weeks were both conscious that "there was no provision covering access to Berlin in the agreement reached by the EAC," and they, therefore, argued strongly for the original requests. General Clay said that they were not "demanding exclusive use of these routes but merely access over them without restrictions other than the normal traffic control regulations which the Soviet administration would establish for its own use.'' He explains in his memoirs that ''We did not wish to accept specific routes which might be interpreted as a denial of our right of access over all routes but there was merit to the Soviet contention that existing routes were needed for demobilization purposes.''[34] And so General Clay did accept the routes that Marshal Zhukov offered, in the understanding that all decisions were subject to revision by the Control Council. The routes agreed were the railroad and the autobahn from Magdeburg to Berlin and an air route from Goslar over Magdeburg to Berlin. General Clay insisted that it was necessary to have ''freedom of access and rights on roads and lanes.'' The Americans, he said, had not asked for exclusive use, but must have rights to use the roads and lanes ''as we need.'' Zhukov replied that he was not rejecting the right but said that the Soviet authorities should not be expected to give any corridor. When General Clay asked for unlimited access on roads, Marshal Zhukov replied that he did not understand just what the British and Americans desired. ''It will be necessary,'' he stated, ''for vehicles to be governed by Russian road signs, military police, document checking, but no inspection of cargo—the Soviet side are not interested in what is being handled, how much, or how many trucks are moving.''

With regard to air traffic, the marshal said he would report to his government that the Americans and British would accept one air lane approximately 20 miles wide from Frankfurt to Berlin via Goslar and Magdeburg, with the understanding that they would operate under U.S. and British regulations, notifying Soviet authorities with the same notice given U.S. and British authorities. The Americans and British would accede to the Soviet request to notify the Soviets one hour before takeoff time or arrival over Soviet territory, giving the number of the aircraft and destination.

The Soviet side offered the Americans and British the use of an underground communications cable from Berlin to Frankfurt via Leipzig on the understanding that it would be maintained and guarded by the Russians in the Soviet Zone and by the Americans in U.S. administered territory. Marshal Zhukov said that whenever the U.S. or British authorities wished to inspect or repair the cable they were welcome to do so and could enter the Soviet Zone ''at any time with a Soviet pass.'' It was also agreed that Tempelhof Airport would be available to the Americans and Gatow to the British.

That night General Clay dictated in his notes, ''It was agreed that all traffic—air, road and rail—would be free from border search or control by customs or military authorities.'' Nothing, however, was put down in writing. There were no agreed minutes, only the unilateral notes taken by the participants to serve as the basis for dealing with future controversies and crises. General Clay recognized the importance of unrestricted Allied access and says that he ''did not want an agreement in writing which established anything less than the right of unrestricted access.''[35] But in the perspective of the subsequent years of harrassment and blockade he concluded that he ''was mistaken in not at this time making free access to Berlin a condition to our withdrawal into our occupation zone."[36]

The oral understanding reached in Marshal Zhukov's headquarters on June 29, 1945, was to remain the major element in Allied access over the years. But it was supplemented by decisions taken subsequently in organs of the Control Council and recorded in writing. The one air corridor very quickly proved inadequate and the Western Allies sought to increase the number to six. They succeeded in gaining Soviet concurrence in the Aviation Committee of the Control Council's Air Directorate, and the committee proposed corridors from Berlin to Hamburg, Hanover (Buckeberg), Frankfurt-on-Main, Warsaw, Prague, and Copenhagen, "which would be used by aircraft of the four Allied Nations with full freedom of action."[37] When this report was considered in the Air Directorate, the Soviet representative stated that the directorate could request the Control Council coordinating committee to confirm the three corridors to Frankfurt-on-Main, Hamburg, and Hanover that were necessary to provide for the needs of the occupation troops in Greater Berlin, but the other proposed corridors were not for this purpose and therefore could only be discussed on decision of higher authority. The Control Council, at its thirteenth meeting on November 30, 1945, approved the three corridors to Frankfurt, Hamburg, and Hanover. At this meeting Marshal Zhukov expressed confidence that in due course the other air corridors would be opened. They never were. He also expressed the assumption that "his colleagues would give the Soviet military authorities the right to fly along these air corridors into the Western Zones" and therefore would put appropriate airfields at Soviet disposal for landing Soviet aircraft, or at least allow Soviet ground staff on terminal and intermediate fields to facilitate the servicing of Soviet aircraft. The Western military governors assured the marshal that they would "afford every facility" to Soviet aircraft but like the three additional corridors, the allocation of airfields to Soviet authorities in the Western zones never materialized, nor did authorization for Soviet ground staff to be stationed at Western airfields.

After the corridors from Hamburg, Hanover, and Frankfurt-on-Main were approved, the aviation committee agreed on the establishment of the Berlin Air Safety Center (BASC) and on flight rules for the corridors. The BASC, which is the only quadripartite body that continued to function during the blockade and continues to do so today, was founded to establish security of flights of aircraft in the control zone during bad weather conditions and at night. It was to provide unified control over flights of all aircraft in the control zone at the control center. The Berlin control zone was defined as

the air space height up to 10,000 feet above sea level in a radius of 20 English miles from the building of the Allied Control Authority. Also an air space height of 10,000 feet above sea level in agreed air corridors which go out in a radius from Berlin to the borders of the territory of occupied Germany.

The flight rules were approved by the air directorate on December 31—less than two weeks after the BASC organization had been approved. The air corridors are defined separately as being 20 English miles wide, that is, 10 miles each side of the center line. No ceiling is given. According to flight rules

arriving aircraft will contact the airfield of destination in the Berlin Control Zone at a distance of 75 miles (120 kilometers) from Berlin, giving their estimated time of arrival, altitude and other information as appears necessary. (This communications contact is not mandatory but is desirable). The airfield at which the aircraft arrives will inform BASC of such arrival.

A flight plan was to be filed with BASC through the national air traffic center prior to entering a "Control Area or Control Zone." Reckless flying in the corridors was prohibited as were "flight in formation" and acrobatics. It was provided that "an aircraft shall give way to another aircraft if a class different from its own in the following order: (a) mechanically driven aircraft; (b) airships; (c) gliders; (d) balloons."

The two documents in which the BASC organization and the flight rules are contained, DAIR/P (45)67 Second Revision and AAIR/P(45)71 revised, are quite detailed, providing full procedural regulations for flights.[38] It is largely the provisions that have been described, however, that bear directly on freedom of access and were to be the source of controversy within this context. Both documents were approved by the quadripartite air directorate of the Allied control authority but not by the Control Council itself. It has never been contended by any one of the parties that they are any less binding as a result.

In the first months of the Allied occupation of Berlin numerous problems arose in organizing railroad traffic over the single line from the Western zones. It was especially urgent to improve the situation before winter since the Western Allies had to bring in coal as well as food to supply their sectors. The coordinating committee, in August of 1945, instructed the transport directorate to study and report on the technical transport problems. As a result of this study, the directorate, in a memorandum of September 10, 1945, set forth its agreement that sixteen trains per day in each direction would be required, divided as follows:

British maintenance (military)	1
U.S. French (military)	2
Coal (U.S., British, French, civil and military combined)	8
Civil food (U.S., British, French)	5

The daily freight trains were to move eastward "over the Russian L of C" (presumably line of communications), under Soviet control and supervision on the route Helmstedt–Magdeburg–Berlin. The empties would return on the route Berlin–Stendal–Hanover, also under Soviet control and supervision. The specification of *freight* trains was presumably intended to differentiate them from Allied passenger trains, over which the Soviets would not have control and supervision.[39] The manner in which the daily trains were divided between Allied military and freight intended for the civilian population was never very precise. When in December the U.S. representative in the transport directorate indicated that the Americans intended to increase passenger trains to one a day, the Soviet representative pointed out that the Western Allies were free to run passenger or freight trains as desired up to the agreed limit of sixteen train paths a day. The meeting formally agreed "that the U.S., British and French should jointly work out the division of the 16 available train paths between freight and passenger trains, and that this requirement should then be agreed between the British and Soviet delegations."[40] The sixteen daily trains were pulled to Berlin by West German locomotives and manned by West German crews.

There was at this time one German civilian passenger train daily from Cologne to Berlin via Helmstedt. This was not included in the sixteen train paths since German interzonal passenger trains then and later were arranged between the German railway authorities in the East and the West.

In 1946 informal arrangements were made for an alternate rail route via Oebisfelde for trains going to north Berlin, and the number of train paths was augmented to cover an increase in Allied passenger trains. These were not officially agreed, however, and were therefore not subject to restoration as part of the understanding that ended the blockade.

Inland waterway traffic to and from Berlin was not distinguished in the agreements of the Allied control authority from interzonal waterway traffic in general. The number of barges was never controlled in the way that trains were. Similarly, German civilian road traffic was dealt with as interzonal traffic, regulated by German authorities. The Allied control authority issued general principles for the control of navigation between zones on the inland waterways and on the movement of self-propelled road vehicles in Germany, but there were no specific quadripartite agreements with regard to German civilian water and road traffic to Berlin. The trains carrying freight for the use of the German population of the Western sectors were included in the sixteen quadripartitely agreed daily train paths because the Western Allies had reluctantly agreed, at Soviet insistence, that the necessary food and coal to sustain the population in their sectors should be brought from the Western occupation zones. This has been cited as a clear indication that Soviet authorities did not consider Berlin to be economically part of the Soviet zone, although they were later to insist that it was.

The first official meeting of the Allied *Kommandatura* in Berlin took place on July 11, 1945. Its Order No. 1 began with the sentence: "The Inter-Allied *Kommandatura* has today assumed control over the City of Berlin." The last quadripartite meeting was held on June 16, 1948, when at 11:20 p.m. the entire Soviet delegation walked out of a meeting that had begun at ten o'clock that morning. Two weeks later on July 1, 1948, the Soviet chief of staff stated officially that Soviet representatives would no longer participate in the quadripartite meetings. "In other words," he said, "there is no Allied *Kommandatura*." In reply to a question, he further stated that "since all decisions [taken until then] were taken on basis of initial agreement, these agreements and these decisions are valid for us."[41] This has also been the position of the three Western Allies, who have consistently held that the *Kommandatura* orders and laws that were agreed quadripartitely could be repealed or amended only by quadripartite action. Despite the Soviet declaration, the *Kommandatura* has continued to function, albeit on a tripartite basis. When it has been necessary, because of changed conditions, to remove the laws or orders from effect in West Berlin, the three Western powers have "suspended" them, leaving them technically on the books pending the resumption of quadripartite administration. Thus the decisions made during the three years that the Allied *Kommandatura* functioned quadripartitely constitute Four Power agreements affecting Berlin. Many of these decisions dealt with the administration of the heavily damaged city and are of no enduring relevance. Some were of importance in the development of the Berlin city government, including its constitutional foundation. These are considered in a separate chapter on postwar municipal government in Berlin. In this first chapter we are concerned with agreements that determined the status of the city and defined the rights of the occupying powers. Several laws enacted by the Allied Control Council for Germany and made applicable in Berlin have had a continuing effect on the city's status. The most notable of these were on the demilitarization of Germany, especially Control Council Law No. 8 on the Elimination and Prohibition of Military Training and Law No. 43 on the Prohibition of the Manufacture, Import, Export, Transport and Storage of War Materials. The three Western powers have respected the continuing validity of these laws by maintaining the prohibition against military training or recruitment and against the manufacture of military equipment in the Western sectors and by protesting (without noticeable effect) against military manifestations in East Berlin. They are disregarded in East Berlin on the ground that, as claimed by the Soviets and East Germans, East Berlin is part of the German Democratic Republic.

FRENCH PARTICIPATION

When the quadripartite administration of Berlin began, France was a full participant—but only just. It had been agreed by Stalin, Roosevelt, and Churchill at Yalta that

a zone in Germany, to be occupied by the French Forces, should be allocated to France. This zone would be formed out of the British and American Zones and its extent would be settled by the British and Americans in consultation with the French Provisional Government.

Agreement on the French zone did not become final until July 26, 1945, when the Protocol of September 12, 1944, on Zones of Occupation was amended to delineate a French zone and to include France as one of the occupying powers in Berlin. The borders of the French sector in Berlin, which was made up of two boroughs orginally allocated to the British sector, were not agreed until after the *Kommandatura* had begun to function. France was not invited to participate in any of the major conferences dealing with the future status of Germany and Berlin, even though French participation in the occupation had been accepted before the meeting in Potsdam. French representatives were in close contact with the United States and Britain during late 1944 and 1945 on German matters, but mainly on the extent of the French zone. There is no indication that French suggestions concerning Berlin's status or access to the city were either requested or offered prior to the assumption by France of its position as one of the four occupying powers in Germany.

The sparse and seemingly fragile complex of agreements and understandings that have been described in this chapter were to serve as the foundation of the Western position in Berlin through repeated crises. They did not emerge as a logical progression from a well-conceived plan for Berlin—as far as the United States was concerned—primarily because the United States did not perceive until quite late that Berlin would be a special area apart from the rest of Germany. Even if it had, the War Department would almost certainly have opposed detailed planning at the diplomatic level on the ground that occupation was a military matter to be handled by the military commanders in the field. President Roosevelt held similar views as we have seen, and seldom sought the advice of his secretary of state. It is easy in retrospect to condemn such short-sightedness, to marvel at the ineffective coordination in Washington on a subject of major importance. Before blaming the future difficulties on the inadequacy of these agreements, however, it is well to keep in mind that they had one great advantage—the elasticity of the broadly defined. They provided an adequate basis for the legal position that the Western powers, when challenged, would develop on the status of Berlin and the broad rights they claimed there. It could have been disadvantageous to have had detailed and written agreements with the Soviet Union on access if they had carried with them the implications that such access was legally dependent on Soviet acquiescence. The point on which a very clear written agreement existed—the status of Greater Berlin as an area of Allied administration separate from the zones of occupation—was the first to be denied as a matter of principle by the Soviet Union. As we deal in the coming pages with Berlin's crisis years it will be well to resist attributing these crises to the confusion that characterized the early U.S. approach to the occupation of Berlin. The primary causes lay elsewhere.

NOTES

1. Secretary of War.

2. For a summary of the proposal, see Cordell Hull, *Memoirs*, Vol. 2 (New York: Macmillan, 1948), pp. 1285–87.

3. See, for example, briefing papers prepared for the First Quebec Conference, Appendices 28 and 29, in a Department of State paper contained in records of Dr. Harley Notter, file no. 1043 (Washington, D.C.: Department of State archives).

4. Austria was also included but with the remark that it might have to be considered separately.

5. Letter of October 15, 1943, from C. K. Lloyd, British embassy, Washington, D.C., to Dr. Harley Notter (Washington, D.C.: Department of State archives).

6. A reproduction of the president's map may be found in Earl F. Ziemke, *The U.S. Army in the Occupation of Germany, 1944–1948* (Washington, D.C.: Center of Military History, 1975), Chapter 10.

7. Memorandum by the representative of the Soviet Union to the EAC. *Foreign Relations of the USA, 1944*, Vol. 1 (Washington, D.C.: Department of State), p. 186.

8. Ibid.

9. Working Security Committee paper, WS–15 Preliminary H, January 7, 1944 (Washington, D.C.: Department of State archives).

10. Working Security Committee paper WS–15C, January 27, 1944 (Washington, D.C.: Department of State archives).

11. Working Security Committee paper WS–86 Preliminary, March 3, 1944 (Washington, D.C.: Department of State archives).

12. Civil Affairs Committee paper CAC–76, Preliminary, March 3, 1944 (Washington, D.C.: Department of State archives).

13. *Foreign Relations, 1944*, Vol. 1, pp. 179, 184, 195, 207.

14. Ibid., p. 208. In conversation with the authors Kennan said that his meeting with President Roosevelt, being well outside of normal channels, resulted in his removal from the European Adivsory Commission (EAC).

15. This Russian word was spelled in several different ways in English-language documents until *Kommandatura* was standardized in July 1945.

16. *Foreign Relations 1944*, Vol. 1, pp. 237–38.

17. Ironically, when the commandant of the U.S. sector first consulted with his Soviet counterpart, it was the Soviet officer who insisted on joint administrative responsibility for all of Berlin. In reporting a meeting in Marshal Zhukov's headquarters on July 7, 1945, the U.S. political advisor, Robert Murphy, wrote the following:

Prior to our arrival a slight misunderstanding had arisen between the Commandant of our Sector, Major General Parks, and the Soviet Command. Parks had mistakenly believed that the military government of the U.S. Sector was vested solely in the United States. The Soviet Command had referred Parks to the contents of paragraph 5 of the Agreement of September 1944, providing for the joint administration of the district of Greater Berlin. The meeting confirmed the latter point of view. It was agreed that according to the terms of the governmental understanding of September 12, 1944, the Berlin area would be governed by joint direction on a quadripartite basis.

See *Foreign Relations, 1945, Conference of Berlin*, Vol. 1, pp. 630–31.)

18. *Foreign Relations, 1944*, Vol. 1, pp. 240–41.

19.   Memorandum of 13 July 1944, from Military Advisor, EAC, to G–1, G–3, G–4, G–5 SHAEF and E–5 ETOUSA (Washington, D.C.: U.S. Army archives).

20.   U.S. embassy London dispatch, transmitting PS-SHAEF(44)26, State Department archives, file 740.00119 (Germany).

21.   Philip E. Mosely, "The Occupation of Germany," *Foreign Affairs* (July 1950). The authors could not locate the State Department plan in extant files.

22.   Ibid.

23.   This account again is entirely dependent on Mr. Mosely, since no documentary record of Ambassador Winant's conversation can be found. There is a later exchange in the minutes of the EAC, however, confirming that the Soviet representative spoke of access as something to be taken for granted.

24.   *Foreign Relations, 1944*, Vol. 1, p. 384.

25.   For full text, see *Documents on Germany 1944–1970* (Washington, D.C.: Senate Committee on Foreign Relations, 1971), pp. 3–4.

26.   Cordell Hull, *Memoirs*, Vol. 2 (New York: Macmillan, 1948), p. 1621.

27.   For U.S./British exchanges see *Foreign Relations, 1945*, Vol. 3, pp. 304–26.

28.   Harry S. Truman, *Memoirs*, Vol. 1, "Year of Decision" (Garden City, NY: Doubleday, 1955), p. 306.

29.   *Foreign Relations, 1944*, Vol. 3, p. 333.

30.   Full text of Churchill's message is in *Foreign Relations, 1945*, Vol. 3, pp. 136–37.

31.   Ibid., p. 137.

32.   Quoted in Truman, *Memoirs*, Vol. 1, p. 306.

33.   The most complete account of this meeting is provided by the notes taken by General Parks, which were not transmitted to the State Department or the JCS until April 1948. The full text is in *Foreign Relations, 1945*, pp. 353–61. Murphy sent a reporting telegram after returning to headquarters in Hoechst, the text of which is contained in *Foreign Relations, 1945*, Vol. 1, "The Conference of Berlin," p. 135. While the two accounts are similar on major points, they differ in details.

34.   Lucius D. Clay, *Decision in Germany* (Garden City, NY: Doubleday, 1950), pp. 25–26.

35.   Ibid.

36.   Ibid.

37.   CORC(P945)170, quoted in *Foreign Relations, 1945*, Vol. 3, p. 1577.

38.   Full texts are found in *Foreign Affairs, 1945*, Vol. 3, p. 1576.

39.   Text in *Documents on Germany, 1944–1970*, pp. 42–44.

40.   Ibid.

41.   Murphy telegram to Secretary of State, *Foreign Relations, 1948*, Vol. 2, p. 941.

2

The Lines Are Drawn

The Soviet utilization of its advancing armies to ensure the installation of communist regimes in Eastern Europe had already caused deep concern on the part of the Western Allies before the four victorious powers met in Berlin. Stalin, for his part, had expressed even earlier open suspicion that the United States and Britain were plotting to reach a separate peace with Germany in order to turn their combined forces against the Soviet Union. While the military governors were able to find a basis for cooperation and limited understanding in their shared pride and experience as military men dealing with a common and happily defeated enemy, the distrust and the abiding dissimilarity in thinking between the Soviet and the Western sides never disappeared. The Allied Control Council, during the first year and a half of its existence, was able to reach agreement on orders or laws affecting all of Germany in limited fields such as denazification, demilitarization, the abrogation of Nazi legislation, and interzonal movement. Sharp disagreement began early, however, on reparations, the demobilization of German troops (on which the Soviets were especially suspicious of the British), and any kind of a united economic administration for Germany as had been foreseen in the Potsdam Agreements. Each of the four zones of occupation was administered as a separate fiefdom, with the French in stubborn opposition to any move toward a central administration for all of Germany.

The friction, distrust, and dissimilar objectives among the Four Powers in dealing with Germany as a whole inevitably affected their relationship in administering Berlin, including Western access to the city. In his memoirs General Lucius D. Clay writes:

As early as 1945, we experienced our first difficulties in the operation of our train service to Berlin, when Soviet soldiers tried to enter these trains to check the identity of passengers.

I discussed this problem in the Control Council without results, so I determined to see General Sokolovsky about it. I went to his office and reminded him of the discussions relating to our entry into Berlin and said that I would have to place armed guards on our trains to prevent access by others if all else failed. Sokolovsky would not waive his claim to the right of inspection, which he applied in particular to German passengers. I advised him that our military trains would carry only such Germans as were employed by us, and all others would apply for quadripartite-issued permits. I also told him that our use of armed guards could create a most unhappy incident for both of us. Sokolovsky then suggested, without waiving his claim, that we would have no further trouble. I replied in the same spirit that a 'gentlemen's agreement' was satisfactory to me but that I wanted to make it clear we would not recognize any right on their part to inspect our trains.[1]

Even though the *Magistrat,* the central German administration for Greater Berlin, was located in the Soviet sector of Berlin until 1948 and travel between the Soviet and the Western sectors was largely unrestricted, a vastly different atmosphere prevailed in the eastern sector.[2] For Americans in Berlin, trips deep into the Soviet sector had the excitement of trips into enemy territory and entry into the Soviet Zone (other than bus trips to Potsdam) was impossible. This influenced appreciably the attitudes of many Americans (and presumably Russians) as disagreement mounted in the Control Council and in the Allied *Kommandatura.* Similarly, direct and indirect Soviet intervention in the German administration in Berlin to strengthen communist elements and hamper anti-communists created an environment of terror and intimidation. In these circumstances, the initiation of clearly systematic restrictions on access to Berlin and the Soviet walkout from the Control Council and the *Kommandatura* came as no great surprise. The inability of the Four Powers to agree on economic measures that would offer hope of German recovery and the bitter disputes over reparations convinced the U.S. side that Four Power administration would not work and caused them, together with the British, to follow the alternative course of economic amalgamation of their zones, and finally, with the reluctant addition the French, to establish a political structure that would unite the three Western zones. The U.S. secretary of state, James F. Byrnes, expressed the frustration of the United States over the failure of the Control Council to function as foreseen when, in a speech at Stuttgart on September 6, 1946, he outlined a new U.S. policy toward Germany in accordance with which "the German people throughout Germany should now be given the primary responsibility for the running of their own affairs."[3] The progressive steps taken by the Soviet Union to isolate the Western sectors of Berlin can be seen, from their timing, to be in direct response to these Western moves. But in assessing cause and effect it must be kept in mind that the Western moves were in response to the seemingly unbridgeable gap between Soviet and Western attitudes toward the administration of Germany as a whole.

THE GRADUAL IMPOSITION OF BLOCKADE

The fifth session of the Council of Foreign Ministers[4] was held in London from November 27 to December 15, 1947, to deal with postwar settlements for Germany and Austria. Given the basic disagreements already evident in the Allied Control Council, the Western powers had little expectation of success on Germany. They were entirely correct. The meetings were acrimonious and served largely to convince the Western powers that Soviet objectives in Germany were so different from their own as to preclude any real possibility for an all-German settlement—something for which the French still had little enthusiasm, in any event. The Soviet side appears to have reached similar conclusions, since Foreign Minister Molotov was outspoken in attacking the European Recovery Program (Marshall Plan) and in accusing the United States of planning a separate West German state in contravention of the Potsdam Agreements.

Secretary of State Marshall issued a negative report on the Council of Foreign Ministers session on December 19, 1947.[5] Shortly thereafter, in January 1948, Soviet military personnel began systematically to board U.S. military trains to and from Berlin and to insist that they had the right to check the identity of individual passengers. This continued through February and March and trains were frequently subject to lengthy delays since the train commanders would not allow the Soviet personnel to carry out the checks. Also in January the Soviet authorities began to exercise stricter control on the movement by truck of German goods from the Western sectors of Berlin into the Soviet zone.

In late February the British, French, and U.S. foreign ministers met in London for an informal discussion of the German problem. They were joined during the later days of the conference by the Benelux foreign ministers, and on March 6, 1948, a communiqué was issued which declared that the "continuous failure of the Council of Foreign Ministers to reach quadripartite agreement has created a situation in Germany which, if permitted to continue, would have increasingly unfortunate consequences for Western Europe." It was accordingly agreed that

a federal form of government, adequately protecting the rights of the respective States but at the same time providing for adequate control authority, is best adapted for the eventual re-establishment of German unity, at present disrupted. Moreover, in order to facilitate the association of Western Germany with the European Recovery Programme the three delegations concerned further agreed that prompt action should be taken to coordinate as far as possible the economic policies of the three zones.[6]

On March 20, 1948, the Soviet representative in the Allied Control Council, Marshal Sokolovsky, declared that at the London conference the Western powers had decided questions that were directly within the competence of the Control Council, and he accused the Western delegations of "tearing up the agreement on the Control Machinery in Germany." Because of these actions, "the Control Council virtually no longer exists."[7] After this statement the Soviet delegation walked out of the Control Council meeting. Sokolovsky never returned. Ten days later on March 30 the Soviet deputy military governor, General Dratvin, sent a letter to his U.S. counterpart, General Hays, informing him of "certain supplementary provisions, with respect to the regime governing the line of demarcation and communications between the Soviet and U.S. Zones of Occupation in Germany, which will be put into effect from 1 April 1948." These were:

1. All military and civilian employees of the U.S. military administration, having U.S. citizenship, and their dependents, proceeding through the Soviet zone of occupation by the Berlin–Helmstedt Highway, would be obliged to present at both ends of the autobahn documentary proof of their identity and of their affiliation with an agency of the U.S. military administration in Germany.

2. The same requirement would apply also to rail passengers.

3. Freight, belonging to the U.S. military authorities and intended for shipment to the Western zones of Germany would be loaded, and cleared through the control and clearing points at the line of demarcation only upon presentation of a permit issued by the office of the Soviet commandant of Berlin, or the foreign trade administration of the Soviet military administration of Germany. Freight coming from the Western zones into the Soviet zone would be cleared on the basis of the accompanying documents.

4. All belongings of persons passing through the control points would be subject to inspection with the exception of the personal belongings carried in a passenger railway car or automobile by U.S. military or civilian personnel connected with the U.S. military government.

The next day Brigadier General Charles Gailey, the U.S. military government chief of staff, replied as follows:

The agreement under which we entered Berlin clearly provided for our free and unrestricted utilization of the established corridors. This right was a condition precedent to our entry into Berlin and our simultaneous evacuation of Saxony and Thuringia. I do not consider that the provisions you now propose are consistent with this agreement. I must also advise you that we do not propose to accept changes in this agreement.

Gailey went on to say that he recognized the Soviet right to check "the authenticity of travel of passengers proceeding by automobile" but not to inspect personal belongings where proper identification has been established. Moreover, he did not recognize this right

as applicable to our military passenger and freight trains as these trains are clearly identified as official United States Army trains with full right under our agreement of free and unrestricted utilization of the agreed railroad route, subject only to requisite and normal traffic control.

The general expressed willingness to have train commanders on passenger trains provide passenger lists accompanied by copies of the orders of each passenger and, in the case of freight trains, cargo manifests. But Soviet representatives would not be allowed to enter the trains for inspection purposes.

On April 3 General Dratvin wrote back that he saw no possibility of changing "the existing regulation affecting the traffic of freight and personnel through the Soviet Zone of Occupation." He could not help "considering as a misunderstanding and an error the statement that there was some sort of an agreement concerning the free and unrestricted use of the established corridors," since it was obvious that unregulated and uncontrolled traffic could only lead to confusion and provoke unrest in the Soviet zone.

The next day General Gailey sent a further letter reiterating the position he had stated on March 31, emphasizing that U.S. representatives who had been present at the meeting with Marshal Zhukov on June 29, 1945, had clearly understood that "United States forces in Berlin would have free and unrestricted use of the established corridors to meet their requirements, subject only to normal regulation of movements."[8] The positions of the Soviet and the Western sides on Allied access had been clearly stated.

On April 1, 1948, two U.S. and two British passenger trains were turned back at the Soviet zone border when Soviet representatives were not allowed to board them for inspection. One French train was permitted to pass after submitting to inspection. Subsequently no Allied passenger trains were able to travel to Berlin, and no Allied mail cars left Berlin because additional forms were required, the character of which was not clarified.

In the following weeks there was sporadic interference with the various ground transport routes. On April 2 the Soviet authorities requested that the U.S. aid station located midway on the Berlin–Helmstedt autobahn be closed as of May 1. On April 3 the train routes used for German freight between Hamburg and Berlin and Bavaria and Berlin were closed, restricting this traffic to the Helmstedt line. On April 9 U.S. signal personnel who were stationed in the Soviet zone to maintain the telephone cable from Berlin to Frankfurt were ordered to leave, which they did on April 14. Individual clearance was required for barges, and water transport became irregular and subject to long delays. Permission for the inclusion of two international cars on the German passenger train between Berlin and the British zone was withdrawn. Freight and German pasengers continued to reach Berlin, however, by both rail and road until June 15, when the autobahn bridge across the Elbe near Magdeburg was closed. Then on June 19, the day after the law on currency reform in the three Western zones was promulgated, all passenger rail traffic and all vehicular traffic to Berlin from the Western zones was stopped. On June 30 the Soviet military administration ordered all electric power exports to the Western sectors from the Soviet sector and the Soviet zone cut. (In practice this was never fully implemented.) Finally on June 24—the day after a currency reform had been implemented by the Soviet military administration, which according to the legislation was applicable in the Soviet zone and in all of Berlin and the day before the new Western mark, stamped "B," was introduced into the three Western sectors—the Soviet Transport administration ordered all incoming and outgoing freight and passenger traffic stopped.

On June 25 all surface mail shipments to the West were halted, and the agreement under which food was supplied to the Western sectors from the Soviet zone was unilaterally cancelled. Financial measures were also taken to place pressure on West Berlin inhabitants and businesses. Thus by July 1948 all major surface transportation routes between the Western sectors and the Western zones were cut. In retaliation, the Western powers suspended all shipments from the Western zones to the Soviet zone, including reparations. On July 1 the Soviet representative in the Allied *Kommandatura* stated that the

well-known behaviour of Colonel Howley,[9] lack of reaction to protests made by Soviet authorities as well as separate actions of French, U.S. and British authorities in introducing currency reform of Western Zones into Berlin, a city which is part of the economic system of Soviet Zone, have resulted in the fact that the quadripartite meetings in the Allied *Kommandatura* cannot take place any longer. In connection with this, Soviet representatives will no longer participate in the quadripartite meetings of the bodies of the Allied *Kommandatura* in Berlin. . . . In other words, there is no Allied *Kommandatura*.[10]

Within the same time frame as the actions against access and the breakdown of quadripartite administration in the Allied *Kommandatura,* the Soviet military administration and German communist groups, who were patently acting in cooperation with it, created conditions so that the freely elected Berlin government (*Magistrat*) could not operate in the city hall, which was located in the Soviet sector. The result was a split in the city administration between East and West, a condition that was not to end with the end of the blockade—which, indeed, has not ended even now. Details on these developments will be found in the following chapter on the Berlin city government.

By mid-summer 1948, then, the blockade of the access routes between the Western sectors of Berlin and the Western zones of occupation had become broad and effective, although, as was to be the case until the blockade ended, some food, coal, and other supplies reached West Berlin from East Berlin and the Soviet zone through diversion, an active black market, and barter for manufactured goods that went East from West Berlin. Mainly, however, West Berlin had become dependent on supply by air, which was to reach an effectiveness beyond even the highest Western expectations.[11] Tension between the Soviet Union and the Western powers mounted steadily. Reference to the possibility of war occurs frequently in the confidential messages and telecommunications conferences between Washington and U.S. representatives in the field, although General Clay, who in March had warned of an ominous change in the Soviet position in Germany, emphasized in a teleconference with the Secretary of the Army Kenneth Royall on June 25, 1948 (the day on which the Western mark was introduced in the Western sectors) that he did not expect armed conflict. Washington was nervous, however, even to the point of wondering whether the currency change had to be effected in Berlin. When General Clay took umbrage at this and said that it was too late to stop the introduction of the "B mark" in any event, Secretary Royall assured him there was "no thought that decisions on currency were unsound . . . but I do feel strongly that the limited question of Berlin currency is not a good enough question to go to war on."[12] Actually, Secretary Royall had favored withdrawal from Berlin simultaneously with the establishment of a West German government. Ambassador Walter B. Smith, in Moscow, also thought it was foolhardy to try to remain in the city although he was to do a superb job in defending the Western position in the conversations between the three Western ambassadors and Stalin. However, General Clay, although at first doubtful that the basic needs of West Berlin's population could be met by airlift, insisted, with the full support of his foreign service political advisor, Robert Murphy, that it would be disastrous for the future of all of Western Europe if the Americans should abandon Berlin. When he described the situation to President Truman, he found the president despite some reservations in agreement. Clay and Murphy originally proposed that Soviet intentions be tested by military probes on the ground of which the Soviet authorities would be given advance notice. This was opposed as overly risky by the joint chiefs of staff and in the National Security Council. Instead it was decided to meet the Soviet challenge by an airlift to cover the basic needs of the population of the Western sectors. Truman records that he brought up the Berlin situation at the Cabinet meeting of June 25 and on the next day "directed that the improvised airlift be put on a fullscale organized basis and that every plane available to our European Command be impressed into service."[13] On June 28 the Department of State sent out a telegram stating that on the basis of the president's decision the United States intended to remain in Berlin, supply the city by air, maximize propaganda exploitation of the situation, and send a serious note of protest to the Soviet government.

Subsequently, a squadron of B–29 bombers was sent to England as a signal of U.S. determination and readiness to face the Soviet threat. Secretary of Defense James Forrestal, who had entirely agreed with General Clay on the necessity of remaining in Berlin, had from early in the crisis felt the need to know whether the United States would use atomic bombs should war come. On September 13, 1949, Forrestal, together with Generals Omar Bradley and Hoyt Vandenberg, met with President Truman on the subject. Truman was briefed on the state of readiness of the bombs and told that ten days time could be saved in their use against targets in Europe if huts could be constructed for the storage of essential components at the two airfields where the B–29s were stationed. For this British consent would be required. The president stated that he prayed he would not have to make the decision to use the bomb "but if it became necessary, no one need have misgivings but what he would do so."

While the president's response did not really answer the question of whether he would authorize the use of atomic bombs if there should be war with the

Soviet Union over Berlin, Forrestal considered Truman's wording sufficiently clear for him to meet his responsibilities in ensuring the battle readiness of U.S. forces. In a meeting two days later, the president authorized General Norstadt to go to England and sound out the British on construction of the storage huts. Norstadt carried out his mission and the huts were constructed. Meanwhile, Forrestal sought the reaction of various senior colleagues to the possible use of the bomb and found them unanimously in favor if war should come. According to Forrestal's diary, John Foster Dulles told him that the American people "would execute you if you did not use the bomb in the event of war." (Ten years later, in his last meeting with Chancellor Adenauer, Dulles suggested it might be necessary to resort to nuclear war in resisting the Khrushchev ultimatum on Berlin. David Klein, who was note taker at the meeting, records Adenauer as responding *"um Gotteswillen, nicht über Berlin"* (not, for God's sake, on account of Berlin.)

General Clay, again according to Forrestal, said he would not hesitate to use the atomic bomb and would hit Moscow and Leningrad first. Winston Churchill suggested to Forrestal that the United States erred in talking down the destructive power of the bomb "since doing so encouraged Russia."

Forrestal never again raised the utilization of atomic bombs with President Truman. He was satisfied that the planes and bombs were in place. The remaining question in his mind was whether they could be successfully delivered to targets in the Soviet Union. He was informed in an "Eyes Only" memorandum from Secretary of the Air Force Stuart Symington that General Vandenberg was "absolutely certain" the bomb could be dropped where, how, and when it was wanted.[14]

FOUR POWER NEGOTIATIONS

The closing of the access routes and the withdrawal of Soviet participation in the Allied *Kommandatura* and the Allied Control Council did not result in a blockage of communication channels between Moscow and the West. During the entire course of the blockade there was never a time when Soviet and Western representatives were out of touch, contact being maintained either in Moscow, Berlin, or at the United Nations. In reviewing the course of events and reading through the contemporary Western assessments and position papers (the Soviet equivalents are unfortunately not available) one has the impression of a crisis of high drama and of enormous importance in the formulation of Soviet and Western attitudes that were to endure for decades and beyond; but it was a crisis in which the elements were under the full control of the protagonists. The protagonists did not act at the will of uncontrolled parties. Despite the strong recommendation of General Clay, seconded by Ambassador Murphy, Washington never seriously contemplated sending an armed division along the autobahn to Berlin as a possible means of breaking the blockade.[15] The danger of an armed confrontation was considered to be too great.[16] On the Soviet side, Stalin was personally available to speak reassuringly, if somewhat misleadingly, when tension reached its high point. The Soviet imposition of restrictions, as we have seen, was gradual and justified initially on technical grounds, which left an obvious route open for retreat if necessary. Most importantly, just as the Western powers did not challenge the Soviets by the use of force to open the ground access routes, the Soviets never sought to close the air corridors by force—the only way it could have been done—although they did seek through air maneuvres, including barrage balloons, to make corridor flight risky. To have done more would almost certainly have resulted in at least limited armed exchange.

For the purpose of the present volume, it is the positions of principle concerning Berlin that were defined and challenged by the two sides—in some cases for the first time—that are of main concern.[17] As was recorded in the previous chapter, the limited written agreements reached among the Four Powers with regard to Berlin were largely pragmatic in nature—these were on territory and access routes, rather than on rights and principles. The major claim to the right of free Allied access stated by President Truman in his letter to Marshal Stalin was neither contradicted nor confirmed. But the disputes connected with the blockade required that principles be defined. As it turned out, the Soviet and Western definitions were very different, but equally enduring.

It began with General Clay's "gentleman's agreement" with Sokolovsky on the boarding of U.S. military trains by Soviet personnel. Clay thus sought to establish the principle that the wording of his original oral agreement with Marshal Zhukov[18] excluded Soviet entry onto U.S. military trains. Sokolovsky refused to waive the "right" of Soviet entry but agreed not to implement the "right" in order to avoid difficulties.

It was this same "right" that was revived by General Dratvin in his March 30 letter to General Hays, albeit phrased as a requirement of orderly procedure rather than a principle. General Gailey's response, given the need for speed and the ignorance of access agreements that prevailed in Washington at the time, was remarkably precise and authoritative in defining as a matter of principle what Soviet authorities could and could not do in view of the American "right to free and unrestricted utilization of the established corridors," which "was a condition precedent to our entry into Berlin and our simultaneous evacuation of Saxony and Thuringia." General Dratvin was quick to deny that any agreement on such a right existed and sought to expand the extent of regulation by Soviet authorities required for the orderly movement of freight and personnel. Concurrently with the dispute over the principle of free Allied access to Berlin, there emerged another conflict of principle over the status of the city. As was noted in the previous chapter, one of the few things with regard to Berlin that was clearly agreed in writing in the European Advisory Council was that Berlin would be a separate area jointly administered by the Three (subsequently Four) Powers. Nevertheless, as relations deteriorated badly in late 1947, reports reached U.S. authorities that Soviet officers had begun to refer to Berlin as part of the Soviet zone. On November 5, 1947 (that is, well before the March 1948 Conference of the U.S., British, French, and Benelux foreign ministers, which took the decisions that the Soviet authorities later claimed negated the Western rights in Berlin) the office of the political advisor (U.S. POLAD) in Berlin sent the following cable to the Department of State:

According German contact employed ADN (East German News Service), who is believed reliable, Soviets were both considerably surprised and angered by Clay's "declaration of propaganda warfare." SMA officials. . . . indicated particular anger that Clay chose Berlin to make statement, for they regard Berlin as part of Soviet occupation in which Western Powers are present 'only as guests.'[19]

On April 27, 1948, after serious interference with access had begun, USPOLAD reported to Washington that the Soviet commandant, General Kotikov, had "declared following the March 20th meeting: 'the battle for Berlin has begun', adding that the day would come when the Western Powers would be in Berlin 'only as tolerated guests.' "[20]

Such reports appear to have so impressed U.S. authorities that when the first official written Soviet assertion concerning the relationship between Berlin and the Soviet zone was received, they read more into it than was actually there. On June 20, 1948, Marshal Sokolovsky wrote to General Clay:

Everyone understands that the introduction of the foreign currencies in Berlin would disrupt the economy and monetary circulation in the area of Greater Berlin, located in the Soviet Zone of Occupation and economically appearing to be part of it, but it would disrupt the economy of the Soviet Zone as well.

This wording was ominous, but it still made a clear distinction between Greater Berlin and the Soviet zone of occupation. Nevertheless, General Clay replied:

I must advise you that the quadripartite status of Berlin comes as a result of a separate agreement under which each of the occupying powers has equal rights in Berlin and therefore I am unable to accept the implication that Berlin, merely because of its location in the Soviet Zone of Occupation, comes under the direct purview of the Soviet Military Administration.[21]

During the months of the blockade a great deal of attention was focused on the currency question. After introducing the West mark into the Western sectors in June, the Western powers subsequently agreed in principle in conversations which the U.S., British, and French ambassadors had with Stalin in August in Moscow that the East mark would be the sole currency in circulation in all of Berlin, provided issuance and circulation of the currency in Berlin were under quadripartite control, a condition that was never met. When the Berlin question was taken to the United Nations, the currency question was seen by the members of the Security Council as the key to ending the blockade, and an intricate plan was eventually developed by a "neutral commission" that proved satisfactory to neither side. By this time the Western powers were no longer really interested in a solution that would have left all of Berlin in the Eastern currency zone. In reality, the currency issue, like that of control of West Berlin's trade, which also arose in the conversations with Stalin, was important not as a matter of principle in itself, but rather as having a direct bearing on the status of Berlin both de jure and de facto. It was this, together with the principle of free access to the city, which was at issue. These principles were defined clearly but differently by each side for the first time as a result of the crisis. They were debated and challenged in very concrete form but, as will be seen, the end of the blockade did not mean that agreement had been achieved. In the process, however, the United States had placed on record its commitment to the maintenance of the Western position in Berlin and to the preservation of free access to the city.

The United States, Britain, and France, after concluding that the interference with access could not be resolved pragmatically by the four military governors in Germany, sent identical notes to the Soviet government on July 6, 1948, setting forth their legal position, which to the present day has remained unchanged. The main points were (quoting from the U.S. note):

—The rights of the United States as a joint occupying power in Berlin derive from the total defeat and unconditional surrender of Germany. They stem from precisely the same source as those of the Soviet Union. It is impossible to assert the latter and deny the former.

—International agreements undertaken in connection therewith (i.e., the total defeat and unconditional surrender) defined the sectors of Berlin which are occupied by these powers and established quadripartite control of Berlin.

—These agreements implied the right of free access to Berlin, a right that has long been confirmed by usage. The right was specified in the message sent by President Truman to Premier Stalin on June 14, 1945, to which Stalin in his reply of June 16, 1945, took no exception. Commitments entered into in good faith by the Zone Commanders, and subsequently confirmed by the Allied Control Authority, as well as by usage, guarantee the United States together with the other powers, free access to Berlin for the purposes of fulfilling its responsibilities as an occupying power.

—It also results from these undertakings of the Four Powers that Berlin is an international zone of occupation and not part of the Soviet Zone.

The Soviet Union defined its position as follows in its reply of July 14, 1948:

—The United States, the United Kingdom and France violated the agreed decisions of the Four Powers in regard to Germany and Berlin by (1) carrying out a separate currency reform, (2) introducing a special currency in the Western sectors of Berlin, (3) pursuing a policy of dismemberment of Germany, (4) failing to complete the process of demilitarization, and (5) removing the Ruhr from Four Power control.

—The Four Power control mechanism in Germany has thus been destroyed and the Control Council has ceased its activity.

—The exercise of the occupation right of the United States arising out of the defeat and capitulation of Germany is linked to the obligatory exercise by the Four Powers of the agreements concluded among themselves with regard to Germany as a whole. By their actions, the three Western Powers have undermined the legal basis which assured their right to participate in the administration of Berlin.

—Berlin lies in the center of the Soviet Zone and is a part of that Zone.[22]

Thus the Soviet Union did not deny that rights claimed by the Western powers once existed but contended rather that they lapsed because these powers had destroyed the Four Power agreements in which these rights had had their basis. It did not seek to give a legal justification to its assertion that Berlin was part of the Soviet zone. Over the years the Soviet Union has never abandoned this contention but neither has it been consistent in its articulation. For example, only two months later in its note of September 25, 1948, it used the wording, "Berlin, which is in the center of the Soviet Zone," rather than "which is a part of the Soviet Zone"; but it would revert to this latter wording later.

Given the legal position taken by the Soviet Union in its note of July 14, 1948, it was natural that the Soviet side would seek to make any resolution of the crisis dependent on a new agreement that would be the only legal basis for any Western rights in Berlin, that is through the consent of the Soviet Union. The persistent Soviet position as stated by Foreign Minister Molotov during the talks with the three Western ambassadors in August in Moscow was that "quadripartite control had ceased as a result of London decisions. If agreement were reached for the restoration of quadripartite control in Germany as a whole then it might also be restored in Berlin."[23] The Department of State cabled in response:

It is apparent . . . that the Soviet Government is seeking to establish its thesis that quadripartite control of Germany and, consequently, of Berlin as well, has lapsed and therefore whatever agreement may be reached in the Moscow discussions will constitute the only Four Power agreement concerning Berlin. This position . . . is completely unacceptable to this Government. . . . It therefore seems necessary to us clearly to reaffirm that there has been no derogation of our rights in Berlin by our agreement to a practical solution of the blockade and currency problems.

This position was faithfully communicated in the oral statement made by U.S. Ambassador Bedell Smith to Molotov in behalf of the three Western powers on August 12, 1948.[24]

There was considerable internal discussion on the U.S. side as to whether specific Soviet acknowledgement of Western rights in Berlin should be sought. This was the inclination in the Department of State. The U.S. ambassador in Moscow advised against seeking this objective since he was convinced the result was bound to be negative. He recommended instead that the Western side seek to work out a modus vivendi without prejudice to juridical rights. This same discussion was to recur after more than 20 years during the Berlin negotiations in 1969–70. The ambassador's advice would again be followed.

When, after a seemingly encouraging understanding with Marshal Stalin, the negotiations to end the blockade were shifted back to the military governors in Berlin, the talks immediately became deadlocked in tortuous details of currency control and trade. The failure of these discussions contributed to the effective division of Berlin. On the other hand, the successful resistance of the Western side to Soviet or East German control of West Berlin's economy through currency and trade greatly strengthened the Western capacity to stay indefinitely in Berlin. But these lengthy negotiations did not alter the de jure status of the city as seen by either side.

In the course of the negotiations among the military governors, the Soviet side did raise a further matter of principle of great sensitivity to the Western side affecting access. In discussing the lifting of restrictions on Western access, Marshal Sokolovsky referred, almost *en passant,* to the necessity of the other three military governors complying strictly "with the regulations imposed by the Control Council's decision of November 30, 1945, on air traffic for the needs of the occupation forces" and said that air traffic through the corridors to Berlin should be limited to meeting the needs of the military forces of occupation. Nonmilitary traffic would be subject to the usual control and processing of civil air transport entering the Soviet zone. The Western powers reacted strongly against this, asserting that in conversations aimed at removing restrictions on access the Soviet side was, in fact, seeking to impose a new one. The dispute was continued in the notes exchanged between the Soviet Union and the Western powers following the failure of the military governors' talks in Berlin. In an *aide-mémoire* that Foreign Minister Molotov handed to the three Western ambassadors in Moscow on September 18, 1948, it was stated:

the Soviet Military Governor pointed to the necessity of the other three Military Governors complying strictly with the regulations imposed by the Control Council's decision of November 30, 1945, on air traffic for the needs of the occupation forces and this had never been disputed by any of the Military Governors since the adoption of these regulations three years ago. There is no foundation whatsoever for regarding this justified demand of the Soviet Military Governor as an imposition of new restrictions on air traffic, because these regulations had been imposed as far back as 1945 and not after March 30, 1948.[25]

With this the British ambassador, Sir Frank Roberts, immediately took issue and in so doing, made an important clarification that was to remain, in future disputes on air access, an essential element of the Western position. The decision of November 30, 1945, he said, "did not relate to the needs of the occupying forces, *but to those of the occupying powers in regard to Berlin, which naturally included fulfillment of their responsibilities in regard to Berlin* [emphasis added]."[26]

In a note of September 24, 1948, to the Soviet government, the United States expressed the Western position more formally as follows:

Actually during the discussions leading up to the decision of the Control Council of November 1945, to establish air corridors, the Soviet military authorities in Berlin had suggested that the traffic in the corridors should be limited to the needs of the military forces. Neither the Control Council, however, nor any other Four Power body accepted this proposal and the traffic in the corridors has since been subject only to those safety regulations which were agreed on a Four Power basis. Other than these agreed safety regulations, no restrictions whatsoever have been or are in existence on the use by aircraft of the occupying powers of air communications in the corridors between Berlin and the Western Zones of Germany.[27]

The decision of November 30, 1945, of the Allied Control Council, to which the Soviet side had reference and as recorded in the minutes (CONL/M(45)18), says nothing about the utilization of the corridors; it only establishes them. However, the Allied Control Council coordinating committee, on November 27, 1945, approved CORC/P(45)170 and agreed to submit it to the Control Council "for confirmation of that portion which deals with air corridors from Berlin to the West." CORC/P(45)170 contains the sentence: "Flights over these routes (corridors) will be conducted without previous notice being given, by aircraft of the nations governing Germany." The decision of the Control Council of November 30, 1945, can reasonably be understood to incorporate that sentence.

In justification of the Soviet position, it can be said the Western side had voluntarily accepted the distinction that the Soviets were seeking to make with regard to air traffic in the case of surface passenger traffic and to a degree with regard to surface freight traffic. And yet the Control Council agreement on train paths was clearly based on the principle expressed by Sir Frank Roberts, that is, the requirement for the Western occupying powers to fulfil their responsibilities in regard to Berlin—not just to supply their own garrisons. Soviet authorities, despite the vastly increased civilian air traffic that has developed over the years through the corridors, have never abandoned their position de jure and even now object to international flights to West Berlin through the corridors, on the ground that they are not for the supply of Western military garrisons. The Western powers, for their part, continue to limit commercial flights through the corridors to their national carriers. The only non–Four Power aircraft to use the corridors on a regular basis have been those of the Polish Airline, LOT. LOT was already operating a regular service from Berlin to London before the corridors were established and continued to do so with the special agreement of the Allied Control Authority. There have been no LOT flights, however, since December 1981. This reflects a Polish decision, since Allied authorities took no action to deny corridor access to LOT.[28]

THE END OF THE BLOCKADE

The Berlin blockade and the resultant Western airlift did a great deal to solidify the Western orientation of Germans in general and of Berliners in particular. It provided a strong catalyst for Western unity in meeting a Soviet threat that Berlin symbolized in the most vivid terms. The Soviet Union had placed itself in the public position of a villain trying to gain its way by subjecting more than 2 million people to debilitating hardship and ultimate starvation. When it became obvious that the Soviet objective of preventing the establishment of a West German state, or, at least, of forcing the three powers to leave Berlin, could not be achieved through the blockade, it was clearly in the Soviet interest to end it and cut their losses. Once this decision was taken, Moscow haggled about details but not about principles, which were simply set aside.

On January 27, 1949, Kingsbury Smith, European general manager of the International News Service, submitted four questions to Premier Stalin, the third one of which read as follows:

If the Governments of the United States of America, the United Kingdom and France agreed to postpone establishment of a separate Western German Government state pending a meeting of the Council of Foreign Ministers to consider the German problem as a whole, would the Government of the USSR be prepared to remove the restrictions which Soviet authorities have imposed on communications between Berlin and the Western Zones of Germany?

On January 30 Stalin gave the following reply to this question:

Provided the United States of America, Great Britain, and France observe the conditions set forth in the third question, the Soviet Government sees no obstacles in lifting the transport restrictions on the understanding, however, that transport and trade restrictions introduced by the three powers should be lifted simultaneously.

The Department of State noted as possibly significant that Stalin had made no mention of the currency question, the issue on which the long and futile negotiations in Moscow, Berlin, and the United Nations had centered. The Secretary of State, Dean Acheson, consulted with President Truman and with the latter's concurrence stated in a press conference on February 2 that

there are many ways in which a serious proposal by the Soviet Government to restore normal inter-zonal communications and communications with and within Berlin could be made. All channels are open for any suggestions to that end. The United States, together with the other Western occupying powers, would, of course, consider carefully any proposal made to solve the Berlin problem consistent with their rights, their duties and their obligations as occupying powers.[29]

Hearing of the department's interest, the U.S. chargé d'affaires in Moscow, Foy Kohler, repeated his earlier analysis sent to the Department of State on January 30, that "Stalin's reply simply goes back to the Kremlin's initial objectives last summer. . . . Currency problem and blockade could always have been solved overnight if we agreed to make concessions on West Germany satisfactory to Stalin."[30] Acheson nonetheless thought Stalin's reply merited further exploration, and presumably at his suggestion (no written documentation has been found) Dean Rusk, who was then assistant secretary of state for United Nations affairs, suggested to Ambassador Phillip Jessup, the deputy chief of the U.S. mission to the United Nations, that if a suitable occasion should arise he should sound out the Soviet side in New York. The occasion arose on February 15 when Jessup had an informal conversation in the delegates lounge at Lake Success with Soviet Ambassador Jacob Malik. Jessup asked whether Stalin's omission of reference to the currency question had any special significance. Malik said he would inquire. On March 15 he informed Jessup that "Moscow says that the omission of this reference to the currency question was 'not accidental.' " This was the beginning of the Jessup–Malik conversations that were to lay the basis for the end of the blockade.[31] The Soviet side made an effort to obtain agreement on wording that all restrictions on access to West Berlin and on travel and trade between the Western and Soviet zones "instituted after March 28, 1948," would be lifted, which would have implied that the Soviet-imposed restrictions were entirely the result of the decisions taken by the Western powers at the London foreign ministers' conference, and that there had been no earlier harassments. The Western powers insisted that the date be March 1, 1948, which the Soviet side finally accepted. The Soviet Union wished to have assurance that a West German government would not be established while the Council of Foreign Ministers was in session. The Western powers were prepared to give this assurance but without delaying the preparations for the new government. They simply said that given the timetable foreseen, it was unlikely that the new government could come into existence before July 1, 1949. It was added that the establishment of a government in western Germany "does not preclude Four-Power agreement whereby a government for the whole of Germany could be established and the three governments will make a sincere endeavor to ascertain whether there is a real prospect of agreement among the Four Powers."[32] This, too, was accepted and on May 5, 1949, the Four Powers issued a communiqué announcing that:

1. On May 12, 1949, all the restrictions imposed since March 1, 1948, on communications, transportation, and trade between Berlin and the Western zones of Germany and between the Eastern zone and the Western zones would be removed.

2. On the same day all the restrictions imposed since March 1, 1948, by the United States, France, and Britain, or any one of them, on communications, transportation, and trade between Berlin and the Eastern zone and between the Western and Eastern zones would be removed.

3. A meeting of the Council of Foreign Ministers would be convened on May 23, 1949, in Paris to consider questions relating to Germany, and problems arising out of the situation in Berlin, including the question of currency.

The military governors in Berlin were given the task of lifting the restrictions. A great deal of attention was devoted to complications connected with the resumption of trade between the Western zones and the East. Many orders had been placed and paid for before the dual currency reforms. Moreover, during the blockade the Western powers had established lists of products of potential military value, of which the shipment to the East was prohibited. They intended to maintain this restriction notwithstanding the wording of the communiqué. With regard to Berlin, the task was simply to establish what had been the practice as of March 1, 1948. This was to prove an impossible task.

When the military governors had met in September 1948 after the Moscow conversations with Stalin to try to find a solution to the crisis, General Clay, in summarizing the situation that had prevailed prior to March 1, stated:

In March our military passenger trains carried Americans and non-Germans who had been approved for visits to Berlin . . . the only restriction was in an understanding which I had with Marshal Sokolovsky that only Germans working directly for U.S. would be carried on these trains. The removal of restrictions, therefore, for train travel meant to me the return to this condition. At the time the restrictions were imposed, there were no restrictions on airlift and therefore it was not subject to discussion. I was prepared to have a German inspection service, under quadripartite supervision, inspect all German cargo and passengers [moving by surface] to enforce such regulations with respect to movement of goods and currencies that might be agreed, [and] I was further prepared to provide a passenger list for each military train movement and to provide my own inspection service to see that this passenger list was checked and that any regulations which may be agreed with respect to currency and goods was enforced. I stated I was prepared to make the same arrangements for air.[33]

On September 8, 1948, Sokolovsky gave his interpretation of what a return to March would mean: all restrictions imposed on rail and autobahn transport since March 30 would be removed. Rail and highway travel would be via Helmstedt–Berlin routes. Sixteen train paths would be provided daily, of which three would be military. Military personnel, families, and civilian members of military administration could be carried in military trains and use the autobahn subject to producing indentification cards (which, General Clay noted, would mean trains were subject to Soviet inspection). German employees were not to be carried on military trains. Military trains would carry supplies for the occupying powers, and the train commander would present waybills of food and coal with licenses to be produced for commercial cargo.[34]

Given the differences and lack of clarity in this 1948 exchange, difficulties in reaching agreement in 1949 (among the same military governors) were inevitable. In the process of seeking such agreement the Western powers retreated substantially from their original contention as to what a return to the situation prevailing on March 1, 1948 meant.

The following is the text of a paper on rail and water access tabled by the three Western military governors at a quadripartite meeting on May 30, 1949, in the effort to send an agreed report of the four military governors to the council of foreign ministers:

1. Goods consigned to the Western sectors of Berlin from the Western zones will require only interzonal trade permits (*Warenbegleitscheine*) from the appropriate authorities of the Western zones, or in the case of occupation traffic, military warrant or such other documentation as may be established by the Western authorities concerned.

2. Goods consigned to the Western zones from the Western sectors of Berlin will require only an interzonal trade permit (*Warenbegleitschein*) from the *Magistrat* in the Western sectors, or in case of Allied freight, the normal documentation of the Allied authorities of the Western sectors.

3. The documentation provided in accordance with paras 1 and 2 shall be accepted by the competent Soviet zone authorities at all border crossing points between the Soviet zone and the U.S./UK zones and between the Soviet zone and the Western sectors of Berlin as full authorization for the free passage of the goods so documented.

4. Rail traffic to and from Berlin may pass the Soviet zone border at Helmstedt, Buchen, Oebisfelde, Hof and Probstzella as was the case before 1st March 48, and at such other points as may become available.

5. In accordance with practice prevailing before 1st March 48, the number of allied military and *Kommandatura* trains to Berlin, which may pass daily through the Soviet zone over the above crossing points, shall be not less than 25, of which 5 will be accomodated on passenger schedules. These trains are in addition to normal German commercial rail traffic between the Western zones and Berlin, which is not limited.

6. The Western occupying powers shall be responsible for the provision of locomotives and crews to haul the trains for Allied and occupational traffic through the Soviet zone. Locomotives and crews of the Soviet zone will not be used for this purpose.

7. The directions of the Western occupying powers to the Reichsbahn regarding the handling of their rail traffic within the Western sectors shall be given directly to the Reichsbahn and not through intermediaries of the SMA (Soviet Military Administration), or other authority, and shall be carried out by the Reichsbahn.

8. Railway wagons requested by shippers of Western sectors of Berlin for outgoing shipment of goods to the Western zones shall be provided to the shippers immediately and in any case within 24 hours after submission of request to the Reichsbahn.

9. Certificates authorizing the operation in the Soviet zone of IWT [Interzonal Water Transport] craft from the Western zones shall be issued on the same basis as on 1 March 48. The submission of crew lists in connection with the issuance of such certificates is therefore not necessary. Applications for such certificates shall be finally acted upon by the Soviet authorities within seven days of their submission to the Soviet authorities. All waterways in the Soviet zone will be open to IWT craft carrying these documents.

10. The above arrangements are subject to modifications arising from decisions of the CFM.

The Soviet military governor immediately accused his Western colleagues of "arbitrarily injecting new points."[35] On June 13 the Western military governors reported to the Western delegations at Paris "their impression" that the Soviet military administration would pursue the following courses[36]:

(a) Rail traffic to and from Berlin will be handled via Helmstedt, but authorization for the use of other crossing points for specific movements may be given.

(b) Nineteen trains will be scheduled for daily operation via Helmstedt into Berlin from the Western zones.

(c) Locomotives and crews for the movement of these trains through the Soviet zone will be provided by the Reichsbahn of the Soviet zone following usual railway operating procedures.

(d) Requests of the Western Occupation Powers regarding the handling of their railway traffic within the Western sectors will be made to the Reichsbahn representatives with simultaneous notification to the SMA [Soviet Military Administration] rail representative.

(e) Railway wagons for shipments out of Berlin will be provided promptly by the Reichsbahn. The SMA has issued instructions that wagons sent to Berlin from the Western zones shall be returned promptly, and will not be diverted for use in the Soviet zone.

(f) Certificates permitting the operation of IWT [Interzonal Water Transport] craft of the Western zones in the Soviet zone will be issued promptly by the SMA. The SMA will require the submission of full crew lists before issuing such certificates, but will recognize later amendments to such crew lists as authorized by the Western Occupation Powers.

(g) Road traffic will be authorized to move in accordance with practices in effect on 1st March 1948.[37]

The foreign ministers in Paris were no more successful than the military governors in reaching a written understanding defining the conditions of access to the Western sectors. Somewhat surprisingly, the Americans for the first (and last) time formally proposed that "the Western Powers operate and maintain the Autobahn from Helmstedt to Berlin."[38] Soviet Foreign Minister Vyshinsky interrupted to ask that the translation of this part of Secretary Acheson's presentation be repeated. The secretary of state subsequently handed him a memorandum incorporating this idea, along with the proposal that the occupation authorities, yet once again, negotiate an agreement on the details of access. Mr. Vyshinsky ignored the autobhan suggestion and proposed that instead of negotiating a new agreement the occupation authorities, "each in its zone," undertake "to take measures for ensuring the normal functioning of the rail, water and road transport and that of the postal, telephone and telegraph communications."[39] It was Vyshinsky's wording that was incorporated in the final communiqué of the Council of Foreign Ministers meeting, although it was also stated that the occupation authorities would consult together in Berlin on facilitation of the movement of persons and goods and the exchange of information between the Western zones and the Eastern zone and between Berlin and the zones.

The foreign ministers were even less successful in restoring the quadripartite administration of Berlin and the unity of the city. The Western powers wished to retain quadripartite control only in restricted fields, delegating wide authority to the German municipal government for the city's administration. The Soviet side insisted that most fields be reserved to the *Kommandatura* and that all actions of the city government be subject to the veto of any one of the four commandants. The discussion of currency was hardly serious. By this time the Western powers were not really interested in a solution that would place West Berlin in the East mark area, even if the original Western conditions were met. Since the Soviet representatives did not offer to do this, the Western powers were not put to the test. In sum, with regard to Berlin the Paris meeting of the Council of Foreign Ministers simply (a) reconfirmed the New York agreement on lifting the blockade without defining the status of access that the lifting of restrictions would restore; and (b) clarified beyond any real doubt that there was no prospect of restoring Berlin's unity.

Recognizing that the Berlin situation was likely to remain highly unsatisfactory, the Western powers, during the course of the conference, began a process that had been completely lacking in the pre-blockade period. They undertook contingency planning for a recurrence of restrictions on access. Over the years these plans were to assume elaborate proportions. Planning was begun for stockpiling essential supplies in West Berlin, and Secretary Acheson put forward the idea of a probe by Western military forces should Allied access be obstructed. On June 17, 1949, President Truman approved the following formulation:

Traffic to Berlin would not be halted by the Western Powers on a mere administrative order or notification by the Soviets that movement would not be permitted; vehicles would continue to attempt to transit the corridor until confronted by a physical barrier, an armed guard, or other evidence of force; and we should make no show of force such as 'mounting an armed convoy on the highway.'[40]

Where Did This Leave Things?

Since no agreed definition was achieved of what access procedures and agreements were in effect on March 1, 1948, both sides were left to interpret in their own way the meaning of the lifting of all restrictions imposed since March 1, 1948. The effective means of control being in Soviet rather than Western hands, the Soviet interpretation tended to prevail. Thus while it is demonstrably true that prior to March 1, 1948 Allied trains were pulled to and from Berlin by West German engines and crews, this was not to happen again after the blockade was lifted. The Americans no longer sought to transport Germans, even if they were employed in an official capacity, in U.S. military trains. The extra train paths and routes that had been informally agreed by local military authorities in the early days of occupation were not restored. The requirement for the submission of crew lists to Soviet zonal authorities in order to obtain certificates of operation for Western barges in the Soviet zone was retained. None of these blockade "holdovers" proved particularly onerous, although the necessary reliance on East German locomotives and crews was a source of considerable difficulties in subsequent periods of access harassment.

In comparison with these relatively limited losses the wording of the Four

Power communiqué ending the blockade was a very large achievement. It constituted the first comprehensive quadripartite agreement on unhindered access to Berlin, since access prior to March 1, 1948 was relatively unhindered within the agreed routes. Henceforth the Three Powers could cite the New York and Paris communiqués as a Soviet commitment to abide by the practices and procedures in effect on March 1, whether or not they had been the subject of formal quadripartite agreements. This proved of enormous importance in the ensuing years.

If the manner in which the blockade was ended came close to restoring the status quo ante in terms of Berlin access, it did nothing at all to restore Greater Berlin as an area of joint quadripartite administration, something, as we have seen, that had been actually provided for in a written agreement among the occupying powers. The Paris communiqué made the gesture of referring the subject back to the military governors; but the lack of conviction was apparent. Neither side was really interested in the restoration of a united Berlin administration under conditions that the other could even remotely be expected to accept. Thus while the end of the blockade marked the preservation of quadripartite agreement that access to Berlin remained a responsibility of the Four Powers, it ended the agreement that they had a similar responsibility for the unity of the city. Berlin was a very different place at the end of the blockade than it had been at the beginning. The *Kommandatura* was never to function again on a Four Power basis and the division of the city was to deepen.

Why Did It Happen?

The Berlin blockade not only dramatized the division of Berlin, but also the division of Germany. The Soviet government maintained then, as it does now, that the interference with access was intended to prevent the dismemberment of Germany by dissuading the Western powers from proceeding with the establishment of a separate West German state in contravention to the Potsdam Agreements. At the time U.S. officials were quite clear in their own minds as to the nature of Soviet intentions. In his memoirs, President Truman writes:

General Lucius Clay later blamed himself for not having insisted on a confirmation of the agreement [on access] in writing. It is my opinion that it would have made very little difference to the Russians whether or not there was an agreement in writing. What was at stake in Berlin was not a contest over legal rights, although our position was entirely sound under international law, but a struggle over Germany, and in a larger sense, over Europe. In the face of our launching of the Marshall Plan, the Kremlin tried to mislead the people of Europe into believing that our interest and support would not extend beyond economic matters and that we would back away from any military risks. What the Russians were trying to do was to get us out of Berlin.[41]

The Department of State's perception of Soviet intentions as stated in a briefing paper prepared for the Council of Foreign Ministers Paris meeting was similar although stated somewhat differently: "The ultimate Soviet objective in Germany is complete economic and political domination. The immediate prerequisite to the attainment of this objective is the prevention of West Germany's integration into the economic and political structure of Western Europe."[42] Nothing has emerged during the past thirty years that would discredit this analysis. Pending the opening of Soviet archives it seems reasonable to make the following further assumptions concerning Soviet objectives that led to the blockade:

1. For Moscow, the first priority after the defeat of Germany was to ensure that the part of Europe that had come under its military control would remain associated with the Soviet Union both ideologically and politically. This included the Soviet zone of Germany. (Only in Austria did this policy eventually change.)

2. In agreeing at Potsdam that Germany should be administered as an economic unit, the Soviets were thinking largely in terms of Germany as a reparations pool with greater assets in the West than in the East and as an area of commonly shared control of German economic potential, especially the Ruhr.

3. The potential of Germany as an element of power in Europe was clearly perceived, but this had to be weighed against the immediate requirement of seizing every available German resource for the reconstruction of the devastated Soviet economy. The latter came first, and this brought the Soviets into conflict with the United States and Britain and compromised the attractiveness of close association with the Soviet Union in the eyes of most Germans.

4. The Soviet leadership had no special interest in German unity *per se*, but they had a strong interest in preventing the accretion of German potential to the strength of the Western community. An ineffective Four Power administration of Germany served this objective and gave the Soviet Union time to consolidate a communist-dominated economic and political structure in the Soviet zone.

5. U.S. and British plans first to join their zones in an economic union and then, with the French, to form a West German state threatened to produce exactly what Moscow did not want. The only effective lever available to prevent this was Berlin.

6. The Soviet Union therefore gradually imposed restrictions, seeking to make clear that the Western powers could not expect to remain in Berlin under the wartime agreements if they proceeded with the separate economic and political development of the Western zones. The Soviets recognized the separate Western currency reform to be of crucial importance in this development.

7. The at times ambivalent Soviet attitude during the blockade resulted from their recognition that they might not be able to prevent the creation of a separate Western-oriented German state, or even, short of war, to force the Western powers out of Berlin. They had, therefore, to prepare for the contingency that the Western powers would remain at least for an indefinite while in the city. This required isolating Western influence to the extent possible from the area of Soviet control, including East Berlin. The destruction of the democratic (and in Soviet eyes therefore Western-oriented) united city government was essential to ensure this minimum requirement. Thus while pressure through access blockage,

demonstrations, and arrests in the Western sectors was imposed first in the hope (probably early abandoned) of preventing a West German state, and second with the intention (which the airlift foiled) of forcing the Western Allies out of Berlin, action was pursued to split the city administration in order, if the other objectives failed, that the Soviet sector would be under full Soviet control and the influence of the Western Allies and the Western-oriented city administration severely circumscribed outside the Western Sectors.

Since most of the documentation concerning the development of U.S. policy is now in the public domain, the reasons why Washington, together with its British and French allies, acted as it did in the period leading up to and during the blockade are fairly clear. It can first be confirmed that Washington, despite its earlier advocacy of dismemberment, entered into the occupation of Germany committed to the restoration of a united German state, especially for economic reasons. One of the U.S. briefing papers for the Potsdam Conference stated, for example,

The economy of Eastern Germany can be readily assimilated into an Eastern economic sphere. In contrast, acceptance by the Western Powers of the task of finding a place for a Western German economy would create extreme difficulties and would greatly intensify the post-war economic problems of the United States, Great Britain and Western Europe.[43]

President Truman was personally opposed to dismemberment. Thus, while the Americans recognized that the zonal organization constituted a kind of division, which U.S. military authorities found convenient, the Americans left Potsdam in the belief that the way had been prepared for the reestablishment of a central German administration. At the same time, the Americans, always mindful of their experience after World War I, were determined that they would not bear the full economic burden of supporting a devastated Germany. This intensified as they saw the Soviets trying to take reparations from current production, which meant that the United States would, in effect, be subsidizing the Soviet Union. The clearer it became that Germany would remain an economic burden as long as economic reform was dependent on Four Power agreement in the Control Council and that without recovery in Germany a healthy Western European economy would not be possible, the more the Americans were attracted to the independent economic and political development of the area of Germany under Western control. By mid–1947 Washington had reached the conclusion that the recovery of Western Europe required the restoration of a productive, self-sustaining economy in West Germany and this became the U.S. goal. While the United States consistently maintained that the establishment of a West German state need not interfere with eventual Four Power agreement on a unified German state, beginning in 1947 priority was clearly given to the former. George Kennan stated that "we will not favor a united Germany in a divided Europe,"[44] but Kennan was perennially skeptical as to whether German unity would be in the best interests of Europe. The U.S. philosophy was probably best stated in the following sentences from a memorandum drafted by Dean Acheson in May 1949:

Our major premise is that our concern is with the future of Europe and not with Germany as a problem by itself. We are concerned with the integration of Germany into a free and democratic Europe. . . . Just as the unification of Germany is not an end in itself, so the division of Germany is not an end in itself.[45]

When plans moved forward from the economic union of the British and U.S. zones, to a Western currency reform and a West German political structure, U.S. officials were conscious that the Soviets might, in retaliation, step up their pressure against the Western position in Berlin. (Why they prepared no contingency plans remains unfathomable.) When the pressure came, the policy of the Western powers was determined, as Mr. Acheson put it, neither by the objective of preserving or destroying the option of German unity, but rather by the objective of developing a stable, economically prosperous Western Europe that could resist communist domination. General Clay's strongest argument to President Truman was that if the United States abandoned Berlin all of Western Europe would be lost. The major U.S. concern when the end of the blockade seemed in sight was that nothing should be done in the negotiations with the Soviets that might prejudice the development of the West German state.

When viewed in this perspective the Western side dealt successfully with the challenge posed by the blockade. They retained their position in Berlin, gained for the first time a written commitment on access, and the Federal Republic became a major element in the restoration of Western Europe and the development of the Atlantic alliance. But the Soviets achieved the definitive consolidation of their control in East Berlin and East Germany and ensured that East Germany would remain firmly within the communist-controlled area of Europe.

NOTES

1. Lucius D. Clay, *Decision in Germany* (New York: Doubleday and Co., 1950), p. 115.

2. The author of this chapter was vice-counsul in Berlin at the time, having arrived in October 1946 in the U.S. military train and experienced one of those Soviet military inspections to which General Clay took exception. In mid–1947 the Danish-American tenor Lauritz Melchior came to Berlin with the endorsement of several important U.S. officials, determined to look into the condition of a hunting estate that he had owned in what was now the Soviet zone. With great difficulty, telephone contact was established with the Soviet consulate general, which was located in Karlshorst (also the location of the Soviet military administration) and an appointment was made for Mr. Melchoir to see the Soviet consul general. Sutterlin accompanied him in a U.S. consular car, with a German driver who knew the way. They were stopped repeatedly by Soviet soldiers and finally, on entering Karlshorst, a young soldier halted the car with drawn automatic carbine. Efforts to explain their mission in German were without effect and the young,

rather disheveled soldier opened the door of the car and forced his way in, with the carbine pressing against the ample flank of Mr. Melchior, who kept protesting in Wagnerian German that he had "sung for the Russian troops." The Russian soldier only left the car when it finally reached the consular office. There the consul general professed total ignorance of any appointment and showed no understanding of why they had come. He did agree to look into Mr. Melchoir's problem and suggested that he return the next day. When the two returned after a less perilous trip, they were shown into the same office only to be confronted by a different Soviet official who said he knew nothing of the case or of the previous call. Despite its comic overtones, this incident illustrates the distinctly non-Allied relationship which prevailed outside the limited circle of Control Council and Allied *Kommandatura* officials from the beginning of the Berlin occupation.

3. The full text may be found in *Documents on Germany, 1944–1970*, Senate Committee on Foreign Relations, May 17, 1971, p. 59ff.

4. The foreign ministers of France, Britain, the Soviet Union, and the United States, who were to meet periodically to deal with postwar settlements.

5. *Documents on Germany, 1944–1970*, p. 86.

6. Ibid., p. 91.

7. Ibid., pp. 92–93.

8. Texts of the Dratvin–Gailey correspondence are in *The Berlin Crisis: A Report on the Moscow Discussions 1948* (Washington, D.C.: Department of State publication 3298, 1949), pp. 1–6.

9. The U.S. commandant. He had left the previous fruitless meeting at 11 p.m., leaving his deputy in charge, an action that earned General Clay's displeasure.

10. Quoted in a telegram from Murphy to Secstate. *Foreign Relations of the United States of America, 1948*, Vol. 2 (Washington, D.C.: Dept. of State), pp. 930–31.

11. Descriptions of the situation in late October and in mid-December may be found in *OMGUS Weekly Intelligence, no. 128*, 23 October 1948, and in a memorandum of 13 December 1948 from the acting secretary of the army to General Wedemeyer (Washington, D.C.: Department of Army Archives).

12. DA-TT–9667, June 25, 1947, (Washington, D.C.: Department of State archives).

13. *Truman Memoirs*, Vol. 2 (Garden City, N.Y.: Doubleday, 1955), pp. 122–23.

14. See the papers of George Elsey, Special Assistant to Secretary of Defense Forrestal, The Truman Library, Independence, MO, File (R)304A, pp. 27–34.

15. Clay's proposal is contained in CINCEUR Message CC–5118, quoted in *Foreign Relations of the United States of America, 1948*, Vol. 2, pp. 956–58.

16. On July 28, 1948, the secretary of defense informed the secretary of state by letter that the joint chiefs did not recommend an effort to supply Berlin by armed convoy, "in view of the risk of war involved and the inadequacy of U.S. preparation for global war." *Foreign Relations of the United States of America, 1948*, Vol. 2, p. 944.

17. The use of the term "two sides" would be inaccurate if it implied consistent unity among the three Western powers on how to deal with the Berlin crisis. However, on questions of the status of Berlin and of the rights and responsibilities of the Allies, the British, French, and Americans were united. In this limited framework, it is accurate to refer to "the two sides," as will frequently be done.

18. Recorded somewhat differently by Ambassador Murphy and General Parks, both of whom were present.

19. 740.00019 Control (Germany)/11–547 (Washington, D.C.: Department of State archives).

20. The March 20 meeting is not identified but presumably was in East Berlin. See 740.00119 (Germany)/4–548, Box C–162 (Washington, D.C.: Department of State archives).

21. *Foreign Relations of the United States, 1948*, Vol. 2, p. 910.

22. Texts of exchange are in *Documents on Germany, 1944–1970*, pp. 104–110.

23. Quoted in a telegram of August 9, 1948, from the U.S. embassy Moscow to the secretary of state. *Foreign Relations of the United States, 1948*, Vol. 2, p. 1024.

24. For the text see *The Berlin Crisis, A Report on the Moscow Discussions* (Washington, D.C.: Department of State publication 3258, 1948), p. 27.

25. Ibid., p. 48.

26. *Foreign Relations of the United States, 1948*, Vol. 2, p. 1168.

27. Full texts of the exchange may be found in *The Berlin Crisis*, pp. 44–61.

28. A French airline with part West German ownership received Allied authorization in November 1988 for flights between Berlin and West Germany.

29. For texts and references to further source material see *Foreign Relations of the United States, 1949*, Vol. 3, pp. 666–67.

30. Moscow 261 to secretary of state February 2. *Foreign Relations of the United States*, Vol. 2, pp. 667–68.

31. Ambassador Jessup's reports of the conversations are quoted in *Foreign Relations of the United States, 1949*, Vol. 3, beginning on p. 694.

32. Ibid., p. 736.

33. Ibid., p. 1120.

34. Ibid., p. 1136.

35. Ibid., pp. 801–3.

36. *Foreign Relations of the United States of America, 1944*, Vol. 3, pp. 815–16.

37. It should be noted that a strike of Reichsbahn workers in West Berlin that began with the lifting of the blockade because of payment questions connected with the dual currency situation made it impossible to assess the effect on railroad traffic of the lifting of Soviet restrictions. The strike did not end until June 26.

38. *Foreign Relations of the United States of America, 1944*, Vol. 3, p. 987.

39. Ibid., p. 1053.

40. Ibid., p. 836.

41. *Truman Memoirs*, Vol. 2, pp. 122–23.

42. *Foreign Relations of the United States of America, 1949*, Vol. 2, p. 909.

43. *Foreign Relations of the United States of America, 1945: The Conference of Berlin*, p. 440.

44. *Foreign Relations, 1949*, Vol. 3, p. 861.

45. Ibid., p. 872.

3

The Khrushchev Years and the Next Crisis

The inauguration of the Eisenhower administration in Washington in January 1953, followed by the death of Stalin in Moscow almost 60 days later, created political uncertainty and ushered in a period of reassessment on both sides. John Foster Dulles, the newly appointed secretary of state and principal foreign policy spokesperson for the Eisenhower government, had already suggested that U.S. foreign policy would seek a rollback and liberation rather than the containment of communist influence in Eastern Europe. In Moscow there was political disarray and no assurance that turmoil could be avoided in the Soviet Union and its satellites. A collective leadership emerged with Malenkov *seemingly* in the top positions as Premier and First Secretary as Stalin's designated successor. The U.S. ambassador in Moscow, Charles E. Bohlen, mistakenly concluded that he would remain the decisive figure in the leadership. But by replacing Malenkov in the post of first secretary in the Communist party of the Soviet Union, Nikita Khrushchev obtained control of the levers of power that would make him Stalin's real successor.

Initially the conduct of the collective leadership on the international scene was careful and circumspect, seemingly reflecting more the inclinations of Malenkov than of Khrushchev. The new leadership's first attention was understandably devoted to gaining effective control of the government and party machinery. Clear signals were sent that the new regime would use all its resources to preserve full control of subject lands and peoples. Berlin, the perennial area of contention between the Soviet Union and the Western powers, provided one of the first tests of will and intentions for the new Soviet leadership.

What began as a series of protests by residents of East Germany against the prevailing living conditions on June 17, 1953, suddenly, erupted as a full-scale rebellion in East Berlin—in the open sight of Western observers. Responding to the challenge and determined to contain its consequences, the Soviet authorities applied substantial military force.

The Soviet action resulted not only in large numbers of German casualties but also in a series of measures intended to cauterize the political situation by separating the two parts of the divided city of Berlin more effectively through the erection of physical barriers. When order was restored in East Germany, Soviet power was clearly fully in place. In the protests issued by both sides regarding the situation, the words were strong but carefully selected. The Western commandants in Berlin on June 17, 1953, in a communication to their Soviet counterpart, condemned "the irresponsible [Soviet] recourse to military force which had as its result the killing or serious wounding of a considerable number of citizens of Berlin, including some from our own sectors." They also protested arbitrary measures that "resulted in the interruption of traffic between the sectors and free circulation throughout Berlin" and called for the immediate lifting of "harsh restrictions" and the reestablishment of "free circulation within Berlin."

On June 20, 1953, in his reply the Soviet commandant told his Western colleagues that the measures taken were needed to "curtail the burnings and other disturbances caused by groups of provocateurs and fascist agents from the Western sectors of Berlin who were sent here." He went on to ask how the three Western powers would have responded if *agents provocateurs* had been sent out from East Berlin to set fires, conduct pogroms, commit murders and other disturbances, and instigate other acts of violence in West Berlin?

As for the reestablishment of communication between the two parts of the city, the Soviet commandant saw no "hindrances either as to transport or other communication . . . on the condition that the [Western] Commandants . . . take all the measures necessary to guarantee the curtailment of forays by provocateurs and other criminal elements onto the territory of East Berlin."[1]

German Chancellor Konrad Adenauer's appeal to President Eisenhower of June 21, 1953 was also couched in careful language. He asked the U.S. government "to do everything in its power to do away with the conditions that caused the revolt, that the human rights which have been violated may be restored and the entire German people may be given back the unity and freedom which alone guarantee a lasting peaceful development in Europe."[2] Responding, President Eisenhower told the chancellor that the events in East Berlin and East Germany had "stirred the hearts and hopes of people." He went on to assure the chancellor that the U.S. government was convinced that a way could and must be found "to satisfy the just aspirations of the German people for freedom and unity . . . on the basis of free elections as we urged the Soviets to agree in the notes of September 23, 1952."[3] The Western Allies did not seek to use the occasion to press back the frontier of Soviet control, and the Soviet Union did not threaten retaliation for alleged Western subversion. Clearly both sides preferred to avoid the risks of armed confrontation or of undoing the status quo already implicit in the agreement of 1949 ending the Berlin blockade. For the Soviet side, there presumably remained, also, the continuing hope that the divided city could continue to provide Moscow with possibly useful political leverage on the Western powers in dealing with other East–West issues.

Against the backdrop of the East German uprising and of the political changes in Moscow and Washington, the Western powers on July 14, 1953 again proposed a meeting of the Four Powers on "first steps to lead to a satisfactory solution of the German problem."[4] (The Soviet Union had not responded to an earlier proposal in 1952.) It took Moscow six months and thirteen notes to agree to confer in Berlin beginning January 25, 1954. An early indication of the probable Soviet position was Moscow's insistence that the conference site be rotated between the Allied Control Authority building in West Berlin and the Soviet embassy to the German Democratic Republic in East Berlin, thus emphasizing that the existence of the GDR would have to be taken into account.

After twenty days of difficult and inconclusive meetings, the four foreign ministers issued a communiqué, the final paragraph of which stated: "The four Ministers have had a full exchange of views on the German question, on the problems of European security and on the Austrian question. They were unable to reach agreement on these matters."[5]

The following day the three Western foreign ministers issued their own communiqué, which stated among other things that

The major problem facing the Berlin Conference was that of Germany. The three Western delegations urged that the reunification of Germany should be achieved through free elections, leading to the creation of an all-German government with which a peace treaty could be concluded. They put forward a practical plan to this end. Their proposals were not accepted by the Soviet delegation, even as a basis for discussion and they were forced to the conclusion that the Soviet government was not ready to permit free all-German elections or to abandon its control over East Germany.[6]

Reporting to the American people over radio and television five days later, U.S. Secretary of State John Foster Dulles said, "As far as Europe was concerned, we brought Mr. Molotov to show Russia's hand. It was seen as a hand that held fast to everything it had, including East Germany."[7] For its part, the Soviet Union, which during the conference had proposed a peace treaty providing for a united, neutral, and demilitarized Germany, on March 25, 1954 issued a statement attributing "full sovereignty" to the German Democratic Republic.[8]

Over the next three years, as intermittent harassment on the access routes, including Allied military movements, persisted, the Western powers, now joined by the Federal Republic of Germany, repeatedly proposed the reunification of Germany on the basis of free elections. The Soviet Union supported, instead, the suggestion put forward by Walter Ulbricht for a confederation of the two German states and the plan developed by Polish Foreign Minister Rapacki for a demilitarized zone in Central Europe. More importantly for the future course of events, diplomatic relations were established between the Federal Republic of Germany and the Soviet Union on September 13, 1955.

On February 28, 1958 the Soviet Union proposed that a new summit meeting be held to discuss a German peace treaty and other issues. The Western powers countered on September 30, 1958, by insisting on the creation of an all-German government through free elections prior to the negotiation of a German peace treaty. Six weeks later Nikita Khrushchev, speaking at a friendship meeting in Moscow in honor of a Polish delegation headed by the then first secretary of the Polish Communist party, Wladeslaw Gomulka, bluntly charged the Western powers and Bonn with continued violations of the Potsdam Agreement, and warned:

The time has evidently come for the powers which signed the Potsdam Agreement to give up the remnants of the occupation regime in Berlin and thus make it possible to create a normal atmosphere in the capital of the German Democratic Republic. The Soviet Union, for its part, will hand over those functions which are still in the hands of Soviet organs to the sovereign German Democratic Republic. . . . Let the United States, France and Britain themselves build their own relations with the German Democratic Republic, let them reach agreement with it themselves if they are interested in any questions concerning Berlin.[9]

The Soviet Union followed up the Khrushchev pronouncement on November 27, 1958 with diplomatic notes to the three Western powers and a separate message to the Federal Republic of Germany. In its note to the Allies, the Soviet government stated:

[T]he Soviet Government regards as null and void the Protocol of the Agreement between the Governments of the Union of Soviet Socialist Republics, the United States of America, and the United Kingdom on the zones of occupation in Germany and the administration of Greater Berlin of September 12, 1944, and the related supplementary agreements including the agreement of . . . May 1, 1945. . . . Pursuant to the foregoing . . . the Soviet Government will enter into negotiations with the Government of the German Democratic Republic at an appropriate time with a view to transferring to the German Democratic Republic the functions temporarily performed by the Soviet authorities by virtue of the above-mentioned Allied agreements and under the agreement between the USSR and the GDR of September 20, 1955. . . . The Soviet Government for its part would consider it possible to solve the West Berlin question at the present time by the conversion of West Berlin into an independent political unit—a free city which could have its own government, run its own economic, administrative, and other affairs.

Having made a variety of charges and threats, the Soviet note then went on to say:

At the same time the Soviet Government is prepared to enter into negotiations with the Governments of the United States of America and with those of the other states concerned on granting West Berlin the status of a free city. The Soviet Government moreover hopes the necessary change in Berlin's situation takes place in a cool atmosphere without hostile and unnecessary friction, with maximum possible consideration for the interests of the parties concerned. . . . The Soviet Government proposes to make no changes in the present procedure in military traffic of the United States of America, Great Britain and France for half a year. If the above-mentioned period is not utilized to reach an adequate agreement, the Soviet Union will then carry out planned measures through an agreement with the German Democratic Republic.[10]

A new Berlin crisis had begun. Reacting to the Soviet demands, the foreign ministers of the three Western governments, after meeting in Paris together with the foreign minister of the FRG and the governing mayor of Berlin, publicly affirmed on December 14, 1958 their determination "to maintain their position and rights with respect to Berlin, including the right of free access." They "found unacceptable a unilateral repudiation by the Soviet Government of its obligations." In their formal replies delivered to the Soviets on December 31, 1958, the three Western governments stated they were not prepared "to give up or in any way endanger their rights in Berlin or the rights of the Berliners." However, they were prepared "in an atmosphere devoid of coercion or threats to discuss Berlin in the wider framework of negotiations for the solution of the German problem as well as that of European security."[11]

While many Allied officials were exercised by the Soviet challenge, which became known as the "Khrushchev ultimatum," President Eisenhower remained fairly relaxed. In a meeting with General Twining, the then chairman of the joint chiefs of staff, the president stressed the need to avoid overreaction. Eisenhower said the United States must address the problem in terms not of six months but of forty years. During this time the Soviets would attempt continually to throw the Allies off balance. "The Soviets," he said, "would like for the U.S. to become frantic every time Moscow created difficulties." He therefore considered "it essential for the United States to carry on with existing programs to assure deterrence. And while he understood the need to consider the possibility of miscalculation, he questioned the need, or indeed the desirability, of any crash measures."[12]

Elaborating on this theme at a subsequent cabinet meeting, President Eisenhower referred to Khrushchev's ultimatum on Berlin as "an incident in a continuing series." "The United States," he said,

must rely on a long range plan, looking to the continuation of the Cold War for the next twenty, thirty, forty or however more years. . . . The Russians [in Berlin] had the advantage of pressing the issue by doing nothing instead of engaging in some overt action. Hence the United States had to be careful to avoid doing anything that could be regarded as aggressive.

"The United States," he stressed, "had to stand firm even should the situation come down to the last and ultimate decision," although neither he (nor the State Department) believed it would ever be allowed to go to that terrible climax. The president thought the cabinet should not regard this as the beginning of the end, nor should it think it possible to end tension by walking away from it. This would cause "the destruction of . . . peace." The president said that in his view, "There was good reason to believe that the Russians did not want war, especially since they had, in their view, reason to think they were winning under present developments short of war."[13]

In a subsequent discussion, Eisenhower told his advisers:

To keep our Allies together, we must hold to a positive position and follow it through no matter whether the strain in any particular moment happens to be acute in Berlin or elsewhere. The easiest thing in the world is to confuse strength with bad deportment. We must always emphasize strength and yet always hold out the hand of friendship, otherwise the world is liable to run away from us.

The president also "advised of his belief that hostilities will not ensue . . . [for] should hostilities begin, the Soviets know that they will suffer unacceptable damage." The president on this occasion suggested that an invitation to Khrushchev was "still a possible ace in the hole in dealing with the Berlin crisis."[14]

THE GENEVA CONFERENCE

The Khrushchev ultimatum eventually produced the 1959 Four Power foreign ministers conference in Geneva. There, after spending considerable time arguing about seating arrangements for the two German delegations (which eventually were seated two pencil widths away from the main conference table, to reflect the difference in status and responsibility between the Four Powers and the two German governments), the two sides talked past each other on the substance of the German problem, including Berlin. The Western Peace Plan, an updated version of the earlier Eden Plan for German reunification and European security first introduced at the 1954 Berlin conference of foreign ministers, was tabled at the very outset of the conference by the new U.S. secretary of state, Christian Herter.[15] It was promptly rejected by the Soviets. Instead, the Soviet side reiterated its call for an immediate peace treaty with a divided Germany and for the withdrawal of all protective forces from West Berlin.[16] No basis for agreement could be found. However, despite its lack of concrete achievements, the conference provided the possibility for the Soviet Union to delay the deadline for implementing its 1958 "ultimatum," thus serving to defuse the Berlin crisis. The fact that the conference took place at all, and perhaps more importantly that it was followed by Khrushchev's meeting with Eisenhower in the United States in the fall of 1959, enabled the Soviet Union to back away from its initial positions without unacceptable loss of face. Secretary Herter reported to President Eisenhower from the conference on June 25, 1959 that "the Soviets keep stressing that the specific time set is not a matter of importance or principle, but it is intended simply to keep the present situation from dragging on indefinitely." An additional comment by Secretary Herter is of interest in light of the subsequent erection of the Berlin Wall. "The Soviets," he said, "in complaining about 'subversive' activities in West Berlin, have never mentioned the flight of the refugees to the West. They seemed too embarrassed about this.''[17]

In looking back at this period, it is worth noting that the Soviet Union did not try, during the crisis, to inject the East Germans forcibly into the West Berlin situation. In particular, they did not seek to replace Soviet military personnel by East Germans to control Allied access on the ground routes to Berlin, although there is good reason to believe the Soviet side was aware of a Western decision to accept such a change if necessary on the rationale that East German guards would be acting as agents of Soviet authorities. Perhaps this was an indication of underlying Soviet caution, or of a continuing Soviet preference to retain direct control over Allied access to Berlin.

Given the substantive failure of the Geneva conference and the still outstanding, if delayed, Khrushchev ultimatum, thought was given on the Western side to the possibility of a meeting of the heads of government of the Four Powers. In considering the matter, President Eisenhower recalled that both British Prime Minister Macmillan and Khrushchev had made statements that if no progress were made in the foreign ministers' meeting, a summit meeting would be all the more necessary. Eisenhower, however, was reluctant to agree to such an arrangement so long as the matter of the ultimatum was unresolved. The president, therefore, agreed that a summit could be held only after a satisfactory outcome of a visit by Khrushchev to the United States, an event that became of major political importance to the Soviet leader, since he would be the first head of the Soviet government to be so honored. In the words of Alexei Adzhubei, Khrushchev's son-in-law, ''The Head of the Soviet Government's accepting the invitation made it possible for . . . the Head of the government of one great power to meet the head of another.''[18] During the visit Khrushchev and Eisenhower agreed at their Camp David meetings that negotiations on Berlin would be reopened. Khrushchev promised that the Soviet Union meanwhile would take no unilateral action. The president agreed that the negotiations would not be prolonged indefinitely. Thus, in effect, the Soviet ultimatum was lifted and the way opened for the summit meeting, but further negotiations on Berlin were not to occur during the remainder of the Eisenhower administration. The Four Power summit, scheduled for Paris in May 1960, was aborted following the Soviet downing of the American U-2 aircraft flying over Soviet territory. The Soviets nonetheless chose to continue the moratorium on the Berlin ultimatum. Speaking in Berlin on May 20, 1960, en route to Moscow from Paris, Khrushchev stated that the summit conference would have to be postponed six to eight months until after the U.S. presidential elections. During that period nothing significant happened affecting Berlin.

The transition paper handed to President-elect Kennedy by President Eisenhower, dictated by Eisenhower himself, was curiously uninformative about Berlin. It only warned the incoming new chief executive of a probable early Soviet move for negotiations leading to the establishment of a ''free city'' of West Berlin, the Soviet euphemism for removing West Berlin from Western control.

It also contained cryptic advice that the best hope may lie in agreement with the Soviets on more basic issues. President Kennedy nonetheless seemingly gained the impression from President Eisenhower that the Soviet Union meant to move ahead with its intention to conclude a separate peace treaty with East Germany. This was reinforced by Khrushchev, himself, in a speech on January 6, 1961, in Moscow. The new secretary of state, Dean Rusk, warned the president a little over a week after his inauguration that Khrushchev would be returning to the Berlin question in due course. The new administration braced itself for a renewed Soviet thrust. The problem for the Kennedy government was intensified to some extent by its own activist style. There were those around President Kennedy who, critical of the Eisenhower administration's foreign policy generally, and specifically of its tactics and policy toward the Soviet Union, were convinced that urgent negotiations on Berlin were essential if peace with the Soviet Union was to be preserved. This underlay the possibly excessive attention given to the January 6 Khrushchev speech. Berlin was put at the top of the Kennedy foreign policy agenda.

Assessing the Berlin problem at that time, Ambassador Llewellyn Thompson telegraphed from Moscow on February 4, 1961:

Soviet Union [was] interested in stabilization of its Western front and Communist regimes in East Europe, particularly East Germany which probably was most vulnerable. . . . Even if the Berlin question were settled to Soviet satisfaction, problem of Germany would remain major issue between East and West. . . . In the Soviet Union, Berlin was of great importance since:

1. It is convenient and forceful means of leverage for Soviets.

2. Khrushchev's prestige personally involved.

3. Soviets under some pressure from Ulbricht regime.

4. Present situation in Berlin threatens stability of East German regime because of its use as escape route, base for espionage, and propaganda activities, etc.

Although admittedly uncertain of Khrushchev's real intentions, Thompson speculated that

if there was some activity on the German problem indicating that some real progress could be made . . . he [Khrushchev] would be disposed not to bring matters to a head. . . . If there is no progress . . . Khrushchev will almost certainly proceed with a separate peace treaty.

Positing the possibility of successful negotiations, Thompson urged a modification of the earlier Western proposals for dealing with the German problem as put forward at the Berlin and Geneva foreign ministers conferences by extending the period before free elections would be held throughout Germany.[19] The conclusion was surprising given the clear and repeated Soviet rejection of German reunification on Western terms and Thompson's own analysis of Soviet interest in stabilizing East Germany. But for a new Washington administration interested in early fruitful negotiations with the Soviet Union, Thompson's advice urging negotiations was picked up eagerly. The president himself took the initiative for a meeting with Khrushchev. On instructions from the White House, Ambassador Thompson was sent in pursuit of Khrushchev, then on a tour of Siberia, with a letter of invitation from the president suggesting a bilateral summit meeting in the late spring either in Vienna or Stockholm. Khrushchev was actually handed the message on March 9, 1961, but did not reply until May 12, 1961, after the Bay of Pigs.

The Vienna summit began on June 4, 1961. Arthur Schlesinger, Jr. wrote several years after the event that "by 1961 local considerations in East Germany were giving Khrushchev an almost desperate feeling that he had to do something."[20] Whether President Kennedy shared this particular view is not clear. He had received sounder advice from President de Gaulle, who on the eve of the meeting in Vienna told Kennedy "that Khrushchev had been threatening actions on Berlin and laying down six month deadlines for two and a half years. Surely if he had planned to go to war over Berlin he would have done so already."[21]

Khrushchev, no doubt intending to intimidate the young American president, again insisted West Berlin should become a free city. The Western occupation rights would terminate on the signing by the Soviet Union of a peace treaty with the GDR. This time, however, no specific deadline accompanied the Soviet threat. Returning from Vienna, President Kennedy reported to the American people the sober terms. With regard to the subject of Berlin he stated:

Our most somber talks were on the subject of Germany and Berlin. I made it clear to Mr. Khrushchev that the security of Western Europe and therefore our own security are deeply involved in our presence and our access rights to West Berlin, that those rights are based on law and not on sufferance, and that we are determined to maintain those rights at any risk, and thus meet our obligation to the people of West Berlin, and their right to choose their own future.

Mr. Khrushchev, in turn, presented his views in detail, and his presentation will be the subject of further communications. But we are not seeking to change the present situation. A binding German peace treaty is a matter for all who were at war with Germany, and we and our Allies cannot abandon our obligations to the people of West Berlin.

Generally, Mr. Khrushchev did not talk in terms of war. He believes the world will move his way without resort to force. He spoke of his nation's achievements in space. He stressed his intention to outdo us in industrial production, to outtrade us, to prove to the world the superiority of his system over ours.[22]

In response to the Soviet *aide-mémoire* on Berlin and Germany handed to Kennedy by Khrushchev at the Vienna meeting,[23] the president made the following public statement on July 19, 1961:

The Soviet *aide-mémoire* is a document which speaks of peace but threatens to disturb it. It speaks of ending the abnormal situation in Germany but insists on making permanent it abnormal division. It refers to the Four Power Alliance of World War II but seeks the unilateral abrogation of the rights of the other three powers. It calls for new international agreements while preparing to violate existing ones. It offers certain assurances while making it plain that previous Soviet assurances are not to be relied upon. It professes concern for the rights of the citizens of West Berlin while seeking to expose them to the immediate or eventual domination of a regime which permits no self-determination. Three simple facts are clear:

1. Today there is peace in Berlin, in Germany and in Europe. If that peace is destroyed by the unilateral actions of the Soviet Union, its leaders will bear a heavy responsibility before world opinion and history.

2. Today the people of West Berlin are free. In that sense it is already a 'free city'—free to determine its own leaders and free to enjoy the fundamental human rights reaffirmed in the United Nations Charter.

3. Today the continued presence in West Berlin of the United States, the United Kingdom and France is by clear legal right, arising from war, acknowledged in many agreements signed by the Soviet Union, and strongly supported by the overwhelming majority of the people of that city. Their freedom is dependent upon our exercise of these rights—an exercise which is thus a political and moral obligation as well as a legal right. Inasmuch as these rights, including the right of access to Berlin, are not held from the Soviet Government, they cannot be ended by any unilateral action of the Soviet Union. They cannot be affected by a so-called "peace treaty," covering only a part of Germany, with a regime of the Soviet Union's own creation—a regime which is not freely representative of all or any part of Germany, and does not enjoy the confidence of the 17 million East Germans. The steady stream of German refugees from East to West is eloquent testimony to that fact.[24]

Once again the by-now somewhat threadbare Soviet ultimatum was overtaken by events. Frightened at the prospect of being completely shut off in the near future from any possibility of leaving East Germany, East Germans fled to West Berlin in massive numbers. In response, and in continuing pursuit of the objective of ensuring the stability of the GDR as a loyal client state, the Berlin wall was constructed on August 13, 1961, as authorized by the Soviet Union. With that act, the Soviet Union pulled out its chips from the larger game, which had lasted since before the Berlin blockade, of removing from West Berlin the military presence and protection of the three Western powers.

Although the Western powers were expecting drastic communist action to stem the East German refugee flow, the draconian act of building the wall took them by surprise. There were no contingency plans for such an event. The Berlin garrison was strengthened. Otherwise, the Western reaction was largely limited to spirited but totally ineffective protests. An internal State Department memorandum prepared in conjunction with Vice President Johnnson's hurried trip to Germany after the wall's construction contained the remarkably candid statement that "in short, we have determined that our only *vital* interest is to stay where we are, and our only irrevocable commitment is to *defend the people already behind our lines*" (italics added).[25]

On August 20, 1961, in a conversation in Berlin with then Governing Mayor

The Berlin Wall. Photo courtesy of the German Information Center, New York.

Willy Brandt, just a week after East Berlin was sealed off from the West, Ambassador Charles E. Bohlen mentioned that President Kennedy took the view that apart from Vice President Lyndon Johnson's visit to West Berlin, and the strengthening of the Berlin garrison, no other actions needed to be contemplated. Additional actions, he explained, "would not bring about the un-sealing of the city. They would be unproductive and might lead only to counter-measures by the other side." Moreover, he continued, "in our [American] view, this was not the real Berlin crisis; that will come only when the Russians try to interfere with the rights of the Allied powers."[26]

The West took comfort in the belief that the wall reflected basic Soviet weakness rather than strength. Communism, far from being on the march, could only maintain its dominance by holding a people captive. Moreover, it was quickly perceived that the wall might increase stability in an otherwise volatile area, thereby reducing the risk of armed confrontation.

Former governing mayor of Berlin, Klaus Schütz, reminiscing about the wall, said at a gathering in Berlin in June 1981 that although the wall was an ugly scar in the center of Berlin, it had enabled the Western sectors to live in greater security and prosperity than anyone could have imagined twenty years before. While the wall had not really changed anything in the city—the two parts had been separated for some time—it had ended illusions in both East and West and forced the people and leaders on both sides to concentrate on improving the status quo. In Mayor Schütz's words, "German *Ostpolitik* began on August 13, 1961."[27]

Washington's comforting assumption that the building of the wall signalled the willingness of the Soviet Union to live with the political status quo in Berlin was shortly to come into doubt when the Soviet Union attempted to install nuclear weapons in Cuba aimed at the continental United States. The Kennedy administration became convinced that the challenge to the United States in Cuba in October 1962 could have implications for Berlin. The reasoning was that Soviet geographic advantage in Berlin was not unlike the U.S. geographic advantage in Cuba. Secretary of Defense Robert S. McNamara, speaking before the House of Representatives Subcommittee on Defense Appropriations on February 6, 1963, put it succinctly:

Our sharp confrontation with the Soviets in the Caribbean no doubt upset their [the Soviet] agenda for Berlin. Their stationing of nuclear armed ballistic missiles in Cuba was directly related to that agenda. The psychological if not the military threat that these missiles would have posed to our homeland was apparently the trump card which Mr. Khrushchev intended to play in the next round of negotiations on the state of Berlin.[28]

Subsequently, President Kennedy, in a note on October 23, 1962 to President Charles de Gaulle, said:

I have now had Mr. Acheson's entire report on his conversations with you and I want you to know how much I value your understanding of our position. I quite understand your comment that what we have undertaken so far may not prove to be all that is necessary in the end, but I can assure you of determination to see this matter through. I fully agree with you that there may be a particular test in Berlin, and I feel as you do that at this point we must and will all stand together.[29]

From the outset of the Cuban missile crisis, Berlin contingency planning was intensified. The Berlin contingency group under the codirection of Assistant Secretary of Defense Paul Nitze and Ambassador Llewellyn Thompson, who had been replaced in Moscow and returned to Washington in time to help the president in this crisis, was established as a subordinate part of the executive committee of the National Security Council to deal with the "Berlin–Cuba problem." This group considered not only defensive responses to possible Soviet moves against Berlin; it also worked on possible offensive actions to improve the Allied position in and around the city. It actually began to consider a proposal entailing the possible seizure of territory under East German control to establish a defensible land bridge between West Berlin and West Germany to stabilize the Western position in Berlin and to provide the means for bringing this about. The early end to the Cuban missile crisis ended that phase of Berlin contingency planning. But there was, after all, a connection between the construction of the wall and the Cuban missile crisis. Khrushchev had sought to alter the political and strategic balance in what at the time were perhaps the two most sensitive points in the world for the United States. His effort failed but it did not leave the world unchanged. In Berlin the wall delineated a status quo, which opened the possibility of a more constructive East–West relationship in Europe. In Cuba the crisis produced a new set of rules for what, as each side came to realize, must be a game without victory. Subsequently in his American University speech of June 11, 1963 and in pronouncements during his European trip that followed, President Kennedy offered the prospect of peaceful cooperation with the Soviet Union. In eastern Europe the dominant theme became security and cooperation between East and West. The testing of the Khrushchev years had identified firm ground on which a definitive European settlement would be constructed, including the German *Ostpolitik* and the first formal, written quadripartite agreement on Berlin.

NOTES

1. *Documents on the Status of Berlin, 1944–1959* (Munich: R. Oldenbourg Verlag, 1959), pp. 155–56.

2. Ibid., p. 157.

3. *Department of State Bulletin*, July 6, 1953, pp. 9–11.

4. *Documents on Germany, 1945–70*, (Washington, U.S. Government Printing Office, 1971), p. 226.

5. "Foreign Ministers' Meeting, Berlin Discussions, January 25–February 18, 1954," Department of State Publication 5399, *International Organization and Conference Series 1*, March 26, 1954, p. 218.

6. Ibid., p. 219.

7. Ibid., p. 5.

8. TASS statement, March 25, 1954.

9. *New York Times,* November 12, 1958.

10. *Documents on the Status of Berlin,* pp. 183–84.

11. Ibid., p. 185.

12. White House memo, March 9, 1959.

13. White House memo, March 13, 1959.

14. White House memo, March 26, 1959.

15. "Foreign Ministers' Meeting, Geneva, May–August 1959," Department of State publication 6882, *International Organization and Conference Series 8,* September 1959, pp. 134–45.

16. Ibid., pp. 146–57.

17. Geneva conference (1959) paper, p. 3, quoted in John Eisenhower, June 25, 1959, White House memorandum, Eisenhower Library archives, Abilene, Kansas.

18. Alexei Adzhubei, *Face to Face with America—the Story of the Voyage of N.S. Khrushchev to the U.S.A.* (Moscow: Moscow Foreign Language Publishing House, 1960).

19. Thompson message from Moscow, February 4, 1961.

20. Arthur Schlesinger, *A Thousand Days,* (Boston, MA: Houghton Mifflin Company, 1965), p. 347.

21. Ibid., p. 350.

22. Ibid., p. 377.

23. *Public Papers of the Presidents,* John F. Kennedy, 1961 (Washington, D.C., 1962), pp. 521–22.

24. Ibid., pp. 533–36.

25. Schlesinger, *A Thousand Days,* p. 396.

26. Memorandum of conversation between Governing Mayor Willy Brandt and Ambassador Charles E. Bohlen, dated August 20, 1961.

27. Notes taken by David Klein at a meeting on Berlin, at the Aspen Institute Berlin, June 3–5, 1981.

28. *Congressional Record,* February 6, 1963.

29. Letter from President Kennedy to General de Gaulle, October 23, 1962.

4

The Development of Local Government in Berlin

The view that Berlin presented after the surrender of German General Weidling and his troops on May 2, 1945, can hardly be described adequately in words or numbers. At first sight the city looked like a mammoth ruin. More than 70 percent of the city's 250,000 buildings were damaged; about 10 percent were completely destroyed; and another 10 percent were so badly hit that rebuilding seemed impossible. The city was covered by more than 70 million cubic meters of rubble. There was no light or public transportation, or mail or telephone service. The gas, water, and electrical systems had virtually collapsed. Buses, trolleys, railways, and subways were mostly destroyed. Despite these chaotic conditions, however, about 3 million people (of a prewar 4.3 million) still lived in the city, and they were joined by a growing number of refugees—a total of 1.5 million by 1946. Only half of the 1.45 million living accommodations that had existed in 1939 were still habitable at the end of the war. The building of new infrastructure, the provision of food and medical care for the population, and the construction of new housing as well as the restoration of public security were urgent tasks that permitted no delay. It required a functioning local government that the occupation regime alone could not provide. The help of Germans with administrative skills and knowledge of local conditions was absolutely essential.

THE NEW BEGINNING OF LOCAL ADMINISTRATION

On April 21, 1945, when the battle of Berlin was at its peak (eleven days before the Nazi forces in the city surrendered) the first local mayor was appointed in Hermsdorf, a northern suburb of Berlin, where the fighting had ended. Thus began the rebuilding of the Berlin administration. Moreover, social democrats and communists who had survived the Nazi regime founded on their own initiative *Volkskomitees* (people committees) and *antifaschistische Komitees* (anti-Fascist committees) in which representatives of many civic associations were represented. The supply of electricity, gas, and water began to be slowly restored; organized transportation began to work again; and limited food supplies began to be distributed.

This spontaneous development of order, however, was soon brought under the control of the Soviet military administration (SMA). As early as May 30—still before the capitulation of the city—a group of German communist returnees under the leadership of Walter Ulbricht arrived at Bruchmühle near Berlin on a plane from Moscow. The principal members of this group constituted the political core of the Komitee Freies Deutschland (Committee of Free Germany), which had been founded in the Soviet Union after the battle of Stalingrad. Now, with the backing of the Soviet military administration, the Gruppe Ulbricht (Ulbricht Group) took charge of the administrative rebuilding of Berlin.

The offices of the people's committees and anti-Fascist committees, which had been opened spontaneously, were promptly closed. New administrative departments were established and selection of the staff was determined by the Ulbricht Group. Although there was an instruction to the effect that no more than a third of the newly established administrative positions could be filled by members of the former Communist party of Germany, Marshall Zhukov guaranteed that these members would hold the key positions. Wolfgang Leonhard (then a member of the Ulbricht group who later fled to the West) reports that Ulbricht himself had given the directive: "It is quite clear that it must look democratic, but we must control everything."[1]

Thus only a few days after the capitulation of Berlin, the Soviety military authorities installed *antifaschistisch-demokratische Bezirksverwaltungen* (anti-fascist–democratic district administrations), which, through a system of street, block, and house representatives, provided a link between the local authorities and the population. As early as May 17, 1945, the first postwar *Magistrat* (city government) of Berlin was formed, with Dr. Arthur Werner as mayor. An architect by profession, he was not distinguished politically. Three of his four deputies were communists. First among them was Karl Maron, who later became minister of the interior of the German Democratic Republic. All in all only eight of the twenty departments of the new city government were led by communists, but among them they controlled the important divisions of administration and personnel, education, postal and telephone service, social welfare, and finance and taxes.

The communist influence was further strengthened by the fact that the Ulbricht group filled important positions in the security operations with people in whom they had confidence, particularly in the leadership of the police. Moreover, the communist influence was reinforced by the Soviet authorities, who had to approve appointments to the leading positions in the German administration.

Yet respected representatives of the upper middle class were prepared to collaborate with the communists in order to search for joint ways out of the general distress. Ferdinand Friedensburg, a cofounder of the Christian Democratic party, recalled: "Everywhere there was a strong yearning to begin again, to make some money, to clear away the ruins and the chaos, to provide again, to regain hope."[2] Former Reichsminister Dr. Andreas Hermes became responsible for nutrition; Professor Ferdinand Sauerbruch, a surgeon, for public health; and Hans Scharoun, an architect, for housing. After twelve years of Nazi terror, they, like many other members of the upper middle class, were not unwilling to revise their former assessments and dislike concerning the communists. Together they wanted to take advantage of the opportunity for a new beginning, to avoid the mistakes of the Weimar Republic, where conservatives, social democrats, and communists fought one another, and unwittingly prepared the way for the Nazis.

Social democrats were not part of the new Berlin city government. Old rivalries remained. The Ulbricht Group obviously realized that the communists were in a weak position compared with the social democrats. Backed by the decisive might of the Soviet occupation forces, the communists prepared for a "democratic" takeover of power in order to implement "Nach Hitler—wir!" (After Hitler—we!), the old slogan of the KPD. They did not want to be under the pressure of the moral claims of the social democrats to share power after having suffered so much under the Hitler regime. The "threat" that the social democrats posed to the communists possibly seemed more dangerous than that of the bourgeois forces, which were divided and partly discredited because of their behavior during the Weimar Republic and the Third Reich. The communists were therefore prepared to (and did) cooperate with representatives of the upper middle class quite easily, but were less willing to do so with social democrats.

Even after the Western Allies took control of their sectors in Berlin on July 5, 1945, and when the Allied *Kommandatura* started to work on July 11, the structure of the Berlin administration, as developed until then, did not greatly change. The *Kommandatura* immediately passed a resolution to keep fully in force the orders issued by the Soviet command. Moreover, subsequent revision of individual regulations was possible only with Soviet agreement since decisions in the *Kommandatura* had to be unanimous. Given this Soviet veto right in the *Kommandatura*, the influence of the communists in the local government of Berlin was promoted, not only in the eastern part of the city but also in the Western sectors. The Soviets were able to expand their influence throughout local administration offices in Berlin. This led the British historian Philip Windsor to suggest that at this point the Russian conquest of Berlin had become complete.[3] It took some time—until the clashes in June and July 1948—for the Western powers to alter fully the arrangements imposed during the very first hours of the Soviet occupation in Berlin.

THE FOUNDATION OF PARTIES AND TRADE UNIONS

The Western Allies acquiesced in the initiative of Marshall Zhukov who, by his Order no. 2 of June 10, 1945, more than a month before the opening of the Potsdam Conference, had stimulated the establishment of "anti-fascist–democratic" parties and trade unions in Berlin, as well as in the Soviet occupation zone (SOZ), even though the London Agreements of September 12, 1944 made clear that Berlin did not belong exclusively to the Soviet sphere of influence. Consequently, under direction of the Soviet military administration, four parties were founded, all of them active in the Soviet Zone and in Berlin: the Communist party of Germany (KPD) on June 11; the Social Democratic party of Germany (SPD) on June 15; somewhat later, the Christian Democratic Union (CDU) on June 26; and the Liberal Democratic party (LDP) on July 5. In addition, the Ulbricht Group established a communist-dominated trade union organization, the Free German Trade Union League (FDGB) on July 15, 1945.

These initiatives, which resulted in the mobilization and concentration of political forces in Berlin and in the Soviet zone of occupation earlier than in other parts of Germany, were not viewed as suspect by those of various political orientations who took an active part in this process. On the contrary, the founding of parties and trade unions seemed to demonstrate the readiness of the Soviet Union to promote seriously and expeditiously the development of German democracy. The social democrats would even have liked to have taken the process a step further and to continue the *Kampfgemeinschaft* (joint struggle) that they had formed with the communists during the time of Nazi persecution between 1933 and 1945. The social democrats thereby hoped to overcome the divisions within the German labor movement that had developed after the foundation of the KPD in 1919, with disastrous results for German politics. For many social democrats in Berlin and East Germany, the reestablishment of the traditional SPD on June 15, 1945 was, therefore, a "founding against their wills," necessary only because of the refusal of the KPD to agree to a merger at that time. The KPD felt it could afford to risk a merger only after a period of internal consolidation and the clarification of political conditions in Germany.

In contrast with the situation that existed prior to World War I and during the Weimar Republic, the bourgeois parties were no longer insistent upon disassociating themselves from the social democrats and the communists. Instead they favored cooperation among all democratic forces. The Soviet military administration and KPD consequently were able to form a United Front of Anti-fascist–Democratic Parties (*Einheitsfront*) as early as July 14, 1945, and the KPD and SPD along with the CDU and LDP became members. Within this *Einheitsfront* resolutions were adopted not by voting, but through consensus. Gradually, however, the readiness of social democrats and the bourgeois politicians to cooperate lessened as they began to understand better the practice of the Soviet administration and the behavior of the German communists, who were dependent upon the Soviet occupation force for their strength and clearly were acting on Soviet instructions.

BERLIN DURING THE PERIOD OF TRANSITION

During this period, Berlin was not geographically a completely isolated territory. As a result of the close historical, economic, and technical connections, special relations existed between Berlin and the surrounding areas. New arrangements were set up between the city under Four Power control and the Soviet zone of occupation (SOZ). While the Soviet zone was hermetically closed to the Western zones, the border between Berlin and the SOZ remained open until 1952. Berliners from all the four sectors of the city could travel into the SOZ, and the inhabitants of the Soviet zone could come to Berlin. Not until July 1, 1952, was entry to the Soviet zone closed for inhabitants of the Western sectors. But even then, entry to East Berlin was open, and remained so until the city was divided by the building of the wall in August 1961. Moreover, as a result of the integration of transportation facilities between Berlin and the surrounding administrative units, the Soviet zone administration had authority to manage the railways and the canal locks in all of Berlin. Until the blockade of West Berlin in 1948–49, the supplies of food, fuel, and electricity for the city came mostly from the surrounding area. This gave the Soviet Union substantial leverage on the Western side which led from time to time to the disruption and, finally, the almost complete interruption of the supplies.

The extent to which Berlin was regarded by the Soviet Union, at least in the beginning, as the "natural capital" of the surrounding Soviet zone could be seen from several developments. In July 1945 the Berlin *Magistrat* had to participate in a conference of provincial officials and chief mayors of the province of Brandenburg. Time and again workers from Berlin were ordered by the Soviet military administration to help with the harvest and to dismantle plants in the Soviet zone. At the end of 1945 Soviet plans for revitalizing Berlin industry totally neglected the presence of the Western Allies in the still undivided Four Power city.

The dismantling of West Berlin industry was carried on until the arrival of the Americans and the British on July 1, 1945. By then about 85 percent of the production capacity that had been intact at the end of the war in the Western sectors had been removed. In the same time frame only 35 percent had been dismantled in the Eastern sector. Even after the arrival of the Western forces, Soviet intervention in the Western sectors continued. With the assistance of the Berlin police, who were directed from the Eastern sector, German skilled workers, technicians, and scientists were deported to the SOZ or to the Soviet Union. These and other encroachments, especially by the police under its president, Paul Markgraf, a former member of the *Komitee Freies Deutschland,* early gave rise to a feeling of general insecurity. As late as February 1948 the Department for Social Affairs of the Magistrat was involved in the compulsory removal of 9,000 workers to the Soviet occupation zone, most of whom were sent to the uranium mines at Aue.

The degree to which the Berlin police in particular had come under communist influence is evident by the fact that in 1946, fifteen out of twenty-one leading officials (*Dezernenten*) of the criminal police and almost 70 percent of the district chiefs of the regular police (*Schutzpolizei*) were members of the Socialist Unity party (SED). Their central offices were located in the Soviet sector. Similarly, all other central offices of the parties and the trade unions as well as the *Magistrat* and the *Stadtverordnetenversammlung* (city parliament) were requested to establish their headquarters in the Eastern sector. For a considerable time the Soviets also maintained a monopoly in Berlin broadcasting. But in February 1946 the Americans established their own radio station, the *Rundfunk im Amerikanischen Sektor* (RIAS), in order to break the Soviet monopoly. The *Haus des Rundfunks,* the home of Radio Free Berlin, located in the British sector, remained under Soviet control even after the blockade of West Berlin in 1948–49. Only in July 1956 were Governing Mayor Otto Suhr and the then British commandant able to induce the Soviets to vacate the premises.

The press also offered little opportunity for the expression of divergent views. Until the summer of 1945 only Soviet organs and German newspapers operating under Soviet licenses and editorial guidelines were available. The first press license in the Western sectors was granted by U.S. authorities at the end of September 1945 to the *Tagesspiegel*. Under the leadership of Erik Reger, the *Tagesspiegel* tried, with U.S. backing, to provide independent coverage according to Western standards of press freedom. This was followed by establishment of the social democratic *Telegraf* under a British license in April 1946.

Education development followed a similar pattern. With few exceptions the major institutes, including the former Friedrich-Wilhelm University, were located in the Eastern sector of the city. So was the Prussian State Library, the largest library in Germany. Therefore, the Soviet military authorities, by a unilateral administrative order, were able to bring these institutions under control of the Soviet occupation authority without encountering Western objections. The Berlin University was denied the right to self-administration after it reopened on January 20, 1946. Professors and students, overwhelmingly non-communist, soon came into conflict with the university administration and leadership, which were controlled by the Soviet military administration and the German communists. Clearly, academic freedom could not survive under these conditions. Continuing clashes at the university in 1947 led to the establishment in 1948 of the Free University Berlin in Berlin-Dahlem, in the U.S. sector of the city.

Soviet behavior had already come under critical Western scrutiny late in the summer of 1945. The Western powers expressed concern about the institution of street, block, and house representatives as agents of the city administration. Instruments for expanding communist influence, they began to appear in the Western sectors without authorization.[4] On August 21, 1945, the U.S. command in Berlin-Neukoelln ordered their immediate abolition. This order was subsequently extended to the entire U.S. sector on September 9. The British followed the U.S. example on October 12, 1945, and the French on August 2, 1946.

The Unity Front (*Einheitsfront*) of the communist-dominated parties and the Soviet broadcasting monopoly also were rejected by the U.S. occupation authorities. In a report of September 20, 1945, the military governor of the U.S. occupation zone, General Dwight D. Eisenhower, stated that the system of party "block building" was not compatible with the American understanding of democracy, and therefore would not be tolerated in the U.S. zone. He also expressed concern about Soviet action to force the concentration of the press and radio facilities into the Eastern sector of Berlin, thus removing them from the influence of the other occupying powers.

The first serious clashes within the newly founded parties occurred at the end of 1945 after a period of earnest effort for inter-party cooperation. In December 1945 the Christian Democrats (CDU) in the Soviet occupation zone were faced with the abrupt dismissal by the Soviet authorities of their freely elected leadership, since they had dared to express "serious concern" about the management of the land reform program in the Soviet occupation zone and had warned against the failure to provide some help in dealing with the reduced availability of food. Colonel Sergei Tulpanov then announced that the two CDU chairmen, Dr. Andreas Hermes and Dr. Walther Schreiber, had lost the confidence of their party members (even though this was untrue, as information from the regional CDU organization in the Soviet zone revealed). They were asked to resign voluntarily. When Dr. Hermes and Dr. Schreiber refused to do so, the Soviet authorities forced them to give up their posts. Their successors, Jakob Kaiser and Ernst Lemmer, both of whom came from the trade union movement, met a similar fate. They were forced to resign at the end of 1947.

THE CONFLICT SURROUNDING EFFORTS TO MERGE SPD AND KPD

Among social democrats, skepticism toward the communists increased sharply in the autumn of 1945. The communist methods of administration were especially disliked. However, the social democrats were not completely united, as could be seen particularly during the struggle for the merging of the SPD and the KPD into a "Unity Party" (*Einheitspartei*). The SPD in the Western zones, under the leadership of Dr. Kurt Schumacher, was strongly opposed to such a merger, arguing that there were "incompatible differences" between the two parties because of the lack of democracy within the Communist party. However, the SPD in the Soviet occupation zone under Otto Grotewohl favored unification, believing that the social democrats could play a leading role in a united party.

These differences within the SPD became clear when the KPD, which at first opposed the merger, shifted position following the elections in Hungary and Austria in November 1945. In those elections the Communists suffered devastating defeats. The Communist party in Austria won only 5 percent of the vote and, in Hungary only 16 percent. The KPD leadership, therefore, began to press for a merger with the Social Democrats in order to be able to use the Social Democratic party for their purposes. At a turbulent conference of SPD representatives in Berlin on March 1, 1946, the inner-party opposition around Franz Neumann, Kurt Swolinzky, and Karl Germer managed to carry through a resolution which stated that all SPD members should decide about the proposed unification with the KDP in a special vote (*Urabstimmung*) on March 31. It had to be restricted to Berlin, however, for the political pressure for a merger had already become very strong in the Soviet zone.

In Berlin, too, the opponents of a unification were intimidated by the Communists. When the vote finally took place, the booths in the Soviet sector were closed by motorized patrols only half an hour after opening, and the ballot boxes were confiscated. In the Western sectors 72.9 percent of the more than 33,000 SPD members who participated in the balloting rejected unification, while only 2,938 were in favor of it. In response to a second question, a substantial majority of 14,600 against 5,559 supported an alliance of the two parties to ensure cooperation and prevent a "fight among brothers." The result showed clearly that most of the Social Democrats were against merger with the KPD, but many were still prepared to regard the KPD as a *Bruderpartei*.

The unification of the SPD and the KPD into the United Socialist party (SED) proceeded as planned in the Soviet occupation zone after March 31. The process was completed at a joint party congress on April 21–22, 1946. (This was the first and last party congress of the SED at which resolutions were not adopted unanimously.) However, the results of the special voting (*Urabstimmung*) in the Western sectors provided the impulse for many social Democrats to join the ranks of the inner-party opposition. During a party meeting in Berlin-Zehlendorf on April 7, 1946, the "Berlin SPD" was formed and asked the occupying powers for permission to be active in all four sectors. The coordinating committee of the Allied Control Council approved the application on May 28. The *Kommandatura* announced on May 31 the recognition of both the SED and the SPD in Berlin. This legal situation, which also provided the basis for the existence of the SED in West Berlin, continues to the present day.

Thus, the SPD in the Soviet occupation zone was destroyed, and in Berlin it was divided. The resistance of the Social Democrats in Berlin to a forced unification with the KPD became a symbol of their struggle for freedom and independence against communist *Gleichschaltung* and suppression. Their partial success—the maintenance of an independent Social Democratic party in West Berlin—was due largely to the presence of the Western Allies, who ensured the possibility of a free decision. The common cause of Germans on the one hand, and of Americans, British, and French on the other, became evident in an unmistakable manner for the first time, even if the division between conquered and conquerors had not yet been overcome.

THE TEMPORARY CONSTITUTION AND THE ELECTIONS OF OCTOBER 20, 1946

Despite growing differences among the occupying powers, Four Power administration continued in Berlin until 1948. In the spring of 1946 the *Kommandatura* decided to bring an end to the situation in which Berlin was without a constitution. The reason such absence had not created chaotic conditions was that all major decisions were taken by the occupation authorities. Preparatory work for a new constitution had already been started by the *Magistrat* back in October 1945. After some difficulty the deliberations were completed so that the *Kommandatura*, through BK/O (46) 326 of August 14, 1946, could approve a provisional constitution for Greater Berlin.[5] This went into effect in October 1946 and remained so until 1950. Free elections for the Berlin city assembly (*Berliner Stadtverordnetenversammlung*) were scheduled for October 20, 1946. Thereafter, the city assembly was supposed to work out a new constitution (as provided for in Article 35, paragraph 2 of the Temporary Constitution), which was to be submitted to the occupying powers for approval by May 1, 1948.

The elections scheduled for October 20, 1946 led to a heated electoral contest, during which the SED was openly supported by the Soviet occupation authorities, while the SPD, CDU, and LDP, which were campaigning for a democratic system in the Western sense, worked hard to resist Communist pressure. It was during this time that the Western powers' patience with Soviet aggressiveness began to wear thin. In August 1946 General Lucius D. Clay declared that the quadripartite rules would no longer be applicable if the Soviet Union continued its behavior.[6] More important, the Stuttgart speech of U.S. Secretary of State James F. Byrnes on September 6, 1946 signaled a major change in policy toward Germany. The elections of October 20, which were the first and last free postwar elections in Greater Berlin, thus came at a critical moment. They amounted to a referendum on the choice of a Western or a Soviet course.

The outcome was clear, as it had been when the Social Democrats in the Western sectors voted on the unification of the SPD and the KPD. The SPD received 48.7 percent of the votes, the CDU 22.2 percent, and the LDP 9.3 percent. The SED, despite massive Soviet backing and interference in the campaigns of the other parties in the Soviet sector, won only 19.8 percent of the vote, far behind the SPD and the CDU. Taking into account the combined support for the "bourgeois parties," represented by the CDU and the LDP, the defeat of the SED was even more disastrous. Even in the Soviet sector of Berlin, the SED received only 29.9 percent of the votes cast. Given the participation of 92.3 percent of the electorate, the Berliners clearly opted decisively for a free Western-style political order and against yet another system of suppression and dictatorship. That decision was not the consequence of momentary happenstance, but the logical result of historical experience in Berlin, and Germany as a whole, as well as in the development of world politics, which was characterized by growing tension, conflict, and division between East and West. After the Soviet occupation authorities and the SED had experienced the shock of the electoral defeat of October 20, they tried to achieve in another way what they had not been able to accomplish by the ballot: to seize full power in Berlin, and push the Western Allies out of West Berlin.

THE DIVISION OF LOCAL GOVERNMENT

In the period immediately following the elections, political, economic, and cultural life in Berlin was greatly disturbed. The police, directed by President

Paul Markgraf and operating throughout Berlin, played a notorious role. The geographic situation of the city, too, was exploited to increase various kinds of pressures. Following the foreign ministers' conference in London in the autumn of 1947, there were growing difficulties on the transit routes between Berlin and West Germany. As already mentioned in Chapter 2, the Soviet supreme commander, Marshall Vassily Sokolovsky, left the Allied Control Council on March 20, 1948, and on June 16, 1948 the Soviet delegates left the Allied *Kommandatura* as well, thereby ending any pretense at joint Four Power government control over Germany and Berlin. And at the end of June 1948 the blockade of surface access to Berlin began.

All this had far-reaching consequences for the development of local government in Berlin. The city assembly was able to meet in the *Stadthaus* in the Eastern sector for just about two months more. The city government was now under constant threat and pressure from the Soviet occupation authorities. Journalists from the Western sectors, covering the city assembly, were arrested in the *Stadthaus*. The situation ultimately became totally untenable with the consequence that on September 6, 1948 the city assembly (except for the SED faction) found it necessary to move to the Western sectors. The *Magistrat* followed in the beginning of October 1948. The trade unions and the CDU and LDP split later in the same year.

The SED faction of the city assembly, which did not participate in the sessions in West Berlin, now insisted that all resolutions adopted outside the Soviet sector were invalid. This controversy reached its climax in November 1948 when an "extraordinary city assembly" met in the Eastern Sector with the participation not only of its 23 SED city assembly delegates (of a total membership of 127), but also of another 1,616 delegates from factories in Berlin, and from other mass organizations under communist control, which formed the so-called Democratic Bloc. This institution (*Gremium*), for which there was no provision in the provisional constitution, terminated the elected *Magistrat* and in its stead elected a "provisional democratic *Magistrat*" with Fritz Ebert (SED) as mayor. The resolutions passed at this gathering, which was essentially a mass meeting, were adopted not by the usual voting process, but rather by a show of hands. They were immediately approved by the Soviet military government, although the Western Commandants sharply protested against the "contrived" measures taken by the "extraordinary city assembly." The Soviet authorities insisted that the "provisional *Magistrat*" in the Eastern sector now was the only legitimate municipal city government for all of Berlin. They considered the *Magistrat* in the Western sectors dissolved. This marked the formal split of the local administration of Berlin. Five days later, general elections for a new city assembly took place in the Western sectors on the basis of the Provisional Constitution. Despite a call for a boycott by the SED, 86.3 percent of the electorate participated in this election. The Allied *Kommandatura* resumed its work on December 21, 1948, six months after the 1948 walkout of the Soviet representative, who henceforth was counted as temporarily absent. A dissolution of the *Komman-*

datura was, in the option of the three Western powers, only possible by the unanimous agreement of the Four Powers.

Developments in the Eastern and Western parts of Berlin now moved on different tracks and in different directions. The Soviet Union failed both to prevent the establishment of a separate West German state and to force the withdrawal of the Western powers from Berlin. Neither the blockade nor the pressure on the local government in Berlin was successful. After the lifting of the blockade on May 12, 1949, the establishment of the Federal Republic of Germany on May 23, 1949, and the founding of the German Democratic Republic (GDR) on October 7, 1949, the Berlin situation stabilized until the end of the 1950s. However, the difficulties that resulted from the division of the city, Berlin's precarious geographical situation, and intermittent Soviet and East German harassment persisted. The local government had to concentrate heavily on resolving the problems resulting from the division of the city and on ensuring political and economic viability in an area that had become the frontline of the cold war between East and West.

EAST BERLIN: "THE CAPITAL OF THE GDR"

With the division of Berlin and the establishment of both the Federal Republic of Germany and the German Democratic Republic, questions arose of the future status of the two parts of the city and of their relationship to the two German states—questions involving profound legal and political principles. In East Berlin a factual situation was created rather early, since the Soviet Union had from the beginning regarded and administered the Eastern sector of Berlin and the surrounding Soviet zone of occupation as a single entity. Consequently, already in the first constitution of the GDR (October 7, 1949) "Berlin" was declared to be the German capital, with all-German pretensions.[7] The major organs of the GDR were set up in East Berlin: the president of the republic, the government departments, the People's Chamber (*Volkskammer*), the Chamber of States (*Länderkammer*) (until its dissolution in 1958), the Supreme Court, and, of course, the party headquarters (*Parteileitung*) of the SED. Thus, the course of the integration of East Berlin into the state system of the GDR was set very early.[8] This process clearly was favored by the geographical situation as well as by the administrative control of the area by a single occupation power, and by the predominant role of the SED both in East Berlin and in the GDR as a whole.

Legally, however, the special status of East Berlin was maintained at first in a fashion that somewhat paralleled that which prevailed in West Berlin. Legislation adopted by the *Volkskammer* for the GDR had to be taken over by the Berlin authorities, and Berlin representatives in the parliament sat separately from other members. But after 1953 such distinctions began to diminish. For instance, in November 1953 the inhabitants of "Greater Berlin (East)" received GDR identification cards. GDR laws and directives of GDR institutions increasingly applied directly to "the democratic sector of Greater Berlin." The Soviet

Union first officially referred to Berlin as the capital of the GDR in a note of January 6, 1958, sent to the secretary general of the United Nations, in which Moscow protested against the integration of West Berlin in international treaties of the Federal Republic of Germany. Even before that it had taken the position that East Berlin was the concern only of the GDR, and pursuant to this principle the Soviet side rejected all Western protests against parades of the East German People's Army (*Volksarmee*) in East Berlin.

In January 1957 the municipal offices of East Berlin were placed under the jurisdiction of the *Volkskammer*. The city was thereby given a status similar to that of other cities and communities of the GDR. Laws and regulations still had to be taken over explicitly by the East Berlin *Magistrat,* but even in that respect the number of exceptions was growing. Many decrees of the GDR State Chamber were applicable directly to East Berlin. After the Eastern sector was cut off from the West in August 1961, even the defense regulations and conscription laws of the GDR were extended to East Berlin. At the same time, the office of the Soviet commandant for East Berlin was abolished, and a GDR commander was appointed in his place.

WEST BERLIN—INTEGRATION UNDER ALLIED RESERVATIONS

Due to geography and Allied reservations, the integration of West Berlin into the political system and administration of the Federal Republic of Germany proved to be more complicated than the integration of East Berlin into the GDR.[9] In September 1948 the five Berlin representatives at the parliamentary council in Frankfurt who took part in drafting the Basic Law of the Federal Republic (the Federal Republic's constitution) were identified only as advisors, since the Western military governments were concerned about protecting the Four Power status of the city, and opposed their full participation with the right of voting. The Western Allies intervened again when the principal committee (*Hauptausschuss*) of the parliamentary council decided on February 9, 1948 to include Greater Berlin as the twelfth state in the area governed by the Basic Law. In a memorandum of March 2, 1949, the Western military governors stated that "with respect to the present situation, the part of Article 23 referring to Berlin must be suspended." There were no reservations against the proposal, "that the responsible authorities in Berlin appoint a small number of representatives to attend sessions of the Parliament,"[10] but the Western Allies prevented these representatives from having the right to vote on substantive issues, a subject discussed further in Chapter 6.

After a conference of the three Western foreign ministers in Washington in April 1949, the Allied position on the status of Berlin was explicitly confirmed in a letter from the Western military governors, dated April 22, 1949, which stated: "The Foreign Ministers at present cannot agree to include Berlin as a state into the original organization of the German Federal Republic."[11]

All attempts undertaken subsequently by the Federal Republic or by the Berlin authorities to induce the Western powers to withdraw this reservation were fruitless and, in fact, led to repeated reaffirmations of the Western Allies' position. Paragraphs 2 and 3 of Article 1 of the Berlin constitution, adopted by the city assembly (*Stadtverordnetenversammlung*) on August 4, 1950, were suspended by the Allied *Kommandatura* on August 29, 1950, because they asserted that Berlin was a state of the Federal Republic of Germany and that the Basic Law and the federal laws of the Federal Republic were binding for Berlin. The Allies declared that Berlin "during the transition period" possessed none of the attributes of a state of the Federal Republic.[12] The reference to a "transition period" (which was repeated in other communications of the Three Powers) implied, at least the Germans believed, that a solution to the German problem was still expected which in some undefined way would permit West Berlin to become part of the Federal Republic.

Meanwhile, to avoid jeopardizing the Four Power status of the city, the Western powers took special care to ensure that their "supreme authority" in Berlin remained intact. Even now German courts are not permitted to question Allied law. Additionally, sentences of occupation courts remain binding for German courts and German authorities. Occupation law is considered superior to German law in Berlin.

This legal situation, which contrasts sharply with the virtually complete integration of East Berlin into the GDR, has not prevented the extensive de facto integration of West Berlin into the Federal Republic. With very few exceptions (e.g., the law on conscription and the emergency law, *Notstandsgesetz*) all Federal laws contain a Berlin clause stating that the law can also be valid in Berlin. The Berlin House of Representatives almost always adopts these laws through the device of a covering law (*Mantelgesetz*), and if the Allies do not object within a certain period of time, the law then becomes effective in Berlin. The same procedure is followed for Federal decrees. The Allied *Kommandatura* did object to the application in Berlin of the Federal Constitutional Court Law. In a letter to the governing mayor of December 20, 1952, the commandants argued that the Federal Constitutional Court embodied the supreme authority of the Federal Republic, and therefore its extension to Berlin would be contradictory to the reservations registered by the Western powers when they had approved the Basic Law in 1949.

Representation of Berlin in foreign affairs was originally reserved exclusively to the occupation powers. In a Declaration on the Integration of Berlin in International Treaties and Obligations of the Federal Government of May 21, 1952, the Allied *Kommandatura* stated that under certain circumstances the *Kommandatura* would not object to Berlin's inclusion in international treaties subscribed to by the Federal Republic. The Soviet Union, as will be seen, acknowledged the legitimacy of the procedure in the Four Power agreement of September 13, 1971, as long as matters affecting status and security were not involved. Since the 1950s ties in every field of daily life—economic, social, and cultural—have been developed between West Berlin and the Federal Republic. As a result the social and economic environment in the Western sectors of Berlin is similar to that in the other major cities of the Federal Republic. The legal and political systems are very similar, and West Berlin has been fully integrated financially into the Federal system through the so-called Third Transition Law (*Drittes Überleitungsgesetz*). The Federal government is present in West Berlin in the form of some 85 offices, courts, and institutes, with more than 20,000 employees. Among these are the Federal Administration Court, the Fifth Penal Senate of the Federal Law Court, the Federal Cartel Office, the Federal Health Office, and the Federal Environmental Office. West Berlin residents can easily feel themselves to be part of the Federal Republic even if legally this is not the case.

Even with this de facto integration of West Berlin into the life of the Federal Republic, however, the city long remained under the shadow of intermittent interference with access, of physical encirclement by a communist, Soviet-dominated state, and of confrontation with an oppressive political system symbolized by the wall that divided not only the city but also families and friends. The headquarters of most major German corporations left Berlin for the West. The population of the Western sectors declined, leaving the city with a disproportionate number of pensioners. Only slowly after the trauma of the wall did this shadow lighten. Gradually in the course of the 1960s, as Soviet and East German harassment declined, a sense of normalcy replaced the former mood of *Frontstadt*. Younger Germans and new industry were attracted to the city by tax and other inducements, along with a more problematic infusion of foreign workers. By 1969, when the Four Power talks began on a Berlin Agreement, the atmosphere in Berlin was devoid of crisis. Crisis and confrontation were not the spurs that brought the Four Powers to seek a more solid and promising *modus vivendi* for the city, where they had met as victors and ruled as antagonists.

NOTES

1. Wolfgang Leonhard, *Die Revolution entlässt ihre Kinder* (Cologne and Berlin: Kiepenheuer & Witsch Verlag, 1974), p. 317.

2. Ferdinand Friedensburg, *Es ging um Deutschlands Einheit, Ruckschau eines Berliners auf die Jahre nach 1945* (Berlin: Haude & Spenersche Verlagsbuchhandlung, 1971), p. 67.

3. Philip Windsor, *City on Leave: A History of Berlin, 1945–1962* (New York: Praeger, 1963), p. 50.

4. See Senat von Berlin (ed.), *Berlin, Quellen und Dokumente, 1945–1951*, Vol. 1 (Berlin: Spitzing Verlag, 1964), pp. 237–49.

5. With regard to the Provisional Constitution, see ibid., Vol. 1, pp. 1071–1111.

6. Lucius D. Clay, *Decision in Germany* (New York: Doubleday, 1950), p. 135. See also Michael Balfour and John Mair, *Four-Power Control in Germany and Austria, 1945–1956* (London: Oxford University Press, 1956), p. 212.

7. *Dokumente zur Berlin-Frage, 1944–1966*, 3rd edn (Munich and Vienna: Oldenbourg Verlag, 1967), pp. 139.

8. See Dieter Mahncke, *Berlin im geteilten Deutschland*, Schriften des Forschungsinstituts der Deutschen Gesellschaft für Auswärtige Politik, Vol. 34 (Munich and Vienna: Oldenbourg Verlag, 1973), beginning at p. 49.

9. For a detailed description, see Ernst R. Zivier, *Der Rechtesstatus des Landes Berlin, Eine Untersuchung nach dem Viermächte-Abkommen vom 3 September 1971*, 3rd edn (Berlin: Berlin Verlag, 1977).

10. *Dokumente zur Berlin-Frage, 1944–1966*, p. 112.

11. Ibid., p. 113.

12. Ibid., p. 153.

5

From Crisis to Negotiations

In the period following the climactic construction of the wall in Berlin two paths were followed in an effort to reduce East–West tension, and to ameliorate the hardships resulting from the division of Berlin and the geographic isolation of the Western sectors. The first path, followed by the United States and the Soviet Union, was marked by continued efforts to define an altered arrangement for Berlin as the Soviets, especially before the wall, had insisted must be done. These exchanges, which took place in Moscow, Washington, and Geneva during late 1961 and early 1962, were no longer carried out under the threat of Khrushchev's ultimatum, but the Soviet objectives were largely unchanged. They were first, to establish, through formal agreement, West Berlin as a separate entity or "free city" where the U.S., British, and French troops would be replaced either by neutral troops, contingents from Eastern and Western Europe, or from the United Nations; and second, to subject access to Berlin to the sovereign control of the GDR. The United States was totally unwilling to contemplate the withdrawal of the Allied troops from Berlin in the absence of an overall German settlement, but it developed the concept of an international access authority that would administer the air and surface routes to Berlin and that would be compatible with "free access and the local responsibilities and authority of those in the area through which access would move."[1] The Soviet side interpreted this as a U.S. willingness to combine free access with respect for the sovereignty of the GDR and reacted positively. The Adenauer government in Bonn, which was deeply suspicious of President Kennedy's intentions at this point because of a set of "Draft Principles" on Germany that had been given to the Soviet side by the Americans as a basis for discussions without Bonn's clearance, interpreted the international access idea in the same way as Moscow with precisely the opposite reaction. Bonn refused to concur in the presentation to the Soviet Union of a formal proposal on the authority, and Chancellor Konrad Adenauer did his best to bring the U.S.–Soviet discussions to an early end. In a press conference on May 7, 1962, he commented that "if it should turn out in the course of negotiations that an authority . . . is to be newly created, it will be our primary task to see to it that this cannot be regarded as a first step toward a recognition of the Soviet Zone under international law." He added:

I am not convinced, and I don't even have the slightest hope, that these soundings will lead to a result. I think they have been going on for nine months now, and for us poor people—I may include myself—it really is no pleasure to read all these telegrams. This is extremely boring because there is absolutely nothing in them.[2]

This marked the effective end of the U.S.–Soviet discussions. The episode contributed to a lasting distrust of the Kennedy administration by Chancellor Adenauer and his subsequent increasing orientation toward President de Gaulle of France. Thus, the path followed by the United States and the Soviet Union led nowhere.

The second path, which was to lead not only to a new understanding on Berlin but also to a new order between East and West in Europe, was first perceived and explored by Willy Brandt, then governing mayor of Berlin, the SPD's chancellor candidate in 1960, and beginning in February 1964, chairman of the German Social Democratic party. Brandt was not alone. Unquestionably, he gained ideas and suggestions from the ingenious and articulate Egon Bahr who then, and later in Bonn, was Brandt's closest advisor on dealing with the division of Berlin and Germany and with the countries most closely involved, especially the Soviet Union. A gifted and thoughtful journalist, Peter Bender, in articles and in the book *Offensive Entspannung,* expressed and refined many ideas that would be incorporated into Brandt's thinking. Yet when one reads the mass of Brandt's writings and lectures from the early 1960s and traces his conversations and expostulations through the rest of the decade, he emerges as a man of extraordinary foresight, perceptive of the forces that must be dealt with and capable of bringing together in one relatively simple concept the many, complex factors that had to be taken into account if clearly understood objectives were to be achieved. Brandt, more than any other individual, charted the course of developments in Germany in the crucial decade following the construction of the wall.

Shattered as he was by the cruelty of the wall, Brandt emerged with the conviction that while the wall was an admission of defeat by the communists, one could lessen its effect only through negotiations. Already in a lecture at Harvard in October 1962, Brandt said, "Khrushchev can draw no benefit at all from the Wall." In four years "the balance for Khrushchev would be even more negative than it is now. That is why I believe conversations with the Soviets about Berlin can be meaningful."[3] Brandt rejected Adenauer's suspicions that President Kennedy was seeking an understanding with the Soviets at German expense and, quite to the contrary, "felt emboldened [by Kennedy's ideas] to explore 'new frontiers' in a divided world at my own post of responsibility."[4] He might well have added not only "emboldened" but "compelled," for while Brandt considered that there was no contradiction between U.S. and German interests in Central Europe, he also concluded that the United States would not use its power in pursuit of German interests to bring about an improvement in the status quo. Brandt had noted even before the wall that John Foster Dulles "had made it drastically clear that, for all his fundamental anti-Communism, neither he nor the United States would take a gamble on Germany's account. It became evident . . . that Moscow and Washington subscribed to a sort of tacit agreement on the non-violation of European spheres of influence."[5]

The failure of the United States to prevent the construction of the wall was definitive proof for Brandt that if anything was to be done to mitigate the results of the sealing off of one part of Germany from the other, it would have to be undertaken by the Germans themselves. That is what he set out to do, first by means of small steps (*kleine Schritte*) aimed at bringing about change by coming closer together (*Wandlung durch Annäherung*). This concept was viewed with suspicion in Bonn and, to a degree, in Washington, since it evidently entailed a willingness to deal in some form with Soviet and East German representatives. Suspicion was heightened in Washington by knowledge, obtained through telephone taps, that Egon Bahr was in direct touch with Soviet embassy officials in East Berlin. The fear in Bonn was twofold: first that Brandt's approach could lead to recognition of the East German regime; and second, that it could result in the separation of West Berlin from the Federal Republic and acceptance of the Soviet and East German concept of West Berlin as a separate political entity. The British and French were, themselves, already eager for trade arrangements with the GDR, but in the so-called Bonn Group, a standing body established to deal with Berlin questions composed of representatives of the German Foreign Office and the political counselors of the U.S., British, and French embassies, the Western powers worked closely with the Bonn government, which was still under CDU leadership, in monitoring Brandt's efforts.

The first notable "small step" was the pass agreement, reached for the Christmas holiday period in 1963, under which West Berlin residents were able, for the first time since the construction of the wall, to visit relatives in East Berlin. This resulted from an East German proposal which, in turn, was presumably inspired by Brandt's willingness for contacts and the East German wish to lessen somewhat the opprobrium that had resulted from the wall. Further agreements were reached in 1964, 1965, and 1966. The possibility of visits then lapsed because of the negative attitude of East German authorities until the Berlin Agreement of 1971.

To avoid recognition of the GDR of any appearance of acceptance of GDR responsibility for West Berlin, negotiations on the pass agreements were conducted between West Berlin and East Berlin municipal representatives; and to avoid any possibility of the exercise by the GDR of authority in West Berlin, the passes for entry into East Berlin were issued by an East Berlin clerical staff functioning as postal personnel. Minute guidance on such points was drafted in the Bonn Group and transmitted, as directives, to the Berlin *Senat* by the Western occupation authorities in Berlin. Brandt and his colleagues in the Berlin government found the legalistic concerns of Bonn excessive and suspected at times that the CDU government was interested in torpedoing the agreements lest they enhance the political strength of the SPD. The Federal foreign minister during this period was Gerhard Schroeder, who was, indeed, a prominent CDU politician, but he left Berlin matters almost entirely to the state secretary, Karl Carstens. While Carstens was later to become the CDU parliamentary leader and eventually president of the Federal Republic, he was at that time a highly competent bureaucrat, and simultaneously a professor of law. The positions taken by the Bonn government and concurred in the Bonn Group by the Western Allies reflected more the caution of Carstens and the legal division of the Foreign Office than the political concerns of the CDU.

Since the detailed and restrictive instructions came from the Western Allies, Brandt at times let his impatience be known to them as well as to the government in Bonn. However, even in the retrospect of universal recognition of the GDR, the Western concern to avoid any appearance of the exercise of authority by the GDR in West Berlin and the insistence on a negotiating apparatus that was highly artificial in order to avoid any implication that the GDR enjoyed responsibility with regard to Berlin appear wise. For these pass negotiations were to be the starting point for the important provisions in the ultimate Four Power agreement of 1971 pertaining to travel by West Berlin residents to East Berlin and the GDR. Any compromise, no matter how small, in the Western legal position on the status of Berlin could have encouraged the East German and Soviet authorities to believe this position was subject to negotiation when the major talks began six years later. If the Western side remained firm under the pressure of the possibility of bringing thousands of families together for Christmas or Easter after many years of separation, the assumption would have to be it could and would do so when such immediate humanitarian concern was absent.

On December 1, 1966, the grand coalition government of the CDU/CSU and SPD was formed in Bonn and Willy Brandt became the foreign minister and vice chancellor. Before this at its Dortmund Congress in June 1966, the SPD had considered and largely defined an eastern policy or *Ostpolitik,* which was aimed at achieving a relaxation of tension and useful exchange between the Federal Republic and the Soviet Union and its European allies based on the acceptance of "realities" on both sides. These realities from the point of view of the Soviet Union were the existence of the GDR as a separate German state, the Western borders of Poland (the so-called Oder–Neisse line), and the non-nuclear weapons status of the FRG. For the Federal Republic the realities were firm adherence to the Western Alliance and the special status of Berlin, including the close economic and political ties between the Western sectors and Bonn.

In his book *Offensive Entspannung* (published in 1964), Peter Bender wrote:

Where this detente takes treaty form, Berlin must be included. Every step through which Bonn *de facto* or *de jure* acknowledges (*respektiert*) the GDR must be tied to a step to enhance *de facto* or *de jure* the security of Berlin. Recognition of the GDR can only be envisioned if on its side, the GDR recognizes the protective rights of the Western Powers in Berlin.

Firmness in Berlin by no means excludes detente in Germany. If Bonn succeeds in making credible its desire for accommodation with the USSR, Moscow will most likely see to it that the Ulbricht clique does not use Berlin to prevent this accommodation. Only a relaxation of tension between the Federal Republic and the GDR holds promise of helping West Berlin in a basic way.[6]

This was the conceptual linkage between *Ostpolitik* and Berlin that Brandt as foreign minister, and then as chancellor, was to pursue. It would be the single most effective factor in bringing about the Four Power agreement of 1971.

Prior to moving to Bonn, Brandt had had a number of extensive conversations with the Soviet ambassador to the GDR, Abrasimov (first in the residence of the Swedish consul general in West Berlin, Sven Baclund, and subsequently in the Soviet embassy in East Berlin and the *Senat* guest house in Berlin-Dahlem). Brandt explained to Abrasimov the SPD policy and his concept of negotiating to achieve pragmatic improvements in the existing situation by blocking out those issues on which agreement was patently not achievable. Abrasimov indicated the Soviet Union would be prepared to accept West Berlin's ties with the Federal Republic and specific steps to stabilize the situation in the Western sectors of the divided city. Swedish Consul General Baclund, who was instrumental in arranging the meetings and was usually present, has stated that Brandt and Herbert Wehner (leader of the SPD in the Bundestag) had agreed to keep the substance of these discussions from the German government as well as from the three Western Allies. Western intelligence agencies were aware that these meetings were being held but the substance was not known. Backlund has stated that the Soviets at that time were interested in discussing outstanding issues with Brandt but not with his Bonn coalition colleagues. Indeed, as Baclund told David Klein, Soviet Ambassador Abrasimov went so far in later conversations as to pass on a suggestion to Brandt through him that Soviet–German discussions could be facilitated through the formation of a coalition of Social Democrats (SPD) and Free Democrats (FDP) in Bonn. Failing that, the Soviets were prepared to work with Brandt in his capacity as head of the Social Democratic party. Brandt, Baclund says, rejected the latter suggestion as totally unacceptable since he was unwilling to give any appearance of Social Democratic and Communist collaboration in dealing with Germany's national interests.[7]

THE SOUNDING

It is the custom for the U.S. and Soviet foreign ministers to meet in New York each year in September at the beginning of the United Nations General

Assembly for a discussion of bilateral issues. In the 1960s Berlin and the German question always figured on the U.S. agenda. Brandt, while still governing mayor and subsequently as foreign minister, urged that Secretary Rusk "sound out" Gromyko on the possibility of bringing about improvements in the Berlin situation. President Johnson was also convinced of the desirability of easing East–West tensions resulting from Berlin. Dean Rusk faithfully raised the subject each year with Gromyko, albeit without putting forward any specific ideas or offering any change that might have been of interest to Moscow. The conversations were consistently unproductive on Berlin, where Soviet and East German authorities were mounting recurrent harassment aimed at political activities of the Federal Republic and of the West German political parties in the city. But Brandt persisted, presumably encouraged by the conversations he had had in 1966 with Abrasimov. As foreign minister he gained the opportunity to pursue the idea within NATO.

The North Atlantic Alliance meets twice a year at the foreign minister level. At these semiannual meetings the foreign ministers of France, Britain, the United States, and the Federal Republic of Germany meet separately over dinner to discuss questions related to Berlin and Germany. At the quadripartite dinner at the Reykjavik NATO meeting in June 1968, Brandt took the initiative in proposing that the Berlin problem be raised as part of East–West discussions aimed at easing tensions in Europe. Brandt told his colleagues of his negotiating concept and informed them of his conversations with Abrasimov, including the latter's positive reaction to Brandt's idea of a lump-sum payment by the FRG to the GDR to cover the use of road access routes to Berlin by residents of West Germany and of the Western sectors of Berlin (who were required by the GDR to pay tolls for each trip). According to Brandt, Dean Rusk "commented that, if this came off, it would be a major step forward."[8] Brandt also made a statement before the full NATO ministerial council outlining the Federal Republic's policy of dismantling inner-German differences and securing peace in Germany. For this purpose the Federal government was prepared to renounce the use of force in inner-German relations if both sides, among other things, recognized the residual rights of the Four Powers with reference to Berlin and Germany as a whole, and the continuing application of Four Power agreements. Since, however, the East German regime just over a week earlier had imposed a new passport and visa requirement for German travel to Berlin and to its own territory, the NATO communiqué had to restate forcefully the Western commitment to Berlin rather than to suggest any kind of accommodation. But the German policy declaration concerning inner-German relations was published.[9]

The following February the newly inaugurated U.S. president, Richard Nixon, paid an official visit to Berlin. Again German access to the city was under harassment because of the scheduled meeting of the Federal Assembly (*Bundesversammlung*) in Berlin to elect a new Federal president. In addressing the workers at the Berlin Siemens factory, President Nixon strongly reiterated the U.S. commitment to the freedom of Berlin in the face of the new Communist pressure. In the middle of his very tough speech, however, he included the following sentences:

> When we say that we reject any unilateral alteration of the *status quo* in Berlin, we do not mean that we consider the status quo to be satisfactory. Nobody benefits in a stalemate, least of all the people of Berlin.
> Let us set behind us the stereotype of Berlin as a "provocation." Let us, all of us, view the situation in Berlin as an invocation, a call to end the tension of the past age here and everywhere.[10]

Willy Brandt states in his memoirs that this sign of a readiness to negotiate was included at his suggestion since he had had various indications that the Soviets, who at that time were particularly worried about the Chinese, would be receptive. Certainly it was not in the text suggested by the Department of State, and while Henry Kissinger, in *The White House Years,* records the speech as a strong reaffirmation of the U.S. commitment to Berlin, he does not allude to the obvious conciliatory signal. Instead he describes Chancellor Kiesinger as favoring a strong line toward the East and Brandt emphasizing nuances of accommodation. He adds that "Kiesinger's views were closer to Nixon's; Brandt's were more compatible with the convictions of our State Department."[11]

In a conversation with Kissinger shortly after the president's return to Washington, Soviet Ambassador Dobrynin suggested that there were "positive possibilities" to negotiate on Berlin. On March 26 in a letter to Kosygin, Nixon repeated his offer to negotiate on Berlin. According to Henry Kissinger,[12] Kosygin replied on May 26 to the effect that "the Soviet Union had no objections to a discussion of Berlin but that the Federal Republic was to blame for any tension there." These were purely bilateral exchanges. There is nothing to indicate that the British, French, or Germans were consulted. Kissinger states that after receipt of the Kosygin reply he recommended against pursuing the subject further in a bilateral channel.

Meanwhile, in the same time frame as Nixon's exchange with Dobrynin, an initiative was taken in NATO at Brandt's instigation and with full Alliance consultation. A NATO ministerial meeting was held in Washington in April 1969, and at the quadripartite dinner on Berlin and Germany, Brandt expressed his belief that during the harassment connected with the holding of the Federal Assembly in Berlin the Soviet Union, without changing its basic objectives with respect to Berlin, had shown a willingness to compromise while the GDR had not. Less than a month before, the Warsaw Pact, in a communiqué issued at Budapest on March 17, 1969, had again proposed the convocation of a European security conference. Brandt presented a German talking paper at the quadripartite dinner suggesting that the time might be opportune for the three Western powers to explore within the context of European security what the Soviet Union was prepared to do on Berlin and other aspects of the German question. The Alliance endorsed the idea, and the communiqué, issued on April 11, stated that the achievement of a peaceful European settlement presupposed progress toward the elimination of existing sources of tension in the center of Europe: "Concrete measures aimed at improving the situation in Berlin, safeguarding free access to the city, and removing restrictions which affect traffic and communications between the two parts of Germany would be a substantial contribution toward this objective." The NATO ministers endorsed continued efforts by the Three Powers in the framework of their special responsibilities for Berlin and Germany as whole, to explore possibilities for negotiated progress in these important questions.[13] The U.S. embassy in Bonn commented to Washington the next day that this was the best possible reaction to the Warsaw Pact proposal since it focused attention on Berlin as an area in which the Soviets should demonstrate their good intentions prior to serious consideration of a major East–West conference.[14]

Thus began the second of the linkages that were to be of critical importance in the achievement of the Berlin agreement of 1971. In light of the impression that subsequently gained currency that linkages originated with Henry Kissinger, as truth with God, it is well to note that the first linkage (between acceptance of the GDR, reflected ultimately in the Four Power Agreement on Berlin, and improvements in Berlin) was proposed by Brandt and the second (tying a European security conference to successful negotiations on Berlin) originated in NATO on the basis of instructions from foreign ministries and the Department of State.

In the next three months extensive consultations were held among the four Western powers, largely in Bonn, on the form and substance of a formal approach to Moscow concerning Berlin and Germany. Fairly broad agreement had been reached on a "tripartite sounding" of the Soviet Union when, on July 10, Foreign Minister Gromyko delivered a speech before the Supreme Soviet in which after again blaming tension in Berlin on "unlawful attempts of the Federal Republic of Germany to use Berlin's territory for hostile purposes," the foreign minister indicated that if the Western powers,

our allies in the war which bear their share of the responsibility for the situation in West Berlin, will approach this question taking into account the interests of Soviet security, they will find the Soviet Union willing to exchange views as to how complications concerning West Berlin can be prevented now and in the future.

Gromyko emphasized that the Soviet Union would not agree to take "any steps harmful to the just interests of the GDR and the special status of West Berlin." He described Berlin's international status as "unique," lying in the center of the GDR. But he did not say it was part of the GDR.[15] Very obviously the tripartite sounding would have to be reworded to take Gromyko's speech into account.

On July 14, four days after Gromyko's speech, the director of the Office of

Central European Affairs in the Department of State, which had responsibility for German matters, sent a memorandum to the assistant secretary for European affairs, Martin Hillenbrand, commenting that Brandt, in his initial proposal for a tripartite initiative with the Soviet Union had had in mind talks, authorized by the Four Powers responsible for Berlin and Germany as a whole, between the two German sides. The talks would cover both inner-German relations and German access to Berlin. In the text that had been at the stage of approval before the Gromyko speech German access to Berlin had been omitted at the insistence of the French, who felt access was an exclusively quadripartite responsibility, and should not be dealt with as a German matter. Gromyko's remarks, however, raised the possibility of quadripartite consultations on how complications regarding West Berlin could be prevented. The internal State Department memorandum suggested that the two subjects, Berlin and inner-German communications, were not really separable and that the two should be combined in a tripartite approach. Advice received from the embassy in Bonn was cited as stating that should the United States be unwilling to respond to Gromyko, the conclusion could easily be reached in the Federal Republic that Washington was fearful of jeopardizing the prospect of successful U.S. bilateral talks with the Soviet Union. The memorandum concluded that while it would be unrealistic to count on Soviet concessions, the United States should not temporize but move quickly to explore Gromyko's proposition.

It was further suggested in the memorandum that the aim in entering talks with the Soviet Union should be: (1) an arrangement for German access to Berlin; (2) pragmatic improvements in the situation of Berlin's inhabitants and reduction of the effects of the wall through such means as the restoration of citywide telephone service and improvement in Berlin's air connections; and (3) provision of a quadripartite framework or "umbrella" that would permit the FRG to negotiate on inner-German questions with the GDR without prejudicing the principle of quadripartite responsibility for Germany as a whole. As part of this concept, the Four Powers—if talks materialized—might agree to refer the problem of German access to the representatives of the two German states for negotiation with any agreements to be submitted to the Four Powers for approval. In this way the West Germans, without direct involvement of the Four Powers, could make economic or political concessions for which they might feel justified in obtaining a better access arrangement.

Assistant Secretary Hillenbrand agreed with the ideas in the memorandum and on July 17 forwarded to the secretary of state for initialing a memorandum to the president recommending Western agreement be sought in Bonn to inform the Soviet government that the United States had noted Gromyko's remarks concerning Berlin and intended to study them together with France, Britain, and the FRG; that the FRG would like to discuss travel and communications problems with the GDR in order to remove points of friction, and the United States believed such talks would be useful; and that the FRG might be willing to make certain compromises concerning its activities in West Berlin if this would promote a constructive Soviet and East German response. These recommendations were approved by the president and appropriate instructions were sent to Bonn.

The last point reflected Brandt's belief that something had to be offered to the Soviet Union if there was to be any prospect of successful talks, and his conviction that a number of the more demonstrative manifestations of the Federal Republic's political presence in West Berlin were more harmful than helpful in strengthening the ties between Berlin and Bonn. Chancellor Kiesinger agreed. Thus the proposal to include this intentionally vague offer originated with the Grand Coalition government, which proposed to the three Allies that it be included in their *démarche*. The offer was considered highly sensitive. Surprisingly, word of it did not reach the press until the negotiations were well advanced, and it was never officially confirmed. Given the readiness of many in the CDU and CSU to attack the Brandt government for selling out to the Soviet Union, it was of great value that this offer originated with the CDU–CSU/SPD government. The three Western Allies did not push for it even though they had never been enthusiastic about activities that the Federal government now appeared willing to renounce.

After agreement among the four Western powers was reached in Bonn, the three Western ambassadors in Moscow communicated the "sounding" to the Soviet government orally on August 6, NATO having been informed the day before. On the occasion of Chancellor Kiesinger's visit to Washington just prior to the sounding, the State Department sent a briefing paper to the White House recommending that the president express satisfaction that the initiative was being taken with the Soviet government, indicate U.S. interest in exploring the possibilities of progress with the Soviets on individual European questions such as Berlin, notwithstanding skepticism as to the likely results, and stress the need for thorough prior consultation among the four Western Allies, as in the case of the initial sounding.

In the subsequent months the impression arose and persisted on the German side that the Department of State was basically opposed to the Berlin negotiations and was frequently responsible for delaying progress. It is true that there were some officers in the department (and more outside) who found it difficult to adjust to the concept of two German states and others who feared that in accepting it, the United States might end up in a weakened position in Berlin and Europe. The U.S. ambassador in Moscow, Jacob Beam, in commenting on the Gromyko speech, thought it suggested that any serious discussion on Berlin could involve high bargaining in which Moscow holds most of the high cards. The Bonn embassy, on the other hand, considered it possible that the Soviet Union might be genuinely interested in defusing the Berlin situation. Such differences were inevitable. What is historically important is that the Department of State took a position promptly to support talks with the Soviet Union and developed the concept of dual Four Power and German roles within one negotiating complex.

As already noted, the president approved the policy, which was presumably reviewed by Henry Kissinger but who, at the time, was not deeply involved.

The Soviet reply of September 12, 1969, was enigmatic. It stated that

the Soviet side would be ready for an exchange of opinions on averting complications now and in the future around West Berlin, if the powers allied with the USSR in the last war which bear their share of responsibility for the situation in West Berlin would proceed from the necessity of an approach toward this question which takes into account the interests of European security. In this connection, of course, the sovereign rights and legitimate interests of the German Democratic Republic should be properly taken into account. It is impossible not to take into account in this connection also that the external ties of West Berlin are carried out along the lines of communication of the GDR.

The response went on to say that with regard to the proposal for discussions between the FRG and the GDR, the position of the Soviet Union found expression in the Bucharest Declaration on the strengthening of peace and security in Europe and in the Budapest appeal of European socialist states.[16] The indicated willingness of the FRG to reduce political manifestations in West Berlin was completely ignored.

The Soviet response, while courteously worded, reaffirmed three principles of the Soviet position that would underlie the Soviet negotiating position: first, that West Berlin was a separate entity; second, that Four Power rights and responsibilities were applicable only in West Berlin; and third, that access routes to Berlin went through the sovereign territory of the GDR. The first two were totally unacceptable to the Western side and the third had been the source of continuing and serious difficulties over the years. Nonetheless, the Department of State decided that the Soviet position warranted further exploration. The Central European Office prepared an analysis pointing out that while it was clear the Soviet Union had no intention of giving away anything at the expense of the GDR, it was making no threats with regard to the Western position. The memorandum concluded that basic Allied rights stem from the defeat of Germany and not from Soviet consent. Therefore the Western powers should not negotiate with the Soviets on these rights. There were, however, three areas where improvements could be sought without negotiating on rights: (1) areas where the Soviets had infringed on quadripartite agreements, (2) areas not adequately covered by quadripartite agreements, (i.e., German access), and (3) areas of concern primarily to East and West Germany that did not directly involve quadripartite responsibilities. If this premise were accepted, a useful way to smoke out Soviet intentions might be to present a list of desired improvements in and around Berlin such as resumption of telephone communications, resumption of travel from West to East Berlin, permission for West Berliners to visit garden areas on Berlin's perimeter, and reestablishment of a citywide planning office for municipal services. The three Western powers might also suggest to the Soviet

Union that East and West German authorities should designate representatives to discuss improved procedures for the movement of German personnel and goods. Guidance along these lines was sent to Bonn, where the Bonn Group was already in the process of formulating an agreed Western position for eventual negotiations.

The East German regime, on September 10—one day before the Soviet reply to the Allies—had informed the FRG that it was prepared to resume talks on traffic matters, including road, rail, water, and postal communications. The timing strongly suggested that the East Germans, though they may have been encouraged by the Soviet Union, wished to avoid the impression that resumed talks between the FRG and GDR were within the framework of the Four Power exchange. Then, on September 12, the Soviet Union replied in notably cordial terms to an FRG note on the renunciation of the use of force, inviting Bonn to hold concrete discussions in Moscow "on the whole range of questions" connected with the subject. The Department of State considered that the Soviet Union wished to give the impression of a serious intention to improve the situation in Central Europe. It was also hardly coincidental that the three Communist moves came during the final stages of the Federal election campaign in West Germany in which Moscow, if not necessarily the GDR, surely wished to see an SPD victory.

The elections took place on September 28, 1969, and while the CDU/CSU won a plurality, it did not gain the majority needed to form a government. It was quickly apparent that the SPD intended to form a coalition government with the small liberal Free Democratic party. This became a reality on October 21 when Willy Brandt was elected Federal chancellor and the leader of the FDP, Walter Scheel, became vice chancellor and foreign minister. In the policy statement of his new government delivered to the Bundestag on October 28, 1969, Willy Brandt expressed the intention to move ahead in negotiations with the GDR with the objective of achieving "contractually agreed cooperation." He stated further that he would advise the United States, Britain, and France "to continue energetically the talks begun with the Soviet Union on easing and improving the situation in Berlin."[17] Immediately after Brandt's speech, Secretary Rogers sent a memorandum to President Nixon on the status of the tripartite initiative on Berlin expressing the conclusion—based partly on a conversation Soviet Ambassador Abrasimov had had with the governing mayor of Berlin, Klaus Schütz—that Moscow seemed prepared to talk to the Three Powers about Berlin and interested in probing the Federal Republic's offer of concessions regarding political activities in Berlin; that the Soviet Union had not ruled out a discussion of German access to Berlin; but that it insisted on taking fully into account the position of the GDR. The secretary indicated that what was now needed was agreement among the four Western powers on a list of topics to be proposed to the Soviet Union for discussion. After the Soviets had responded one could decide whether to proceed further.

On the same day the secretary's memorandum went to the president, the U.S.

embassy in Bonn informed the British and French embassies of Washington's views on pursuit of the sounding, stressing the need to resume consultations rapidly in view of Chancellor Brandt's statement in his policy declaration. (The practice of occasional consultation on Berlin matters among the Three Powers had long been customary in Bonn given their quasi-sovereign status in Berlin, which the FRG did not share. However, consultation with the FRG had always been close and became intense as quadripartite talks on Berlin progressed.) A week later the FRG introduced in the Bonn Group a draft to serve as the basis of a continuation of the exchange of views between the Three Powers and the Soviet Union. This was revised first in the Bonn Group and then in Washington and Paris. On December 11, 1969, the director of Central European Affairs wrote the following in a personal letter to the counselor for political affairs in Bonn, Jonathan Dean:

It looks as if we are getting close to final agreement on the next step in the Berlin probe. I am very pleased with the coordination we have managed to maintain between Bonn and Washington in the past few days. Here we have continued to be plagued by the problem of White House clearance. If we must go through the bureaucratic procedure of referring outgoing cables to the White House under a memorandum from the Secretary or the Under Secretary we can usually count on a week's delay. Having gotten White House clearance earlier on the substance of our reply (to the Soviets), we have been resorting this past week to informal clearance with Sonnenfeldt and this has worked pretty well.

The last difficulty with regard to the tripartite response was French resistance to suggesting ambassadorial level talks in Berlin. The White House at this point gave high priority to cordial relations with Paris and was inclined to accept the French position. However, the State Department, from the beginning, had placed much importance on the symbolic confirmation of the continuing responsibility of the Four Powers for Berlin that Four Power meetings in Berlin would constitute. The White House accepted the idea of a compromise under which the Berlin site would be maintained, but the level of the meetings would be left open. French agreement followed and this allowed the delivery in Moscow on December 16, 1969 of the Western response to the Soviet note of September 12, 1969. In their statements, which were handed separately by the three ambassadors to Soviet Deputy Foreign Minister Kozyrev, the Three Powers:

—referred to (a) the previous exchange with the Soviet Union concerning an improvement of inner-German relations and of the situation as regards Berlin and access to the city, and (b) to discussions between the Soviet Union and the FRG on the renunciation of the use of force, both of which were relevant to European security;

—welcomed the willingness of the Soviet Union to exchange views on avoiding present and future complications as regards Berlin and access to the city;

—suggested that the Four Powers responsible for Berlin and Germany as a whole should agree on practical measures aimed at eliminating such difficulties and proposed that representatives of the Four Powers meet to discuss appropriate measures;

—stated that an important aim of such discussions would be to prevent difficulties in movement between Berlin and the FRG, possibly through an agreement on procedures and practical measures aimed at ensuring free movement of persons and goods between Berlin and the Federal Republic;

—specified that a second aim of the discussions would be the normalization of the internal life of Berlin, including the restoration of the movement of persons, postal and telephonic communications, and commerce between the Western and Eastern sectors;

—welcomed the initiation of talks between the two German sides on transport and postal matters, and hoped that the Soviet Union would be prepared to encourage them; and

—proposed that representatives of the four missions in Berlin meet at an early date to discuss these and other topics that the Soviet side might wish to raise and to agree on an agenda and arrangements for further talks.

The Soviet response was handed to the three ambassadors in Moscow on February 10, 1970. While there was no modification in the previous Soviet positions (in transmitting the text, Ambassador Beam commented that it was calculated to support the assertion that the Soviets along with the Western powers have a special responsibility for West Berlin),[18] the Soviets agreed to meet and proposed that the meetings be held at the ambassadorial level "in the building formerly occupied by the Allied Control Commission for Germany in West Berlin." The next day the protocol officer of the Soviet embassy in East Berlin called on his counterpart in the U.S. mission in Berlin and stated that Ambassador Abrasimov would be prepared to begin the exchange of views on February 18, 1970. The first meeting, in Abrasimov's view, was to be devoted to agreeing on an agenda and on procedural matters. This date was quickly rejected in view of the need for Allied consultation on the Soviet *aide-mémoire*, but the Three Powers said they would be back in touch with the Soviets "as soon as feasible."[19]

On February 13, only three days after receipt of the Soviet response, the acting secretary of state, Elliot Richardson, submitted a memorandum to the president recommending that the United States proceed with substantive preparations for the talks on the assumption that they would take place. The State Department felt that the Soviet *aide-mémoire* still gave no indication of what Moscow was prepared to concede but it gave some hope for reasonable talks. On February 18 Mr. Kissinger informed Acting Secretary Richardson that the president had concurred in the department's recommendation. At the same time, however, the first of the National Security Council Memoranda (NSSM) on the Berlin negotiations was sent to the State Department requesting that a full negotiating paper outlining the background of the talks, the Western and Soviet objectives, possible Western concessions, and the possible outcome of the talks be submitted to the National Security Council for consideration. This NSSM was a clear indication that the White House perceived, albeit rather belatedly, that serious negotiations with the Soviet Union were about to begin and that the time had come to bring the State Department, which until then had had rather free rein, under control.

The detailed response to the Kissinger request was submitted to the president by the secretary of state at the beginning of March and at the same time was sent informally to the embassy in Bonn with the caution that until the president approved the contents it had absolutely no status. In a covering letter to Dean, the director of Central European affairs said that "we have tried to leave a good amount of negotiating flexibility." On March 12 the president approved the position paper submitted by the Department of State without change, and the embassy in Bonn was authorized to proceed with the development of the Western negotiating position in the Bonn Group on that basis. The authoritative formulation of the U.S. negotiating position opened the way for the initiation of the Four Power negotiations—on West Berlin as the Soviets said, on Berlin, as the Western powers insisted.

NOTES

1. Press conference of Secretary Dean Rusk, April 26, 1962. Cited in *Documents on Germany, 1944–1970*, (Washington, D.C.: U.S. Govt. Printing Office, 1971), pp. 598–99. A fuller description of the proposed access authority is in ibid., p. 595.

2. *Documents on Germany, 1944–1970*, p. 600.

3. Willy Brandt, *The Ordeal of Coexistence* (Cambridge, MA: Harvard University Press, 1963), p. 6.

4. Willy Brandt, *People and Politics* (Boston, MA: Little, Brown and Company, 1976), p. 76.

5. Ibid., p. 79.

6. Peter Bender, *Offensive Entspannung* (Berlin and Cologne: Verlag Kiepenheuer und Witsch, 1964), pp. 147–48.

7. Conversation between Sven Baclund and David Klein, November 1981.

8. Willy Brandt, *People and Politics*, p. 155.

9. *Documents on Germany, 1944–1970*, p. 781.

10. The full text of the speech is in *Documents on Germany, 1944–1970*, p. 799–801.

11. Henry Kissinger, *The White House Years* (Boston, MA: Little, Brown and Company, 1979), p. 100.

12. Ibid., p. 407.

13. *Documents on Germany, 1940–1970*, p. 804.

14. Arthur G. Kogan, "The Quadripartite Berlin Negotiations, 1970–71" (Washington, D.C.: Department of State research project no. 1035, Office of the Historian, unpublished), Chapter 1.

15. The full text may be found in the CIA publication, "Foreign Broadcast Information Service for the USSR and Eastern Europe," July 10, 1969.

16. Relevant excerpts from the Budapest Declaration may be found in *Documents on Germany, 1944–1970*, p. 802. In addition to renewing the earlier proposal for a European security conference, the declaration proclaimed that one of the main preconditions for safeguarding European security was the inviolability of frontiers in Europe, including the

Oder–Neisse line and the frontier between the GDR and the FRG. Also essential were recognition of the existence of the GDR and renunciation by the FRG of its claims to represent all the German people.

17. *Documents on Germany, 1944–1970*, pp. 815–16.
18. Quoted in Kogan, ''The Quadripartite Berlin Negotiations,'' p. 59.
19. Ibid.

6

Objectives and Expectations

In describing the circumstances of the prospective Four Power talks, the Department of State emphasized in a position paper submitted to the president in early March that these would be the first negotiations undertaken with the Soviet Union on Berlin since before the blockade that had not been prompted by a crisis or taken place in a crisis atmosphere. There were continuing difficulties and tensions, but the situation was tolerable. With the help of extensive subsidies from Bonn, West Berlin's standard of living was only slightly below that of the Federal Republic. The political leadership was stable and the expenses involved in the continuing Allied military presence in Berlin were covered rather generously by the Federal Republic. The hardship of life in the Western sectors was largely psychological, stemming from the geographic separation from the West, the insecurity of access through the GDR, and the isolation from relatives and friends living in East Berlin and East Germany. But all in all the situation was better than it had been at any time since World War II. Improvements clearly were desirable but, in the department's view, they were not of such urgency as to warrant jeopardizing the present status of the city in an effort to obtain something better.

The leverage available to the Western side in the negotiations was assessed as unimpressive. The State Department concluded that the only Western bargaining counters would be the following:

—a reduction in the FRG's presence in West Berlin

—FRG financial and economic arrangements favorable to the GDR

—an opportunity for the Soviet Union to gain credit for cooperation in improving conditions in Europe and thus increase prospects for a European security conference

—minor increases in the Soviet presence in West Berlin but only in return for an increased Allied presence in East Berlin not dependent on GDR permission.[1]

Under these circumstances, it was concluded in Washington that one should aim at pragmatic improvements within the framework of existing Four Power agreements and understandings rather than seek a new status for the city. Even with this approach, expectations for favorable results from the talks were not very high. In the State Department's analysis there were four possible outcomes of the talks:

—minor improvements in the situation in Berlin such as restoration of telephone service and a liberalized pass system for entry by West Berliners to East Berlin.[2]

—suspension of the talks without achievement of improvements but without a sharp break

—collapse of the talks with a resultant increase in local tension

—substantial results such as free movement of West Berliners into East Berlin and improvement in surface access to Berlin for FRG and West Berlin residents.

The Department of State concluded that the most probable outcome of the negotiations would be either the first or the second. Looking back, it is well to remember that the two most important Western assets were not taken into account in this calculation. The first was the possibility of extending recognition to the GDR and agreeing to its admission, along with the FRG, to the United Nations. (The three Western powers could control the latter since UN membership is subject to their veto as permanent members of the Security Council.) When the talks started, no decision had been made in Washington concerning such recognition and there were some who opposed it even though it was realized that the British and French were anxious to normalize relations with East Berlin for commercial reasons and probably could not be restrained from doing so for very long.

It was not clear whether the Grand Coalition government in Bonn, with a CDU chancellor, would be prepared to recognize the GDR, although the concept of two German states in one nation was already current in the SPD, the other party in the government. Once Brandt assumed the chancellorship, the readiness of the FRG to agree to general recognition of the East German regime became much more likely. Already in March 1970, Hans Georg Wieck, then deputy to Egan Bahr as head of the Policy Planning Staff of the West German Foreign Office, told David Klein, the U.S. political advisor in Berlin, that the Brandt government was moving consistently and inevitably toward full recognition of the GDR. Signals had been given to the East Germans that this was an attainable goal if they would bargain seriously with Bonn. Wieck indicated senior levels in Bonn realized that recognition of the GDR could have serious implications for Berlin but they tended to think that preservation of Berlin's status was an Allied responsibility. Egon Bahr seemed prepared to accept Four Power control of West Berlin, which would safeguard it from the East Germans. The second important negotiating asset came into existence only later when the FRG made ratification of its treaty of August 12, 1970 with the Soviet Union on the non-use of force dependent on a successful outcome of the Berlin negotiations. Had these been taken into account the department might have been more optimistic.

At the same time, the possible dangers entailed in negotiations as foreseen in Washington were also assessed as modest. They were defined as:

—the possibility of friction between the Three Powers and the FRG with regard to the Western negotiating position

—Soviet utilization of the talks to reinforce their contention that quadripartite responsibility is limited to West Berlin

—Soviet utilization of the FRG's willingness to reduce its political presence in Berlin to insist on the elimination of FRG activities essential to West Berlin's viability

—a psychological letdown for Berlin if the talks should fail

—enhancement of the position of the GDR.

All were considered real but manageable. Moreover, it was felt that merely by holding Four Power talks on Berlin the U.S. would gain the following advantages:

1. They could highlight the continuing Four Power responsibility for questions relating to Berlin and Germany as a whole.

2. They could provide a Four Power umbrella for the FRG's talks with the Soviet Union and especially the GDR and reduce the likelihood that these talks could imply a change in the status of Berlin or in the rights and responsibilities of the Four Powers.

3. They would draw renewed attention to the importance of Berlin in the strengthening of European security and world peace.

Taking these various factors into account, the following guidelines were sent to the embassy in Bonn to be used in seeking agreement in the Bonn Group on a negotiating strategy:

1. While publicity was certain to be extensive, the likelihood of dramatic developments should be intentionally downplayed. The Western negotiators should not be under the pressure of extravagant public expectations. The schedule of the talks should be flexible in order to avoid deadlines and apparent climaxes. If progress was not possible, an adjournment *sine die* could provide a quiet and reasonable denouement, since the four chief representatives were stationed in Germany and could reassemble at the request of any one of them.

2. The Western side should seek to place its proposals for improvements on the agenda first and in specific terms. The presentation should be non-polemical, but the point should be clearly made that the improvements sought were in each

case the elimination of unwarranted restrictions imposed by Soviet or East German authorities.

3. It could be anticipated that the Soviets would insist that only the GDR was competent to discuss the processing of German persons and goods between Berlin and the FRG. The Soviet side might take the same position with regard to inter-sector communications. The FRG was quite prepared to deal with the GDR on access and there were precedents for this. The Berlin *Senat*, too, was willing, even eager, to discuss inter-sector matters either with East Berlin representatives, as it did in the earlier Christmas and Easter pass arrangements, or, if necessary, with GDR officials. The Three Powers should be flexible on this question. They would need (a) to establish for the record that unhindered Berlin access and freedom of movement within Berlin remained quadripartite responsibilities and (b) to ensure that they were not left in the quadripartite forum with nothing to talk about but FRG concessions on its political presence, while all positive subjects were transferred to the inner-German level for negotiation. Beyond this, the Three Powers should welcome German contributions to the solution of existing problems, whether through separate FRG–GDR talks or through the participation of German advisers in the quadripartite negotiations; and they should urge that the Soviet Union meet its responsibilities by influencing GDR and East Berlin authorities to take constructive attitudes.

4. Discussion should be directed to specific and pragmatic issues, and arguments over principle should be limited to the minimum required to maintain the Western legal position.

5. No Western concessions should be implemented until there was ample evidence that improvements sought by the West would be realized.

6. If in the course of the talks the Soviets or East Germans should seek to exert pressure by interfering with Berlin access or introducing other harassment, the Western powers should suspend discussions.

Just as the basic position paper including these guidelines was nearing completion in the Department of State for submission to the White House, the FRG had presented a memorandum to the Three Allies, defining the following objectives for the negotiations:

(a) Both sides would recognize the "factual situation" that had developed in East and West Berlin on the basis of decisions taken by the three Western powers in the case of the Western sectors and by the Soviet Union in the case of the Soviet sector.

(b) Within the framework of such an understanding the Soviet Union should agree to respect the ties that have developed between West Berlin and the FRG. Berlin deputies in the Bundestag should be allowed to vote except in the case of legislation that would not be applicable to Berlin.

(c) The Soviet Union should agree to the protection of the foreign interests of West Berlin and its residents by the FRG.

(d) Undisturbed civilian access between West Berlin and the Federal Republic should be ensured.

Points (a) and (b) were rather different from what Washington had in mind. Point (a) represented an extension to Berlin of the principle of accepting existing realities that underlay Brandt's Eastern policy. In the Eastern policy context it meant among other things acknowledgment of the Oder–Neisse line as the Western border of Poland and of the existence of two German states. Washington understood that in the case of the Western sectors, acceptance of the "factual situation" by the Soviet Union would mean acceptance of the extensive ties that had developed between West Berlin and the FRG, with the exception of as yet undefined "demonstrative manifestations," which Bonn was prepared to renounce. From the U.S. point of view this would be very welcome. However, the application of this principle to East Berlin could mean Western acceptance of its incorporation into the GDR, and of the Soviet contention that quadripartite authority was no longer applicable there. This, it was felt in Washington, and in London and Paris as well, was a matter that would require much study before it could be incorporated into the Western negotiating position. It never was, although it can be argued that with the establishment of Western embassies in East Berlin the factual situation, with the necessary legal caveats, was accepted.

Bonn's proposal that Berlin deputies in the Bundestag should be allowed to vote except in the case of legislation that would not be applicable in Berlin was even more problematical. It had a long history. Article 23 of the Basic Law of the Federal Republic of Germany lists Greater Berlin among the *Länder* (states) where the Basic Law would apply. Article 144(2) provides that

insofar as restrictions are imposed on the application of the Basic Law to one of the *Länder* enumerated in Article 23, paragraph (1), or to a part of one of those *Länder, that Land* or a part of that *Land* shall have the right, in accordance with Article 38, to send representatives to the Bundestag and, in accordance with Article 50, to the Bundesrat.[3]

In approving the Basic Law, the three Western military governors made several reservations. "A third reservation," they stated,

concerns the participation of Greater Berlin in the Federation. We interpret the effect of Articles 23 and 144(2) of the Basic Law as constituting acceptance of our previous request that while Berlin may not be accorded voting membership in the Bundestag or Bundesrat nor be governed by the Federation, she may, nevertheless, designate a small number of representatives to attend the meetings of those legislative bodies.[4]

This reservation was maintained when in 1954 the Conventions on Relations between the Three Powers and the Federal Republic transferring sovereignty to the Federal government were signed. At that time the three high commissioners, as successors to the military governors, stated that the reservation made on 12 May, 1949, by the Military Governors concerning Articles 23 and 144(2) of the Basic Law will, owing to the international situation, be formally maintained by the Three Powers in the exercise of their right relating to Berlin after the entry into force of those Conventions.[5]

The Electoral Law for the First Bundestag stated in Article 26 that Greater Berlin would "have the right to send eight delegates to the Bundestag in an advisory capacity, until Land Berlin joins the Federal Republic of Germany."[6] When the Berlin government proposed to hold elections to choose these delegates, the Allied *Kommandatura* objected and ordered that they be chosen by the city assembly.[7] This situation continued to prevail in 1970 (as it does today), although over the years it had been accepted that the Berlin delegates might vote on purely procedural points but not on legislation or on substantive questions such as the election of the chancellor.

Thus while the Federal government, in its memorandum to the three Western powers, worded its proposal as if it were the Soviet Union that should approve voting rights in the Bundestag for the Berlin deputies, it was really the Western powers who had forbidden such rights. Only they could remove the prohibition. The Brandt government had good reason to wish to see this happen. Its majority was razor thin and vulnerable to defections within the ranks of the FDP, the SPD's coalition partner. Of the twenty-two Berlin delegates thirteen were SPD, one was FDP, and eight were CDU. If they were empowered to vote, the Brandt government would be considerably more secure. It was hinted to the Western powers that Brandt had reason to know the Soviet Union, given its interest in preserving the SPD-led government, would not object to allowing the Berlin representatives to vote.

All three Western powers had strong reservations against the proposal. They viewed the withholding of Berlin voting rights as the most important element in maintaining their basic requirement that Berlin would not be governed by the Federation, something that they felt must be maintained regardless of the Soviet attitude on voting. Beyond this there was much concern because the proposal automatically injected the Western powers, especially the Americans in view of their greater influence, directly into the internal political process of the Federal Republic. The CDU, while it could not take an overt stand against Berlin voting rights given the wide public support that Berlin's integration into the Federal structure enjoyed, patently would not be happy with an Allied move that could perpetuate indefinitely SPD control in Bonn. On the other hand, Brandt viewed continuation of the Allied veto on Berlin voting rights as unfriendly and unnecessary.

Despite the importance that the United States attributed to maintaining the best possible relations with the Bonn government, there was no inclination at this time either in the Department of State or in the White House to accept the voting rights proposal. As has been seen, the State Department was more supportive of the Brandt *Ostpolitik* than the White House, but the senior officials in the department were convinced that if the Berlin delegates were allowed to vote, the Allied position in Berlin would become more tenuous. Moreover, it was not something to be taken up with the Soviets, since this was a West Berlin issue to be decided by the Western powers, not the Soviet Union. As for the White House, President Nixon went further. Just prior to Brandt's Washington visit in April 1970, he directed in an internal memorandum circulated by Henry Kissinger that the United States should not become involved in individual aspects of the Brandt government's Eastern policy. The United States should "endorse the objective of a normalization of the FRG's relations with the East" without endorsing or opposing those aspects of this policy that do not relate directly to "our rights and responsibilities." The director of the State Department Office of Central European Affairs wrote to the U.S. minister in Bonn, Russel Fessenden, that the memorandum reflected White House thinking that the United States should not become too associated with the SPD. The White House was receiving many appeals from Germany to stop the SPD from "sliding down the slippery slope toward accommodation with the USSR." In the letter it was noted that by withholding endorsement of the *Ostpolitik,* the United States became just as involved in German domestic politics as by affording it continuing support. The director doubted that the distinction made in the White House memorandum could, as a practical matter, be implemented. There was no doubt, however, that the White House, given the thinking that the memoradum represented, would strongly oppose a move which, in the context of the political situation in Bonn, might indeed amount to an intervention on the SPD's behalf.

Eventually the proposal was rejected. Brandt reacted bitterly and may well have seen this as an indication of a U.S. interest in seeing his government and his Eastern policy fail. (As described in Chapter 13, Brandt again put forward the proposal after the Quadripartite Agreement was completed and Ambassador Rush obtained President Nixon's approval to concur in it.)

There were other ways, too, in which the West German thinking differed from that of the Americans, the British, and the French. Bonn did not give first priority in the negotiating process to the restoration of communications within Berlin, which the three Allies saw as a primary objective of the negotiations. Instead the West German government placed major emphasis on gaining Soviet acknowledgment of the ties between West Berlin and the Federal Republic and Soviet acceptance of the representation abroad of the Western sectors by the Federal Republic. The position paper that President Nixon approved before the talks began noted that while not specifically stated in communications to the Soviets because of drafting problems with the French, the United States (like Britain and the FRG) had been thinking in terms of seeking Soviet endorsement of the economic, juridical, and financial ties between Bonn and West Berlin. The French, however, had traditionally been more restrictive than the Americans or the British in the interpretation of the separation between West Berlin and the Federal Republic. (Hours had been devoted in earlier years in the *Kommandatura,* for example, to French objections to signs pointing the way to outgoing flights in the Berlin airport that said "Übriges Bundesgebiet," meaning "to other points in the Federal Republic.") In the initial phase of developing the Western negotiating position, the French were reluctant to push for Soviet acknowledgment even of non-political ties between the two areas. Later a disagreement was to develop between the U.S. embassy in Bonn (whose views reflected those of the Federal government) and Washington on negotiating tactics with regard to the ties (this will be described in a subsequent chapter). The United States was consistent from the beginning in holding (1) that the ties between West Berlin and Bonn were an essential element in Berlin's viability and (2) that any restrictions on the manifestation of these ties in the form of the Federal presence in Berlin must be first proposed by the FRG before being introduced in the negotiations with the Soviets.

Soviet acquiescence in the representation of Berlin's foreign interests by the Federal Republic was and remained essentially a West German objective and one that they held to tenaciously. The reasons were understandable. The three Allies had authorized the Federal Republic to represent Berlin abroad. This gave rise to no difficulties outside the Soviet bloc. The Western sectors were routinely included in bilateral and multilateral treaties of the Federal Republic, and West Berlin residents encountered no difficulty in traveling on Federal passports or in turning to FRG embassies and consulates for assistance. West Berlin had even been included in many West German commercial agreements with Eastern European countries and with the GDR by reference to the "D-Mark Zone," which obviously included West Berlin. Since 1963, however, the Soviet Union had refused to accept this device. Moreover, it and a number of its allies refused to give visas to West Berliners with West German passports. Since it was a domestic political necessity for the Bonn government to ensure the inclusion of West Berlin in its treaties, it found itself circumscribed in the possibilities of expanding treaty relations with the Soviet Union and, to a lesser degree, with other Eastern European countries in such fields as culture, science, and consular services, since they would not accept a specific reference to the inclusion of West Berlin. Similarly, Warsaw Pact countries refused to participate in international conferences in West Berlin if they were sponsored by the Federal Republic. This interfered with the efforts of Bonn and of the Berlin *Senat* to strengthen West Berlin's viability by promoting it as an international center, in the interest of which ample and expensive facilities had been built.

By June 1, 1970, the Bonn Group had completed a "scope paper," which took over intact large portions of the earlier U.S. position paper while adding further points relating especially to the ties between the Western sectors and the Federal Republic. As regards treatment of the Federal presence in Berlin, and of Berlin–FRG ties, guidance was included that the Allies should rebut Soviet charges of illegality, but not initiate a discussion of principle on the basis of Federal activities in Berlin. If the progress of the talks should justify it, the Western side should be prepared to identify those activities that had for their main purpose the maintenance of Berlin morale in the face of outside pressures and which therefore might be dispensable. The Soviets should be probed to discover which activities they regarded most negatively. *If an understanding could be reached with the Soviets on giving up certain activities, it should be understood that all the remaining Federal activities would be considered by the Soviet Union, even if only tacitly, as compatible with the status of the city.* The Soviets would be required to act accordingly, in particular, by dropping their opposition to the inclusion of West Berlin in commercial agreements concluded by the FRG, and by dropping their objections to FRG consular protection for West Berliners. It was felt that clarification along these lines should also facilitate efforts to stabilize access, since the Soviets had argued that it was "illegal" FRG activities that had promoted difficulties on the access routes. The Western powers agreed to avoid a situation where they would be asking the Soviet Union to approve each specific FRG activity in Berlin or each tie.

The words in italics reflect the concept, taken over from other treaties and agreements, that what is not specifically prohibited is permitted. This concept had by June 1970 assumed much importance on the Western side and was fully accepted in Washington.

The guidelines included in the Bonn Group scope paper also took account of the stultifying formality of the initial ambassadorial talks and proposed that thought be given at an appropriate stage to moving the talks to the working level of the Berlin political advisors, the senior political officers in the Allied missions in Berlin. The Bonn scope paper suggested that the Allies might consider proposing at some future stage the explicit reaffirmation by the Four Powers of quadripartite responsibility for unimpeded access, but noted that for the present the risks of Soviet rebuttal ruled out this course. This reflected one of the few substantive (as opposed to tactical) differences that existed between U.S. authorities in Bonn, Berlin, and Washington. Dean, the political counselor in Bonn, in line with his letter quoted earlier, felt deeply that the Western side should not be restricted by preconceptions, determined by past circumstances, as to the limits of the possible. He thought it was at least conceivable that finally, thirty-five years after the quadripartite occupation of Berlin, it might be possible to negotiate the kind of agreement with the Soviets that had always been lacking, one that would define an agreed status for Berlin and provide for free access. In the Department of State and in the U.S. mission in Berlin this was considered unrealistic and undesirable—undesirable since it could imply Western acceptance that their position in Berlin was dependent on Soviet agreement. For these same reasons Washington was not enthusiastic about proposing a Four Power agreement on access, and such a proposal was never made.

The Bonn Group scope paper defined Allied objectives relative to civilian access to Berlin in the following terms:

(a) To obtain assurances for unimpeded functioning of traffic and communications to and from Berlin.

(b) To induce the Soviets to associate themselves in some form with the general principle of Four Power responsibility for Berlin access.

(c) To exclude the unilateral introduction of new restrictions including administrative, financial, physical, and other measures likely to hamper the present flow of traffic and communications.

(d) To bring about improvements in present access procedures by reducing existing restrictions.

With regard to the representation abroad of Berlin's interests the scope paper stated that the Allies should attempt to obtain the elimination of the "discriminatory treatment against the economy of the Western sectors of Berlin." It would be desirable to obtain the Soviet Union's acceptance of the principle of Berlin's external representation by the FRG as provided for in the Allied/FRG agreements of 1952–54. In light of the known Soviet attitude, it was considered tactically wise to begin by raising specific problems such as West Berlin's inclusion in FRG commercial treaties and consular protection for West Berliners and moving to other subjects if the Soviet response were favorable.

Allied objectives relative to inner-Berlin communications were quite specific by the time the Bonn scope paper was agreed. They were defined as:

(a) *Reestablishing freedom of movement within Berlin for West Berliners.* West Berliners should, as a general rule, be permitted to enter the Eastern sector freely. It was paradoxical that West Berliners were the least favored of all Germans with regard to entering the Eastern part of their own city. While the practical modalities could be discussed, the system applied with regard to West Berliners should not be worse than that which was enjoyed by inhabitants of the Federal Republic. On the contrary the inhabitants of the city should have available to them even better possibilities.

(b) *Amelioration of arrangements necessary to movement within the city.* New entry points should be opened to facilitate inter-sector movement of Berliners. The reopening of the subway stations located in East Berlin, among other things, could serve this end. The Teltow Canal in West Berlin should be reopened for barge traffic. Telecommunications, between the two parts of the city, should be restored.

(c) *Solutions of various problems posed by the sector limits that hampered the life of West Berliners.* Since the almost total isolation of the Western sectors from the areas that surrounded them conformed neither to the letter nor the spirit of quadripartite agreements, nor to conditions prevailing in Europe, measures should be agreed to remedy this situation. Minor changes in sectoral borders should be sought. The question of the enclave of Steinstucken should be solved through an exchange of territory that would link it with its neighboring sector. West Berliners should be permitted to make visits for various motives (religious, humanitarian, familial, cultural, or touristic) to locales or places bordering on the Western sectors.

These were the Western objectives. They endured essentially unchanged throughout the negotiations and, in the end, were in large measure achieved.

Soviet objectives, in entering the negotiations, can only be guessed. Soviet positions were clearly and firmly stated in the preliminary exchange of communications and in the early negotiating sessions on the principal issues, as Moscow saw them. On Berlin access the Soviet side stated in its note of September 12, 1969 that the sovereign rights and the legitimate interests of the GDR should be properly recognized. It was impossible not to take into account that the external ties of West Berlin were carried out along the lines of communication of the GDR. This was interpreted by the Western side as suggesting that a major Soviet objective was to gain greater Western acknowledgment of the sovereign status of the East German regime.

The Soviet interest in weakening the ties between West Berlin and the Federal Republic was stated with even greater clarity. The Soviet side contended that the principal cause of tension in connection with Berlin was not interference with access but the ''illegal activities'' of the Federal Republic in West Berlin. It was stated in the Soviet *aide-mémoire* of February 19, 1970, that ''the Soviet Government considers it important, first and foremost, to reach an understanding on the ruling out of activities incompatible with the international status of West Berlin, which continue to be a source of the tension that exists.'' Especially in the Allied missions in Berlin and in the Berlin *Senat* there was a concern that the Soviet objective was not just to limit the political ties between West Berlin and the Federal Republic but, more importantly, thereby to jeopardize the political viability of the city.

The Soviets made no suggestions concerning West Berlin's relations with the East, but they resisted strongly West Berlin's representation by the FRG. They also left the initiative with the Western side on inner-Berlin communications while giving the impression from the beginning that improvements would be feasible.

Three additional Soviet objectives emerged at an early stage in the talks, although Ambassador Abrasimov chose to introduce them in informal conversations rather than at the negotiating table. They were (1) prohibition in West Berlin of the National Democratic party of Germany (NPD), a small rightist group that the Soviets (like many others) claimed was neo-Nazi; (2) strict observance in West Berlin of quadripartitely agreed rules on the demilitarization of Berlin, meaning for one thing that the West Berlin police should not be given hand grenades or machine guns as was currently under discussion in the Berlin *Senat*; and (3) an increase in Soviet representation in West Berlin. (This was posed initially in terms of Soviet commercial enterprises.) While these seemed relatively minor, with only marginal relevance to the basic issues involved in Berlin's status and viability, two of them—the NPD and the Soviet presence— were to prove difficult to handle and to threaten the unity of the Western side.

One can question whether the Soviet Union entered the Berlin negotiations with quite limited objectives, whether they were aiming at something larger such as the prohibition of all political ties between West Berlin and Bonn, or whether they sought an understanding with the Western powers on Berlin primarily as a necessary element in achieving a European detente based on the acceptance of the realities that had resulted from World War II. It is especially difficult to deduce Soviet intentions since it seems highly likely that like the Western planners, Soviet officials did not at the beginning foresee the linkage that the FRG would establish between ratification of the FRG–Soviet treaty on the non-use of force, which was of major importance to Moscow, and the achievement of a satisfactory Berlin agreement. It is surely suggestive, however, that Soviet willingness to enter talks on "West Berlin" was indicated at a time when the Soviet Union and its allies were mounting a strong campaign for a European Security Conference. The connection was apparent, and NATO had already made clear that there would be no such conference without progress in Berlin. While the Soviets proposed reductions in the West German presence in West Berlin that could have had a serious impact on the political viability of the city, they did not push them with the intensity that would have suggested a serious belief that they were attainable. On the whole it seems most likely that the Soviet leaders concluded that talks with the Western powers would be useful in the achievement of the kind of detente in Europe that would permit the Soviet Union to enjoy the benefits of expanded trade and technological exchange with the West and to broaden its influence there and that there were a number of relatively limited objectives directly relative to Berlin that might be achieved in the process. It will be interesting for scholars at some point in history to locate the Soviet equivalent of the original U.S. position paper and determine what the Soviet side calculated it might have to pay in the form of concessions.

NOTES

1. When the talks began, the Soviet presence in West Berlin consisted of (1) Soviet participation in the Berlin Air Safety Center, (2) Soviet participation in the administration of Spandau Prison, (3) the Soviet military guard posted at the Soviet War Memorial in the British sector, (4) an Intourist Office, (5) a Tass office, (6) the Soviet foreign trade organization for the export and import of films (*Soveksportfilm*), (7) the *Novosty-Izvestiya* press agency, (8) the Russian Orthodox Church establishment in the French sector. The Western powers sent (as they still do) frequent military patrols to East Berlin each day. (The Soviets also sent occasional patrols to West Berlin.) The Western military patrols constituted the main visible evidence of the continuing quadripartite status of Berlin as a whole. The United States and Britain had no permanent presence in East Berlin. The French had an unofficial trade mission.

2. Neither the elimination of the wall nor liberalized travel by East Berliners to the West was ever considered a possible outcome and neither was included among the objectives of any one of the Western powers.

3. The text is in *Germany, 1947–1949: The Story in Documents* (Washington: Department of State, 1950), pp. 283–305.

4. Letter from the three military governments to the president of the West German parliamentary council, May 12, 1949, *Documents on Germany, 1944–1970* (Washington, D.C., U.S. Govt. Printing Office, 1971), p. 156.

5. Letter from the Allied high commissioners to Chancellor Adenauer on relations between the Federal Republic of Germany and Berlin, May 26, 1952, as amended October 23, 1954, *Documents on Germany, 1944–1970,* p. 259.

6. *Germany, 1947–1949: The Story in Documents,* pp. 315–16.

7. BK/O(49)139, 30 June 1949, cited in *Documents on Berlin* (Munich: Oldenbourg Verlag 1963), p. 11.

The U.S. Negotiating Structure

This book is concerned essentially with the substance of the agreements and disagreements among the Four Powers responsible for Berlin and not with operating procedures. Within this framework, an examination of the way the U.S. bureaucracy functioned in connection with the Berlin negotiations might seem superfluous and even irrelevant. To a certain extent it is, since the Quadripatite Agreement itself does not need to be interpreted in the light of which American did what. Such an examination is, nonetheless, being included for two reasons: first, because it provides an opportunity to assess the double-track negotiating procedures pursued in several important instances by the United States during the period that Dr. Kissinger was in the White House and subsequently; and second, because it is essential to an understanding of how the negotiating objectives and principles of policy were dealt with by the various U.S. agencies involved.

In Washington the responsibility for formulation of Berlin negotiation policy lay with the Department of State, but the policy as well as the broad negotiating strategy required the approval of the White House. Within the State Department the vertical structure involved three levels: the secretary, William P. Rogers, the assistant secretary for European affairs, Martin S. Hillenbrand, and the Office of Central European Affairs, of which the director was James S. Sutterlin. The horizontal clearance structure within the department included the Office of the Legal Advisor and the Bureau of Intelligence and Research. An inter-agency Berlin task force had long been in existence to deal with crisis situations in Berlin. For the purposes of the Berlin negotiations it was reconstituted as a restricted Berlin task force and subsequently as a special working committee of the European Interdepartmental Group, both under the chairmanship of Assistant Secretary Hillenbrand. Included, in addition to the various State Department participants, were the Department of Defense (the secretary of defense and the secretary of the army were both represented), CIA, USIA, and occasionally, the NSC (in observer status). All major policy recommendations submitted to the White House for approval were first agreed in the group, which met usually at the working level, with Sutterlin acting as chairman in place of Assistant Secretary Hillenbrand.

The drafting of telegrams and policy memoranda was done for the most part in the Office of Central European Affairs. Day-to-day negotiating guidance sent to the field was signed by Hillenbrand after clearance by the Legal Advisor's Office. Telegrams of a policy nature were signed by the secretary but, in accordance with the request of the White House, were frequently referred to the NSC for signature by the president. In reality this was a device to protect the prestige of the Secretary of State, since these telegrams were usually "signed off" in the White House by a member of the NSC staff (either Helmut Sonnenfeld or William Hyland) after discussion with Mr. Kissinger. The Department of State was seldom informed whether the president had personally reviewed a telegram.

Periodically the Department of State was required to submit recommendations for negotiating policy to the National Security Council. These were in response to National Security memoranda and were developed through consultation in the interdepartmental group. They were submitted either by Hillenbrand, as chairman, to Mr. Kissinger as the assistant for national security affairs, or by the secretary to the president. In either case, the recommendations were approved by the secretary prior to submission to the White House, but as a matter of principle the secretary did not submit recommendations to Henry Kissinger. The eventual responses from the White House were in the form of National Security decision memoranda (NSDM), which constituted binding presidential decisions. The NSDMs were highly classified and restricted in distribution. Theoretically they were not to be communicated to the field. The substance, however, was always transmitted in one form or another to the senior level in the U.S. embassy in Bonn.

The principal figure in the field on the U.S. side was the ambassador to Bonn, Kenneth Rush, who was the senior U.S. representative in the negotiations. He submitted continuing recommendations and assessments to the State Department and maintained direct and indirect channels to the White House. For purposes of the negotiations he was assisted principally by his deputy, Russell Fessenden, and the political counselor, Jonathan Dean. He also utilized the staff of the U.S. mission in Berlin, of which he was chief. This was an uneasy relationship, since like his predecessors, Ambassador Rush did not welcome the submission to the Department of State of independent recommendations and evaluations by the U.S. minister in Berlin, although traditionally this had been the minister's prerogative. The situation was further complicated by distrust and differences in judgment between the Berlin and Bonn staffs.

Coordination of negotiating objectives and tactics among the four Western powers was accomplished mainly in the Bonn Group, which consisted of the political counselors from the U.S., British, and French embassies in Bonn and the head of the Office of Inner-German Affairs in the German Foreign Office. These were supplemented by frequent consultations among the three ambassadors, the state secretary in the German Foreign Office, and Egon Bahr from the chancellor's office. There were also senior level meetings among the responsible assistant secretaries (or directors) of the four foreign ministries, a representative from the Berlin *Senat,* and, usually, Egon Bahr. And there were the biannual meetings of the four Western foreign ministers in conjunction with the NATO ministerial conferences.

In brief, U.S. negotiating positions were formulated in the State Department, account being taken of recommendations from Bonn and, to a lesser extent, Berlin, and of the positions of the other three Western powers. The department coordinated the positions with the other interested agencies and either sent instructions directly to Bonn or submitted them first to the White House for approval and then to Bonn. Once a directive or NSDM was received from the White House the State Department was bound by it and had the responsibility to ensure that the directive was followed in the field. This was a relatively clear-cut bureaucratic structure. The number of persons involved on a day-to-day basis was quite small. Cable and telegraphic communications between the State Department and Bonn and Berlin were constant and extensive. All the principal actors knew each other well. There was never a lack of understanding, never a time when arguments could not be made or clarifications obtained through regular channels of communication. The White House was involved in every major policy decision formulated in the State Department and received all relevant telegraphic communications. Yet, because of the method of operation of Dr. Kissinger, an enormous communications gap developed.

Independently, and in secret from the Secretary of State, the White House intervened directly in the negotiating process. In his memoirs Dr. Kissinger describes the special channel of communication he established with Ambassador Rush through a Navy communications facility in Frankfurt to ensure that the Department of State was not privy to the exchanges. The use of so-called back channel messages is common between Washington and field offices. These messages are usually sent over a communications network used for special intelligence and are hand delivered to the addressee by a specially cleared officer. The messages do not go through State Department communications facilities and are not given any automatic distribution, this being their main attraction. They are, however, usually known to the CIA head of station at an embassy. For this reason the usual back channel was not used in this case since, as Mr. Kissinger explains, Ambassador Rush reported to him that the CIA station chief was "very close to some of the embassy personnel." On the other hand, the Frankfurt Navy Office was, according to the advice that Kissinger received from his assistant, General Haig, "completely reliable" and free from any "responsibility to our embassy or any other intelligence or departmental interests."[1] Kissinger also maintained direct contact with Ambassador Dobrynin in Washington and with

Egon Bahr in Bonn, and in this small circle, which was broadened to include the Soviet ambassador in Bonn, Valentin Falin, carried out a separate set of negotiations with the Soviets from which State Department and the other agencies involved in Washington as well as the British and French were intentionally excluded. The extent of these dealings is described in Dr. Kissinger's memoirs.[2] When agreement in the Four Power talks seemed at hand Ambassador Rush, according to Kissinger, sent a jubilant message through the special channel claiming that the bureaucrats "have been foiled."[3] The seeming implication of the ambassador's unfortunate phrase was that the "bureaucrats" (meaning the Department of State) had been intent on preventing an agreement. This was totally false.

In truth, the special channel communications between Kissinger and Rush and Kissinger's covert meetings with Bahr were not entirely unknown in the Department of State. Knowledge existed that a direct communication channel was being used (Ambassador Rush frequently referred rather openly to it, although only after the negotiations were over did he identify the Frankfurt Navy Office), and officers in the department were aware that Kissinger and Bahr were in direct touch. What was not known to the Secretary of State or to the officers responsible for preparing and clearing the instructions to the embassy in Bonn was the substance—or the extent—of what was being communicated. This, patently, could and did lead at times to confusion. In the later stages of the negotiations, Ambassador Rush had secret bilateral meetings with the Soviet ambassador in Bonn and on the basis of authorization from Dr. Kissinger worked out formulations that were subsequently introduced in the regular Four Power negotiating process by one side or the other on a unilateral basis. Chancellor Brandt and Egon Bahr were kept fully informed and cleared (or originated) the positions presented or agreed to by Ambassador Rush. The Department of State, however, was completely ignorant of the prior U.S.–Soviet agreement on these points, as were the British and the French. Inevitably, the State Department raised questions concerning some of the formulations. This caused the senior West German officials who were aware of the prior U.S.–Soviet agreement to conclude, understandably, that the State Department was seeking to interfere with progress and to slow the negotiating process. Ambassador Rush may honestly have felt the same way at times, forgetting that the State Department had no way of knowing that Dr. Kissinger had already cleared on behalf of the president a formulation that when examined by the State Department legal experts seemed susceptible to further improvement.

This extraordinary procedure led, at the very final stage of negotiations, to a serious misunderstanding between the secretary of state and Ambassador Rush, since the secretary thought the ambassador had conceded an issue on which the president had reserved the U.S. position. The issue was that of a Soviet consulate general in the Western sectors of Berlin. The subject of Soviet representation had been under debate for months. In Washington the CIA was especially reluctant to agree to an official Soviet presence in West Berlin but there was general agreement that it should be conceded if a generally desirable agreement depended on it. A NSDM, which was issued by Dr. Kissinger in the president's name in April 1971, directed specifically that the United States could agree to an expansion in the Soviet presence if (a) it was limited, (b) it did not imply an official Soviet representation, (c) if a final agreement that otherwise advanced Western interests, became dependent on this issue, and (d) if the Soviet presence were counterbalanced by some form of Western presence in East Berlin. The Quadripartite Agreement, itself, should contain nothing on the issue and any expansion should be well distanced from the conclusion and implementation of a Berlin agreement. This last provision was motivated by the concern that if the additional Soviet representation were part of the agreement, it could only be eliminated by revising the agreement, even if the Soviet representatives acted in a way seriously detrimental to the security of West Berlin. If, on the other hand, the presence were authorized separately by one of the Western commandants, he could, in case of need, expel the Soviet representative or close the office, without legally affecting the Quadripartite Agreement.

When, early in August 1971, it became apparent that agreement was in sight but that acceptance of a Soviet consulate general would be a necessary part of it, the State Department sent a lengthy memorandum to the White House, which had been cleared by the CIA, recommending that the April NSDM be amended to exclude the presidential prohibition against any office having the character of an official Soviet representation. The other requirements would be retained. The president concurred and required that no change should be made in these instructions without further reference to him. Nevertheless, Kissinger, through the special Navy channel, apparently authorized Rush to agree to the inclusion of permission for the consulate general in Annex 4 of the agreement. Rush, in any event, agreed to it without the Department of State's prior knowledge or agreement. Thus it appeared to the secretary of state that Ambassador Rush in agreeing to the consulate General and several other points, had failed to comply with a presidential requirement. The secretary called Rush back to Washington for urgent consultations at the very moment when the negotiations were on the point of conclusion. (Fuller details on this sequence of events will be found in Chapter 9.)

Prior to seeing Rush, the secretary received a comprehensive analysis of the negotiated agreement submitted by the acting legal advisor, Charles Brower, in Hillenbrand's absence, but drafted in the Office of Central European Affairs. The memorandum identified imperfections in the text but concluded that, on balance, the agreement was sound and advantageous to Berlin. It advised that the Soviet consulate general was tolerable but pointed out that the president had not concurred in the inclusion of provision for it in the text of the agreement.

The secretary, when he saw Ambassador Rush (for whom he had no great admiration, although he later accepted him as his deputy), was not deeply concerned about the Soviet consulate general, in which he had concurred in the earlier memorandum to the president. Nor did he express reservations about any portion of the text as agreed. He recalled that he had earlier admonished the ambassador to take the final step "with all due deliberation," and noted that the ambassador had done the opposite and in the process exceeded his instructions. The secretary's concern was whether the agreement as reached would leave the president vulnerable to domestic political attack. He considered it a major responsibility, which he bore, to protect the president from such an eventuality. Ambassador Rush gave a spirited defense both of the agreement and his negotiating technique, emphasizing the necessity of taking full advantage of the negotiating momentum that had developed. He did not reveal that he had been acting under separate instructions from the White House. The White House, however, was cognizant of the situation, and the secretary received a call during the conversation with Rush, which he took in private as was his custom. According to Kissinger, Robert Haldeman was given the task of fixing things up with the secretary; so presumably the call was from him.[4] The secretary gave no indication, but he did not return to his earlier questions about possible adverse political fallout from the agreement. Very quickly after this decidedly cool meeting Rush was summoned to see the president in San Clemente. Following this meeting the White House issued a press release stating that the president had reviewed the text of the proposed agreement and found it satisfactory.[5] Rush then returned to Germany to initial the agreement and suffered a severe but, happily, brief collapse as a result of the physical and mental strain to which he had been subjected. His subsequent attitude toward the secretary of state was one of genial superiority rather than hostility, and he was wont to refer to Rogers as "poor Bill." When he was appointed as deputy secretary he let it be known that he was to be the channel to Kissinger in the State Department. He confidently expected eventually to succeed Rogers as secretary since the president had told him that only he could get along with Henry. It turned out that despite his high regard for Ambassador Rush, Kissinger preferred to exercise his influence in the State Department more directly.

The sudden recall of Ambassador Rush, the immense physical stress placed on him, and the last-minute interruption of negotiations resulted not from some high-level disagreement on principles. It was in fact totally unnecessary. A simple telephone call from the president to the Secretary of State indicating approval of inclusion in the agreement of provision for the Soviet consulate general, and a readiness to conclude the agreement would have avoided the entire incident. Even a call from the NSC staff to the Office of Central European Affairs would have resulted in a coordinated telegram authorizing Ambassador Rush to conclude the agreement. Instead the secretary of state and the ambassador were allowed to come to a confrontation because each was complying with different instructions from the president. And again it appeared that the State Department was seeking to prevent completion of the agreement. The secretary of state had earlier cabled Ambassador Rush that he was convinced the Soviets badly wanted an agreement. The Western side should take full advantage of this interest to obtain the best possible terms. The Western side should hold out long enough to be sure it was achieving the maximum in improvements in the situation. This was the real attitude of the department, which was unaware that a rather more anxious Henry Kissinger had by then apparently authorized the text as worked out between Ambassador Rush and Soviet representatives.

As surprising as it may seem, this was the only time during the negotiations that the dual-channel technique led to serious confusion with a high damage potential (although it was to happen again in connection with the Four Power statement on the entry of the two German states into the United Nations). Part of the credit for this must go to Ambassador Rush's capacity to keep lines straight. The essential reason, however, was that except for the instance just described, Kissinger and Rush did not depart substantively from the basic negotiating positions defined and coordinated in the Department of State and approved by the president. And, as has been noted, the formulations that were developed between Rush and his Soviet colleague, with the participation of Willy Brandt and Egon Bahr, were in any event subsequently submitted to the Department of State through regular channels for approval as part of the Four Power negotiating process. The extent of these previously agreed formulations is not yet clear since the White House files are not available, and they contain the only record of the secret bilateral negotiations with the Soviets. What is perfectly clear, however, is that Kissinger and Rush did not embark on some new substantive approach to the negotiations and, through a policy different from that proposed by the Department of State (with a major contribution from the embassy in Bonn), find an otherwise unachievable solution for a Berlin agreement.

Why, then, did Dr. Kissinger and Ambassador Rush, with the knowledge and approval of President Nixon, find it desirable to engage in such an elaborate subterfuge aimed at intentionally deceiving the secretary of state, who is the principal official charged with the conduct of foreign policy and senior advisor to the president on foreign affairs? As has become very evident more recently, this question has an importance going behond the Berlin negotiations or even the Nixon–Kissinger administration. It is easy to conclude from the account of events given in Mr. Kissinger's memoirs that successful diplomacy depends on the secret manipulation by one brilliant individual of all the factors at play within the framework of a global concept in which discrete issues are dealt with for interrelated leverage toward a known comprehensive objective. If this is true, as many certainly believe, it is a technique deserving study and emulation. If it is not, emulation can be dangerous and the enlightenment of the many deceived disciples a matter of some lasting importance.

Ambassador Rush, in explaining the reasons for this negotiation technique, said in a lengthy interview on West German television[6] that on returning to Washington during the six-week recess in the talks at the beginning of 1971 he talked with John Mitchell, the attorney general,

who was really the President's primary advisor. . . . I talked to him and told him that the way we were going, we were not going to make any progress. And then at dinner one night with John Mitchell and Henry Kissinger, we evolved the idea of having secret negotiations with the Soviet Union, because it was obvious that the way we were going now, where you had three or four differing governments, where you had within our own government various serious infighting as to what could be done with regard to Berlin, we weren't going to get anywhere. And the President then authorized me to have private negotiations with either Ambassador Abrasimov or Ambassador Falin in Bonn, or both, and this was to be arranged with the Soviet Union, that is, by President Nixon and through Henry Kissinger, and I assume that Henry Kissinger was the one who got in touch with— through (Ambassador) Dobrynin probably—the Soviet Union. I kept Chancellor Brandt fully informed, he knew about it from the beginning.

Thus, Ambassador Rush's version: He originated the idea of the secret bilateral negotiations because (1) there were too many parties involved in the negotiations and (2) there was serious infighting within the U.S. government on the Berlin question. Taking Ambassador Rush's second justification first, it would strongly suggest that working relations between the White House, the State Department and the embassy in Bonn were tense, unfriendly, distrustful, and marked by substantive conflicts. This was not the case.

As has already been mentioned, the very comprehensive initial negotiating paper prepared by the department was approved without change by the president. No new substantive element was introduced then or later by the National Security Council or by Dr. Kissinger personally. The only suggestion of difference was a cautionary suggestion from Dr. Kissinger's office (Sonnenfeld to Sutterlin) that the Department of State might be too enthusiastic in supporting Brandt's Eastern policy. Working-level relationships were friendly, even though it was obvious that NSC staff members were enjoined from giving information to the State Department about the views or actions of the president or Kissinger. The substantive exchanges with the embassy in Bonn were far more extensive and lively than those with the White House, and there were, at times, sharp differences on tactics, or the soundness of a particular formulation. But in terms of negotiating objectives and the principles of the Western negotiating position there was consistent agreement.

In Washington there was not much room for infighting because the number of agencies and people directly involved was so small. None of these was opposed to the objective of an agreement on Berlin that would bring pragmatic improvements to the life of the city. But, inevitably, there were differences within the Department of State and among the other agencies on particular negotiating points. The responsible officer in the Office of the Legal Advisor was Charles Brower, a very bright and hard-working lawyer, with a fluent knowledge of German and a lively interest in German affairs. He took seriously the need for critical and minute legal analysis of every formulation under consideration, whether developed by the embassy in Bonn or one of the other negotiating partners. While from the perspective of Bonn the extensive legal "commentaries" provided by Washington may have seemed to go beyond the acceptable limits of nit-picking, obstruction was not their intent. Mr. Brower had a good lawyer's healthy suspicion of any potentially binding wording developed in haste by individuals in whom he lacked total confidence; but his efforts were aimed at ensuring an agreement that in legal terms would bring about the achievement of Western negotiating objectives. Sutterlin explained repeatedly to the embassy in Bonn by telephone that the lengthy instructions on legal points were to be seen as legal advice, not as binding requirements.

There were some individuals in the Department of State who had less than full confidence in the reliability of the reporting provided by the political counselor in Bonn, Jonathan Dean, and a good many—especially in the CIA, the Department of Defense, and most vocally in the White House—who had profound doubts as to where the Eastern policy would ultimately lead, who feared that recognition of the GDR by the Western powers, which was increasingly seen as an inevitable part of the process, could weaken the Western position in Berlin. These differences led to no impasses in Washington. The attitude of the Department of State was consistent in (a) favoring the achievement of a sound agreement and (b) resisting subjection to time pressure applied either by the Soviets or the FRG as dangerous (and unnecessary) for the achievement of such an agreement. The department was able to maintain a continuing internal and inter-agency consensus on the negotiations, which was something of a rarity in Washington. No torpedo was ever launched against the negotiations by an agency participating in the interdepartmental group. There were major delays at several stages in the negotiations in providing instructions to Bonn. Without exception these were caused by the absence of requested clearance or guidance from the White House. An early informal exchange between Bonn and Washington is revealing in this respect.

After the election of September 28, 1969, as the new Brandt government was being formed and prior to the initial Four Power meeting in Berlin, the embassy political counselor, Jonathan Dean, who was already playing an important role in the formulation of the Western position as substantive advisor to Ambassador Rush and as the U.S. member of the Bonn Group, expressed his views in a lengthy personal letter to Sutterlin in the Department of State. Like the department at that time, he saw little prospect that the discussions with the Soviets would result in significant changes but thought there had been enough evolution in the FRG position on international recognition of the GDR to justify an effort to find out whether some modest progress could be made. The likely position of the new German government on recognition of the GDR could perhaps be used to advantage. He saw the Western objectives as essentially the same as those the department had outlined, listing them as (1) to maintain the Four Power status of Berlin, (2) to diminish the likelihood of incidents that would involve difficulties with the Soviets, and (3) to improve the viability of Berlin "both to the West and to the East," by which he had in mind primarily access from the Federal Republic to Berlin and West Berlin access to the East. Dean indicated that all three Western embassies felt that German access and inner-Berlin communications should be negotiated with the Soviets, at least initially, rather than being delegated to the German level within a quadripartite framework, as the department had suggested. This was the only difference of substance. Dean's one serious concern was obliquely expressed but clear: he rejected as unwarranted any fear that in the enthusiasm of the negotiating process Western control over the outcome might be weakened. It was not, in his view, dangerous to think about Berlin "differently." Underlying Dean's concern even at this early stage before negotiations had begun was a difference more of perspective than of substance between Washington and the embassy in Bonn, which was to persist and lead to misapprehensions on the German side as well. In Bonn—where consultation with the other three powers was a continuing and dynamic process—Washington's instructions seemed overly restrictive and paternalistic. They were sometimes out of phase with instructions that the British and French received, and the Germans were at the advantage of being on their home territory. Ambassador Rush was to complain at a later point that the department was even trying to tell him when to go to the bathroom.

But if there was a feeling of insufficient latitude in Bonn, there was a strong and not groundless concern in the department that Dean, whose brilliance and total commitment were appreciated, was inclined to go beyond instructions, a concern that was heightened by repeated reports to that effect from the U.S. mission in Berlin. Ambassador Rush was completely inexperienced in diplomcy and had no background in German affairs, although he was to prove a quick learner. The Department of State had a clear responsibility to ensure that positions established by the secretary of state or the president after extensive coordination within the Washington community were adhered to and that the department's instructions, which had the authority of the secretary, were followed and not, as seemed occasionally to be the case, undermined by counterpressures from the FRG inspired by the embassy in Bonn. The result, for the most part, was a creative tension between Washington and Bonn, which kept the major actors at the ends of the cable and telephone lines productively alert, but without the bitterness or abrasiveness that might have resulted had there been serious differences on substantive goals or personality clashes. The situation only got out of hand, as has been seen, when the department sought to ensure adherence to one set of instructions from the president without knowing that the president, through Dr. Kissinger, had given substantially different instructions to Ambassador Rush.

The other reason advanced by Ambassador Rush for embarking on secret bilateral negotiations with the Soviets was the difficulty of reaching agreement when the negotiations involved four Western parties, each with differing views. This, unquestionably, was a complex, time-consuming, at times frustrating process. Yet it must also be said that the Bonn Group proved to be an effective instrument of coordination and agreement among the Western powers. Agreed positions were regularly achieved there and served as the basis of the Western position at each session of the four ambassadors in Berlin. The restricting factor was not really an inability of the Western powers to reach agreement (agreement *had* to be achieved one way or another) but rather that each, including Ambassador Rush, was bound to hold to agreed positions until there was Western agreement to change them. This made it impossible for any one of the Western ambassadors to pursue very far the development of compromise formulations with the Soviet ambassador in the formal meetings. Nevertheless, opportunities for less structured exchanges with the Soviet side did exist within what might be called the "regular" framework of contacts. Each of the three Western ambassadors sought occasions to meet separately with Ambassador Abrasimov, usually for lunch or tea, outside the schedule of Four Power meetings. Abrasimov even visited Washington (he had accompanied Gromyko to the United Nations General Assembly) and had an extensive but uninteresting exchange with Assistant Secretary Hillenbrand. Each ambassador told the others of each informal bilateral meeting in advance and provided a debriefing afterward. These meetings with the Soviet representative were seen as opportunities to explore Soviet thinking and probe for possible areas of progress. No one ambassador was authorized to negotiate on behalf of the others, but neither was there any prohibition against the discussion of possible steps that might be helpful in reaching agreement. There were occasional doubts as to whether the French ambassador was entirely forthcoming in reporting the details of his bilateral conversations. For his initial meetings with Abrasimov, Ambassador Rush was almost always accompanied by a bilingual American interpreter who kept full notes. These were usually sent informally to Washington by the mission in Berlin after the reporting telegram had been sent to the State Department by Ambassador Rush. The notes sometimes provided a somewhat different perspective on the conversations than the ambassador's telegrams, but the discrepancies were not serious. Any free-wheeling under these circumstances would have been difficult. These "legitimate" bilateral meetings with Abrasimov were largely unproductive in the case of Ambassdor Rush and, as far as could be determined, in the case of the other two ambassadors as well.

Besides the ambassadorial meetings, there were both Four Power and bilateral meetings of the political counselors or advisors. The Soviet representative at this level, Yuli Kvitsinsky, was fluent in German as were the three Western counselors. The practice was adopted of holding a preliminary meeting or meetings among the four "advisors" before the ambassadors met in formal sessions. The purpose in these less formal meetings, where communication was easy and the exchange of ideas did not involve commitment, was to explore formulations and concepts that could provide the basis for progress at the ambassadorial level. The U.S. counselor, as well as his British and French colleagues, also had extensive informal talks with Kvitsinsky, which were reported to Washington in considerable detail. Thus there were ample opportunities for informal and free communication and negotiation with the Soviet side at the counselor level, and they proved quite productive when the season of progress arrived.

In reality, what Ambassador Rush obtained from Kissinger and the president was not simply authority to have bilateral exchanges with the Soviet side, since this had long existed; rather, it was authority to negotiate with the Soviets unencumbered by the need to obtain prior agreement with the British and French or the Department of State—this was required only from the White House and Willy Brandt. The Soviet side had repeatedly proposed bilateral U.S.–Soviet negotiations from the beginning of the Four Power talks. This was seen by the Department of State as a probable Soviet effort to create divisions among the Western partners, a view in which the White House concurred, at least on paper. This assumption may have been wrong. Still, quite apart from Soviet motivations, the dangers inherent in dealing secretly with the adversary to the exclusion of two allies whose ultimate agreement would be required are apparent, and would seem justified only if success in achieving a Berlin agreement were dependent upon it. Henry Kissinger contends that this was the case. "The results," he says, "should be judged on their merits, though I recognize a price was paid in the manner of their achievement and though I do not believe it should be repeated."[7]

The views of Henry Kissinger and Kenneth Rush on the need for secret bilateral negotiations with the Soviet side coincided. As recorded earlier in this chapter, while Ambassador Rush has stated that he suggested the idea at a dinner at John Mitchell's, Dr. Kissinger records in *The White House Years* that he arranged to have John Mitchell call Rush to Washington so that he, Kissinger, could establish the secret "channel" between him, Rush, and Egon Bahr for the purposes of the Berlin negotiations. The channel already existed between Kissinger and Ambassador Dobrynin before Rush was brought to Washington. Kissinger, like Rush, cites as justification the unwieldiness of the negotiating procedure, which required decisions within the four Western governments on every point and "weeks of controversy" on every change, "comprehensible only to the few lawyers whose odd specialty was the arcane subject of the Potsdam Agreement of 1945 and its later legal history."[8] For the sake of accuracy it must be stated that on the U.S. side at least, no lawyers with a specialty in the Potsdam Agreement were involved in the policy process. Had there been such, they would have had little opportunity to make use of their arcane knowledge since the Potsdam Agreements do not deal with Berlin. While, in charity, this phraseology can be attributed to literary license, the statement is seriously misleading in a far more important respect. Dr. Kissinger, according to his own account, involved himself directly in the negotiations and activated the channel in February 1971. By this time the negotiations had been under way for almost a year and while progress with the Soviets had been limited in terms of agreement, progress had been very great in precisely the area that Dr. Kissinger singles out for criticism— agreement within the Washington community, and among the Western powers, on the main elements of an agreement.

In December 1970 Dr. Kissinger had forwarded to the secretaries of state and defense and to the director of Central Intelligence the presidential directive to prepare a comprehensive status paper on the Berlin negotiations, including a description of the Western and Soviet positions, negotiating options, and possible fallback positions. The response was agreed in the working committee of the European Interdepartmental Group and submitted to the White House in mid-January. It was an extremely comprehensive document, numbering thirty-three pages plus four appendices. Recalling that a scope paper and an "agreed basis for a Four Power Agreement on Berlin" had been drafted in the Bonn Group, approved by governments and utilized as the basis of written presentations to the Soviets on access, inner-Berlin communications, and Bonn/Berlin ties, the paper stated that there was no disagreement among the Western powers concerning objectives, and while there had been differences on tactics the only substantive issue that remained unresolved on the Western side was that of Soviet representation in West Berlin in which the other powers were more inclined to acquiesce than the United States. This paper was considered at a meeting of the senior review group in the White House chaired by Dr. Kissinger on February 10, 1971. Kissinger did not put forward any new ideas nor did he take exception to anything in the study, which he said was excellent. The meeting was devoted largely to an exchange between Kissinger and Assistant Secretary of State Hillenbrand in which Kissinger was insistent on obtaining a clear fallback position from the West Germans on the Federal presence in Berlin before they ended up "in a romantic *Niebelungen* frenzy." He wanted to ensure that the Americans would no longer be the villain or rather, he said, that "Marty" would no longer be the villain, since he, Kissinger, was now "the good guy."

It was decided that the State Department study did not need to go to the NSC but that, instead, a shorter version with recommendations for a new directive should be submitted to the president. This was done in March 1971, and in April a presidential directive was forwarded by Dr. Kissinger to the secretaries of state and defense. The NSDM was largely in line with the recommendations contained in the memorandum submitted by the State Deprtment. It was this document that defined the U.S. position on a Soviet presence in West Berlin. The NSDM also contained an admonition that the negotiators should continue to make every effort to coordinate U.S. policy with the French, British, and Germans and should not regard themselves as operating under time pressure "outside of the negotiations themselves." In retrospect this would seem an extraordinary example of disingenuity.

So much for Washington infighting.

A complete Western draft test had already been presented to the Soviets on February 5, 1971, after extensive but surely necessary discussions among the Western four. It was destined to undergo extensive change, but it represented the achievement of a broad consensus on the desired elements of an agreement. Had this not been the case no amount of secret negotiations with Ambassador Dobrynin or Ambassador Falin could have achieved very much. They could not take the place of the certainly cumbersome but indispensable task of gaining agreement among the agencies in Washington and among the Allied negotiating partners on the elements of the agreement to be sought from the Soviets. Dr. Kissinger, who, like President Nixon, distrusted the government departments and their staffs, recognizes this to an extent. He states that he would introduce as planning topics issues that were actually being secretly negotiated. "In this manner I could learn the views of the agencies . . . without formally 'clearing' my position with them. What I proposed to Dobrynin would reflect a bureaucratic consensus.''[9] Patently, if there had been a real problem as he suggests in reaching consensus within the U.S. bureaucracy, he would not, under this procedure, have been able to make very rapid progress with Dobrynin. This is an important point to be kept in mind by any negotiators who in the future might disregard Kissinger's advice and seek to follow his model, without understanding the necessity of negotiating on the firm basis of a previously, and often laboriously, achieved U.S. or Western consensus.

In reality, after the NSSM of December 1970 (which preceded the "channel") Dr. Kissinger did not "introduce planning topics" into the inter-agency structure until August, when there was a request from him for a comprehensive study on the single question of a Soviet consulate general in West Berlin.

Given Dr. Kissinger's fondness for conceptualization, it must be said in fairness that his interest in having a secret channel of negotiations may have derived from the enhanced possibility this could provide of relating the tempo and progress of these negotiations with other aspects of the global U.S.–Soviet relationship, a linkage that would be in his control. He relates that on one occasion, in May 1971, he instructed Rush to postpone a meeting with Ambassador Falin because of a negative development in the SALT talks. Similarly, Rush was told to delay a negotiating round until after Kissinger's visit to Peking was announced. Neither appears to have constituted a real linkge or to have had any global consequence. At one point in the negotiations State Secretary Horst Ehmke, a prominent member of the SPD and at that time in the chancellor's office, came to Washington convinced that the United States was tying the Berlin negotiations to Vietnam. Even *post facto,* Kissinger claims no such linkage. In no case were telegrams from the State Department to Bonn containing negotiating instructions cleared with the bureau or office having responsibility for the SALT negotiations or Vietnam. Ratification of the FRG's treaty with the Soviet Union on the non-use of force, as well as the holding of a European security conference, had both already been linked to a successful outcome of the Berlin talks before the "channel" was activated. There can be no question that the former, which was done unilaterally by Brandt, provided very considerable leverage. It is likely that good use was made of this *Junktim* in bilateral contacts between the West Germans and the Soviets.

So, while the desirability of keeping one set of negotiations in phase with another through central management cannot be challenged, there is as yet no evidence that this was done to a meaningful extent in the case of the Berlin negotiations. Even assuming the opposite, however, a grave question arises concerning the wisdom and necessity of excluding the secretary of state from knowledge of the global objectives to which these or other negotiations were linked. Perhaps the most persuasive reason for excluding the secretary and his senior staff in the case of the Berlin negotiations was the likelihood that they would have objected to a procedure that risked alienating two allies whose solidarity in the negotiations was essential for ultimate success. It could have complicated Kissinger's preferred method of operation and perhaps made it more difficult for him subsequently to attribute the success of the negotiations almost solely to himself and his chosen agent—as he has done. The dangers inherent in depriving the secretary of state of knowledge of important foreign policy moves, while leaving with him the responsibility (a) to exercise personal leadership of the major foreign policy instrument of the U.S. government, (b) to deal, at the most senior level, seriously and in good faith with other governments including those directly involved in the negotiations, and (c) to articulate to the public and to the Congress the direction of foreign policy, are so apparent as to raise the most serious doubts concerning the judgment of the instigators of the procedure. Was the achievement of an agreement a few weeks earlier than might otherwise have been the case sufficient to warrant the risk involved? As has been shown, the necessity did not lie in the inability to achieve consensus in the Washington community or among the Western four. There were no substantive differences between the White House and the State Department that made it necessary to go behind the back of the latter. There is no persuasive evidence that the United States was able unilaterally to utilize the Berlin negotiations as a lever in attaining other current objectives. Nor would the State Department have resisted if in the final stage the president had informed the secretary of state that he was no longer concerned about including provision for the Soviet consulate general in the text of the agreement. One must regretfully conclude that the true purposes served were to enhance the ego and power of a man determined to do battle with a secretary of state who, mistakenly, had no taste for this kind of competition; and, in the case of Ambassador Rush, to gain a somewhat illusory escape from what he viewed as well-meaning but tiresome bureaucratic chaperonage. It was, without doubt, marvelously dramatic.

NOTES

1. Henry E. Kissinger, *The White House Years* (Boston: Little, Brown, 1979), p. 810.
2. Ibid., pp. 823–33.
3. Ibid., p. 831.
4. Ibid., p. 822.
5. White House press release, August 27, 1971.
6. *Ein Gespräch mit Kenneth Rush,* ARD Television, March 26, 1979.
7. Henry E. Kissinger, *The White House Years,* p. 806.
8. Ibid., p. 800.
9. Ibid., p. 805.

The Negotiating Process

The opening of the quadripartite talks on March 26, 1970, was an occasion of drama. The Four Powers were meeting to deal with Berlin for the first time since the adjournment of the foreign ministers conference in Geneva in August 1959. The scene of the meetings, the Allied Control Authority building, had last been used for a Four Power conference in 1954. It had otherwise remained largely empty since 1949, aside from the offices of the Berlin Air Safety Center (BASC), the only Four Power mechanism other than Spandau Prison that continued to function during and following the blockade. Originally the site of a Prussian court, the impressive building, one of the few to emerge relatively intact from the wartime bombings, had become a silent symbol of the failure of Four Power cooperation in Germany. It had been hurriedly refurbished by the U.S. military authorities, since it is located in the U.S. sector of Berlin. If history was to be made, it provided a suitable setting.

In accordance with a prior agreement reached through protocol channels, the U.S. ambassador opened the first session. His speech had been cleared by President Nixon and by the British, French, and West German governments. He first expressed the hope that the talks would bring meaningful improvements for the Berliners and reduce the possibilities for misunderstanding that had created dangerous tensions in the past. The main substantive points in the speech were the following:

1. Three specific improvements should be sought: (1) freer movement of people between East Berlin and West Berlin; (2) freer movement of German civilians and goods between the Federal Republic and West Berlin, and (3) an end to the discriminatory restrictions against the economy of West Berlin and against its residents in their relations with the Soviet Union and the countries of Eastern Europe.

2. These improvements would be compatible with the special quadripartite status of the city, which had resulted from the Allied victory in World War II, and the relevant wartime agreements, which remained valid.

3. The Western powers had welcomed the readiness of the FRG to contribute to the economic viability of West Berlin and had permitted for this purpose the establishment of certain economic, financial, and cultural links along with compatible legal and juridical systems between the FRG and the Western sectors; but the Western powers had "prohibited and continued to prohibit the incorporation of the Western Sectors into the political structure of the Federal Republic of Germany."

4. To demonstrate their readiness to contribute to freer movement, the Western powers along with other NATO governments, were immediately dropping the requirement that East German and East Berlin residents obtain temporary travel documents from the Allied travel office in order to travel in their countries. It was hoped that this would be followed by similar initiatives from the Eastern side.[1]

This speech accurately stated the objectives with which the three Western powers entered the negotiations, and they were seconded in the speeches of the British and French ambassadors that followed.

The opening statement of Soviet Ambassador Abrasimov seemed to justify the rather pessimistic Washington assessment of the likely outcome of the talks. While the Western ambassadors emphasized the pragmatic improvements that were needed and limited reference to the principles governing the status of Berlin to the minimum needed to preserve the Western position, Ambassador Abrasimov confronted the principles question head-on by insisting that the talks related only to "West Berlin," since the Soviet Union had relinquished its occupation rights in East Berlin, which was now the capital of the GDR. As for West Berlin, Bonn, through a series of acts that the Western powers had failed to prevent, was seeking illegally to integrate it into the Federal Republic. The control of travel across the territory of the GDR was the responsibility of the GDR as a sovereign state.

These Soviet positions had long been familiar, but since they were so firmly and authoritatively reiterated, the Western ambassadors found it necessary to reply for the record with a more extensive articulation of the Western legal position. Thus the first meetings became bogged down in exchanges on principle that the Western side well knew were bound to be unproductive, since these positions were contradictory and there was no likelihood that they would be altered by either side. The most intriguing challenge of the negotiations was the early realization, on the Western side at least, that any eventual agreement would have to be phrased in such a way as not to prejudice the legal position of either side concerning the status of Berlin and the powers and responsibilities of the Four Powers. Perhaps the early, rather discouraging sessions were essential, since until both sides had fully reaffirmed their legal positions neither could deal with formulas that might, in the absence of such a clear reaffirmation, seem to indicate a change in principle.

The Western delegations included, in addition to the ambassadors, the political counsellors and one or two more junior officers from their embassies in Bonn, the political advisers of the Allied missions in Berlin, and two or three additional representatives from the Berlin missions. The Soviet delegation included comparable officers from the Soviet embassy in East Berlin but also officers seconded from the foreign ministry in Moscow, in particular Yuli Kvitsinsky, who in the negotiating process served as the Soviet counterpart of the Western political counsellors. Kvitsinsky, directly representing the Soviet foreign ministry, had greater authority than that enjoyed by his counterparts from the U.S., British, and French embassies in Bonn. The West Berlin *Senat,* which like the Federal Republic was under SPD leadership, gained informal representation in the Bonn Group, and the governing mayor, Klaus Schütz, stayed in regular touch with the three Western ambassadors, usually meeting with them on the eve of each quadripartite negotiating session.

The formal Western ambassadorial presentations were the work of several hands. On the U.S. side (and presumably for the British and French as well) the first drafts were prepared in the embassy in Bonn. The U.S. mission in Berlin had the right of comment. Clearance by the Department of State was required, after which final coordination took place within the Bonn Group. The links to Washington from Berlin in the context of the negotiations were several and varied and not necessarily coordinated. There were regular classified telegrams to the Department of State reporting each negotiating session in detail, as well as the collateral informal discussions and negotiations. These received normal distribution in Washington, including the White House, the Pentagon, and other interested federal agencies. The U.S. minister in Berlin provided extensive comments either by telegrams or informal letters to Washington, including the White House and the Department of State. The Bonn embassy did the same. When he considered it necessary to gain the president's personal attention, Ambassador Rush communicated through the attorney general, John Mitchell, who was a personal friend. As time went on, the special channel between National Security Assistant Kissinger and Rush was established, as has already been described.

At the first ambassadorial session it was agreed that the substance of the discussions should be kept confidential to avoid arousing public expectations concerning the ultimate outcome of the negotiations. A brief communiqué was issued following the session, which merely stated that "the Ambassadors of the Four Powers met on March 26, 1970, in the building formerly occupied by the Allied Control Council. . . . The Ambassadors agreed to meet again on April 28, 1970."[2] The original intention was to use this format for all the subsequent meetings. However, on occasion, political events intruded and forced some textual modifications. In one instance, for example, when the West German government was deeply involved in its negotiations with the Soviet Union on the bilateral treaty on the non-use of force and under heavy attack from the conservative opposition, the German representative in the Bonn Group insisted on inclusion in the next Berlin communiqué of a phrase suggesting some degree of progress. The three Western ambassadors accredited to the Bonn government found it difficult, if not impossible, to resist such a request, and the Brandt government was accommodated. On another occasion, Kvitsinsky stated frankly that the Soviets wanted something positive in the communiqué in view of an upcoming state election in Hesse where the Bonn coalition parties were under serious challenge. This was done, in what came to be known as "The Hessian Communiqué," following the ambassadorial meeting of November 4, 1970, when it was stated that "progress in the negotiations has taken place".[3]

At the outset, the pace of the negotiations was leisurely. The first phase consisted of six plenary sessions, from March until July 1970. In conjunction with each session one of the ambassadors gave a lunch to which the other three ambassadors were invited. When the Soviet ambassador's tone and rhetoric became strident in the plenary meetings, the lunches, where a friendly, relaxed atmosphere prevailed, provided a useful safety valve. The negotiations followed a familiar Soviet pattern, with shifts in mood and manner to suit the political occasion. Ambassador Abrasimov tried different techniques on each of his colleagues. When they missed their mark, he was usually resourceful enough to pull back and limit the damage. In an early exchange with the U.S. ambassador, Abrasimov made some threatening remarks. As soon as Ambassador Rush understood from the interpreter what his Soviet colleague was about, he stiffened noticeably and, in words that permitted no misunderstanding, told the Soviet ambassador that under no circumstances would he tolerate that kind of negotiating behavior. Abrasimov took the point and avoided that tactic in his future dealings with his American colleague. At the third negotiating session on May 14, 1970, the new French ambassador, Jean Sauvagnargues, appeared. A well-informed but somewhat arrogant career French diplomat, he came in early for his share of the Abrasimov treatment. Having delivered a learned dissertation on how Berlin got to be Berlin, the Frenchman was reminded by his Soviet colleague that the French really were not present in Berlin at the creation but came in through the largesse of others. This remark was repeated on several occasions, but with sufficient restraint to indicate Soviet awareness that the French could be helpful to Soviet purposes, particularly on such issues as Berlin's ties with the Federal Republic. Abrasimov's favorite target was the British ambassador, Sir Roger Jackling. Somewhat insecure and not too difficult to intimidate, Ambassador Jackling had problems coping with and often retreated under Abrasimov's lambasts.

The first six sessions of the ambassadorial meetings served to set the parameters of the negotiations. At the sixth session, the French ambassador, acting on behalf of the Western powers, tabled a paper containing the contents of a possible agreement on Berlin. The rationale for this timing was to give the Soviets a specific set of propositions to consider during the summer recess. There also was the feeling that there might be tactical advantage in tabling a Western paper before confronting a Soviet draft. The Western proposal reflected the objectives described in Chapter 6 and followed Ambassador Rush's initial presentation. The first section called for an agreement to "facilitate the unhampered movement of persons and goods in and out of Berlin." The second covered arrangements to enable the inhabitants of the Western sectors of Berlin to visit the Eastern sector in conditions "not more restrictive than those which apply to inhabitants of the Federal Republic." The third called on the Soviet Union and its allies to acknowledge the Federal Republic's right to represent West Berlin's interests abroad. Responding, the Soviet ambassador told his Western colleagues that

the matter under discussion at our session is the situation in West Berlin and around the city. I do not intend to enter into negotiations or talks regarding the capital of the German Democratic Republic . . . and I would like to make it clear that in September, at the next meeting, we have no intention of discussing the capital of the German Democratic Republic. West Berlin is an occupied city. This is the reason the troops of the three Western Powers are stationed there. The competence of the three Powers is limited to West Berlin."[4]

At the luncheon that followed this plenary meeting, the Soviet ambassador announced that as a gesture of goodwill, the government of the German Democratic Republic would make possible the resumption of telegraph and telephone service between West and East Berlin. Suggesting that this step was a major concession, Abrasimov proposed that perhaps "you could do something, too." As noted earlier, the Western powers had already dropped the requirement that East Germans, when visiting NATO countries, travel on special temporary travel documents issued by the Allied Combined Travel Board, rather than national GDR passports. With reference to the three-part Western proposal, Abrasimov said it would be difficult for the Soviets to respond since they had no idea what the Western powers were prepared to offer in return. Then reverting to a persistent Soviet theme, Abrasimov said he could tell the ambassadors two things: "We do not want any Federal political presence in West Berlin. Also, please stop those West German political demonstrations in Berlin. Having done that, we can then talk about your demands."[5]

Ambassador Rush, coming to grips with Abrasimov's repeated assertions that there was no linkage between treaties negotiated by the Federal Republic with the Soviet Union and Poland on the non-use of force and a Berlin agreement, said that the Bonn government had indicated the Eastern treaties would not be ratified unless there was a satisfactory agreement on Berlin. The Western powers, Rush went on to say, supported this position. The political reality was that West German ratification of the Moscow and Warsaw treaties would be impossible without a Berlin agreement. Thus the linkage or *Junktim* between a satisfactory Berlin agreement and ratification of the Federal Republic's Eastern treaties, which had already been explained by Bahr in conversations in Moscow, was reinforced by the Western powers and made part of the Four Power negotiating equation.

On that note the first phase of the negotiations ended and the Berlin talks adjourned for the summer. All sides seemed committed to reach some form of agreement. Failure had become unacceptable politically for all parties, because more was now at stake than just a Berlin agreement; the future of the Federal Republic's *Ostpolitik* and of the Soviet Union's *Westpolitik* were now tied to the fate of the Berlin negotiations.

THE SECOND PHASE

Early in September the Soviet ambassador met privately with his U.S. counterpart. In this discussion Abrasimov indicated a Soviet preference for a limited, rather than broad, agreement. He also confided that the Soviets were prepared to live with any one of a variety of simple agreement formats such as an extended statement or a communiqué which, among other things, would contain assurances that West Berlin did not belong to the Federal Republic and would have its own external cultural, economic, and political ties. As a concession, he said, he could envisage access by West Berliners to East Berlin. He also said he would not foreclose the possibility of discussing access between West Berlin and the Federal Republic.

Perhaps the most significant political point was Abrasimov's association of the Soviet Union with preference for an "interim solution" providing for practical improvements rather than a comprehensive treaty on the status of Berlin. Abrasimov also used the opportunity of the meeting with Rush to propose bilateral Soviet and U.S. negotiations excluding the British, the French, and the West Germans. Ambassador Rush, on this occasion, categorically rejected the suggestion, reminding Abrasimov not only of British and French involvement in Berlin, but also of West Berlin's dependence on the Federal Republic of Germany.

At the ambassadorial meeting on September 30, agreement was reached that the ambassadors' advisers would meet in advance of each plenary session. This would henceforth be an important part of the negotiating procedure. The first such meeting took place on October 7, two days in advance of the next scheduled ambassadorial session. On the Western side, the U.S. adviser group was initially headed by the Berlin mission's political adviser, David Klein. The British and French groups were always headed by their political counselors in Bonn. The Soviet advisory team was led by Yuli Kvitsinsky of the Soviet foreign ministry. Subsequently, the political counselor of the U.S. embassy in Bonn, Jonathan Dean, became head of the U.S. advisory group. The ostensible reason for the change was Klein's promotion to the rank of minister, with the responsibility to run the U.S. mission in Berlin. A more important reason for the shift was Dean's much closer relationship with Ambassador Rush and his probable knowledge of the secret Kissinger-Rush-Bahr-Falin channel, from which the U.S. minister was excluded. The advisers' meeting quickly became a major negotiating forum and proved indispensable in resolving problems of substance as well as form. The

Soviet adviser, Kvitsinsky, did not indulge in Abrasimov's histrionics. Evidently aware of the Soviet desire for an agreement, he brought to the discussions a broader political focus than Abrasimov, who often seemed to be playing the role of the Soviet overlord in East Berlin, with close ties to the East German regime. (In the later U.S.-Soviet strategic nuclear arms talks in Geneva, it was Kvitsinsky who took the "walk in the woods" with Paul Nitze.) During the negotiations the Soviets sought at times to exploit their geographic advantage in Berlin by applying psychological pressure on the Western negotiators and the West Berlin population. In November 1970, for example, surface traffic between West Berlin and the Federal Republic was harassed in response to a scheduled meeting in West Berlin of the West German Christian Democratic (CDU) and the Christian Social (CSU) parliamentary groups, against which the Soviet Union had protested. The Soviets clearly intended to make a political point, and they did. In the ultimate Quadripartite Agreement the party groups (*Fraktionen*) are prohibited from performing constitutional or official acts in the Western sectors.

On October 22, 1970, Soviet Foreign Minister Gromyko discussed the Berlin negotiations, among other issues, with President Nixon and National Security Assistant Kissinger in Washington. While the record of that meeting is not yet available and the Department of State was not fully informed of the exchange, it is known that at this time President Nixon stated unequivocally that the United States wished to achieve an agreement on Berlin. It became clear that in this same time frame the Soviet side was in close consultation with Egon Bahr on the contents of the ultimate agreement, as was confirmed at a much later date by Bahr himself.[6] The West German government was clearly interested in speedy progress in the Berlin talks because it had tied the ratification of its treaties with Moscow and Warsaw to the achievement of a satisfactory Berlin Agreement. To a certain extent, the linkage that the West used to press the Soviets for a satisfactory agreement gave rise, in turn, to West German pressure on the three Western powers to move more swiftly to reach an accord on Berlin. Brandt and his immediate advisers concluded—or were told by Soviet contacts—that unless agreement was reached by a certain deadline there could be dire consequences in Moscow. In talking with the three Western ambassadors, Brandt and Bahr insisted that the Soviet leader, Leonid Brezhnev, needed a completed Berlin agreement in time for the Communist party (CPSU) congress scheduled to take place in Moscow in March 1971. If that opportunity were missed, the chance for an agreement allegedly could be lost. Brandt told his SPD colleagues in Berlin that support within the Soviet Politburo for an agreement was so thin that all could be lost at any moment. Responding to this argumentation, Henry Kissinger told the governing mayor of West Berlin, Klaus Schütz, when he visited Washington in December 1970, that if the Soviets were really interested in having a Berlin Agreement before the Communist party congress in March, it was up to them to make it possible. In that same conversation President Nixon pointed out to Schütz that there was some possibility for improvement in the Berlin situation, provided the Soviets were convinced that they needed such an arrangement. The Western side should not be overeager. The Soviets would drive as hard a bargain as they could, the president said, and "we must stand up to this. The Soviets must understand that they would not get something for nothing and that our ultimate aim was to end the recurring crises. These crises had to be stopped. If the Soviet Union wanted acceptance of the status quo in Central Europe, there had to be an end to Soviet-initiated crises aimed at undermining the Western position in Berlin."[7]

Before 1970 was over the differences on tactics and timing between U.S. authorities, on the one hand, and the German chancellor and his close advisers, on the other hand, became increasingly sharp. The Soviet side, sensing possible negotiating advantage in this developing difference, did what it could to intensify the problem. In discussions with officials close to the chancellor, Soviet representatives persistently attributed the lack of negotiating progress to what they alleged was U.S. inflexibility. They charged that the U.S. representatives failed to take due account of Soviet concessions; that the United States was responsible for the slow pace of the negotiations; and that the United States complicated the negotiating process by getting NATO to insist on a linkage between the holding of the Conference on European Security and Cooperation and the successful outcome of the Berlin negotiations. In their most telling charge, Soviet representatives asserted the United States wanted the Berlin talks to fail in order to torpedo Bonn's *Ostpolitik,* which some around Brandt were predisposed to believe. State Secretary Horst Ehmke, during his visit to the United States referred to in the previous chapter, told journalists that while the German side considered the Soviet proposals an adequate basis for accelerating the Berlin negotiations, the United States, for its own reasons, was not prepared to go forward.[8]

Brandt, because of his strong interest in an early agreement, sought at this point to have the negotiating mechanism changed. In letters to President Nixon, the French president, and the British prime minister late in December 1970, he proposed that the negotiations take on a "conference character" in order to step up the bargaining tempo and bring senior members of the four governments, who would supersede the four ambassadors, into direct participation in the negotiations. He argued that there would be much advantage in replacing Ambassador Abrasimov, whom he considered too inflexible and under excessive influence of the East German regime. Brandt also questioned, by implication, the competence of the three Western ambassadors in Bonn.

Washington was not entirely unsympathetic to Brandt's suggestion for modifying the negotiating mechanism. However, State Department officials did not believe that the process had been as static as Brandt implied. They saw a distinct advantage in retaining the two-level negotiating structure of ambassadorial meetings and informal advisers' working sessions to facilitate the essential Western coordination. Moreover, it enabled the Western powers to keep public expectations under control until there was solid evidence that an acceptable agreement was in the making. The reaction of Paris and London was similar and Brandt's proposal was not pursued. Since the differences between the FRG and the three Western powers began to leak, the German government found it advisable to issue a statement to the press which said that Chancellor Brandt and his cabinet felt that the watchwords for the Berlin talks were "patience, tenacity, and without feeling under any time pressure."[9] However, the differences on tactics and timing were never really resolved and dogged the Western negotiators to the end.

At the end of December 1970 Ambassador Abrasimov tabled two documents, one on "principles" and the other on "access." His "Principles" paper carefully avoided any mention of the word "Berlin." Abrasimov's proposal contained, however, the crucial phraseology, "the governments of the Union of Soviet Socialist Republics, the United States, the United Kingdom, and France, in accordance with agreements and decisions of the Four Powers in effect, which remain unaffected,"[10] thus meeting Western powers' insistence that past agreements not be modified in any way by a new arrangement. The Soviet draft sought, at the same time, to obtain Western recognition of changes in the status of East Berlin and East Germany through the following wording:

... taking into account the *existing situation* and territorial realities, guided by the desire to contribute *on this basis* to eliminate tensions in the Center of Europe ... [italics added]

a. The Government of the Union of Soviet Socialist Republics, the United States, the United Kingdom, and France are of the unanimous view that in the area of their respective responsibility and competence, the use of force or the threat of the use of force should not take place.

b. the status existing in that area irrespective of the views that exist on political-juridical questions, cannot be changed through unilateral measures ...

... [the Four Powers] are of the unanimous view that anything that in accordance with the generally accepted norms of international law would be tantamount to interference in the internal affairs of the other or could violate their sovereign rights and public safety and order, is to be avoided.[11]

The Soviet text defined West Berlin as a separate political entity, but Abrasimov made the important statement that as a result of an agreement with the German Democratic Republic and within the framework of a possible Four Powers agreement, the Soviet side was prepared to say that "transit" between the Federal Republic of Germany and West Berlin would take place in accordance with generally accepted norms and principles of international law without interference and on a preferential basis. Abrasimov added that East German authorities considered that

if an acceptable agreement could be reached on all issues under discussion, then a number of changes could be made in access arrangements. These included: providing sufficient trains between the Federal Republic and West Berlin to meet actual demand; the scheduling of express trains in and out of Berlin; the use of sealed cargo transport by railroad or water; and the elimination of certain freight documents.[12]

The reference to sealed cargo transport was of much potential significance. If the seals were applied in the Federal Republic and West Berlin, this would constitute a major improvement in access. If the sealing were to take place after East German inspection, the gesture would be meaningless. Additionally, Abrasimov indicated that the Soviets might be prepared to accept in some form the right of the Federal Republic to represent West Berlin abroad. Kvitsinsky at this time assured the Western advisers that if all other issues were resolved, there would be no difficulties in agreeing on improved arrangements permitting controlled visits by West Berlin residents to East Berlin and East Germany.

Summing up the results of the twelve ambassadorial meetings held during 1970, the Department of State concluded that the Soviets had an interest in reaching a Berlin agreement that would permit the further implementation of the Federal Republic's Eastern policy, contribute to detente in Europe, and bring about a reduction in the Federal Republic's political presence in the Western sectors. While not prepared to change their position on matters of principle, they seemingly were willing, in exchange for Western concessions, to bring about some pragmatic improvements in the Berlin situation that were in the Western interest.

In weighing the alternatives for the next stage of negotiations, the decisive consideration would be to determine the minimum elements for a meaningful improvement over the status quo. From the U.S. point of view, these could be defined as follows: (1) pragmatic improvements in access; (2) provisions for entry by West Berlin residents to East Berlin and areas surrounding West Berlin; (3) language and format that in no way would prejudice the Western legal position concerning Berlin, Berlin access, and Germany as a whole; and (4) such express Soviet acknowledgment of Bonn-Berlin ties and acceptance of West Berlin's representation by the Federal Republic as the Federal Republic government considered necessary for a satisfactory agreement.

THE THIRD PHASE OF THE NEGOTIATIONS

When the Four Power negotiations resumed at the beginning of 1971, the secret channel for bilateral U.S.-Soviet negotiations had been established. The structure of the quadripartite negotiations among the four ambassadors and their advisers continued unchanged. The commitment of the three Western powers to maintain a united negotiating front remained in effect. In due course, however, the changed situation was reflected in some of Ambassador Rush's practices. Rush began to dispense with the services of his own interpreter in informal bilateral meetings with Abrasimov. Rush spoke of what he described as a private visit with Abrasimov in Potsdam, again with no other U.S. representatives present. In the interview with German television cited in Chapter 7, Rush said:

I would use only the Russian translator when I talked with him [Abrasimov] about the agreement . . . my translator came from the State Department . . . and that would have blown my cover, so to speak. But there was no point in the Russian Ambassador's interpreter not interpreting accurately. If he did not interpret accurately, we didn't get anywhere.[13]

Bureaucratic complications also increased within the ranks of the U.S. delegation between political counselor Dean, who was presumably privy to the secret Rush negotiations, and the others, who were not. The traditional practice had been for the U.S. Adviser to report to the Department of State the detailed exchanges of the advisers' sessions. To avoid any misunderstanding, the identity of each spokesperson was usually made clear. Some time after the secret channel was activated, however, comments made by Dean in the advisers' meetings that did not fit State Department instructions were attributed to others. When this brought charges of deception by other Americans present, Dean further modified the reporting technique. All remarks were attributed to either "Western" or "Soviet" representatives. The rationale for this altered reporting style was that the telegrams were being made available to the West Germans.

At the advisers' meeting on February 5, 1971, a new draft proposal that had been developed in the Bonn Group was tabled by the Western representatives. The text took account of those elements of the Soviet position that were not unacceptable to the Western side and incorporated the Soviet reference to Four Power agreements and decisions "which remain unaffected." Additionally, it included a commitment by the Four Powers to "mutually respect their individual and joint rights and responsibilities." Part II of the text called for, among other things, improvements in civilian access on surface routes to and from Berlin. The key wording was that "all persons and goods" moving between West Berlin and the Federal Republic, "whether on road, rail, or waterways," would be "unhindered" and treated on a "preferential basis." Specific points were spelled out in a separate annex with the understanding that detailed measures to implement these provisions would be worked out by "the appropriate German authorities." Part III of the Western draft dealt with West Berlin's relationship with the Federal Republic and provided that the Western ambassadors would advise their Soviet counterpart that the three Western governments, "after consulting with the government of the Federal Republic of Germany," would ensure the existence of "special ties between the Western sectors of Berlin and the Federal Republic," making clear at the same time that "the Western sectors are not to be regarded as a *Land* of the Federal Republic and are not governed by it"; that

constitutional organs of the Federal Republic, the Federal President, the Federal Chancellor, the Federal Cabinet and the Bundestag and the Bundesrat in plenary sessions will not perform official constitutional acts in the Western sectors of Berlin; and the Federal Assembly, which elects the Federal President, will no longer meet in West Berlin.

Additionally, the three Western governments would authorize the Federal Republic to represent the Western sectors and their inhabitants abroad. Finally, the

Western powers provided the draft of a Final Quadripartite Protocol, the last part of the overall agreement, which would have the effect of incorporating within the quadripartite framework the understanding to be reached between the German authorities.

During the weeks immediately following the tabling of the Western draft, the Soviet side mainly asked questions. At the behest of the U.S. ambassador, Washington gave the U.S. negotiating team more leeway on certain points. While earlier instructions required that any agreement on Berlin must include a Soviet acknowledgment that quadripartite rights and responsibilities were in no way affected, the new instructions stated that the language and format of the agreement could be such as to in no way prejudice the Western interpretation of the quadripartite rights and responsibilities as they relate to Berlin.

In the case of access, rather than requiring a specific combination of improvements, the revised Washington position called for pragmatic improvements, which afforded reasonable assurance that German access to Berlin would be less susceptible to arbitrary harassments. The improvements should be evident and of a nature to encourage increased confidence in the viability of the Western sectors of Berlin. Instead of calling for regularized access arrangements guaranteed by the Soviet Union to the maximum degree feasible, the modified instructions required that the Soviet Union be directly "involved in their realization" and that a final agreement should contain no provisions that specifically or by implication would constitute Western acknowledgment of the sovereignty of the German Democratic Republic over Berlin's access routes. With regard to the ties between West Berlin and the Federal Republic, the Federal German presence in the Western sectors, and visits by West Berliners to East Berlin and the surrounding areas, the new instructions provided that the judgment and expectations of the West German and West Berlin authorities should be decisive.

To protect the Western negotiating position, two conditions were stipulated for any discussion of access matters between German authorities: (a) the discussions must take place only after an explicit quadripartite understanding had been spelled out; and (b) the results of the German discussions would be encompassed within the eventual Quadripartite Agreement. The position defined in the amended National Security Council directive on an expanded Soviet presence in West Berlin has been described in the previous chapter. It will be recalled that the directive provided specifically that any increased Soviet presence should be covered in a separate understanding and not in the Four Power Berlin Agreement.

Between the presentation of the Western proposal in February and the introduction of a new Soviet text in March, Egon Bahr took the lead in expressing the Bonn government's unhappiness with the pace and format of the negotiations, since he felt this was delaying his negotiations with the East Germans. At a meeting with the Western ambassadors he complained about Allied refusal to let him present the model of a "transit agreement" to his East German interlocutor, Michael Kohl, and disputed the ambassadors' assertions that such a premature exchange could undermine the Four Power talks. He reminded the Western ambassadors that the Allies had absolutely no rights over non-Allied civilian access. Why, he asked, if they had ever had such rights, did they not exercise them when the German Democratic Republic harassed German civilian traffic to and from Berlin? He suggested that Allied insistence on nonexisting rights would be at the expense of the Berliners and the Federal Republic. The end result, he warned, might be an East German move to close access routes entirely just to prove their point.

On March 26, 1971, Ambassador Abrasimov tabled the long-awaited Soviet counter-draft. While still reflecting basic Soviet positions, it generally followed the format of the Western paper of February 5. It foresaw agreement among the Four Powers on the principal improvements to be achieved; an understanding between the German authorities on procedures for access and inter-Berlin communications; and a final protocol under which the Four Powers would bring the results of the German discussions within the framework of quadripartite understanding. In the preamble, the Soviet text retained the earlier Soviet formulation, "taking into account the existing situation," and rather than referring to Berlin, the Soviet draft used the circumlocution, "the area of the situation to be examined." The Soviet draft provided that surface traffic would proceed "without interruption," but it included the phrase, "in accordance with customary international norms." This was less than the clear commitment that the Western side wanted to ensure the movement of people and vehicles over the access routes without hinderance or obstacles. While the Western draft referred to the "suspension" of provisions of the Basic Law of the Federal Republic that described West Berlin as a *Land,* the Soviet draft stated that the reference in the West German constitution to the relationship between West Berlin and the Federation "had no effect." In explaining the Soviet intent, Kvitsinsky argued that the word "suspension" implied the possibility of a restoration, and as far as the Soviet side was concerned the suspension had to be permanent.

Some of the wording of this Soviet draft would suggest collaboration between the U.S. and Soviet sides in its preparation, the first instance of such secret bilateral work. This would follow logically from the initiation of the secret channel a few months earlier. The British and French would have had no knowledge of U.S. participation in the drafting of the text, and Ambassador Rush reported the text to Washington as a purely Soviet text, to various aspects of which he took strong exception. In retrospect, a certain disappointment was evident in the ambassador's comments, which would suggest that the Soviet text, while incorporating some of his wording, did not fully meet his expectations.

At a senior-level Allied meeting in London in May 1971, the German representatives felt that the latest Soviet text promised almost all the improvements the Western side was seeking. The French, too, were optimistic. Like the Germans, they foresaw intensified quadripartite negotiations. The British and the Americans, while also seeing a prospect of success, were more cautious about predicting the final outcome of the negotiations. The main difference among the participants at this meeting was on the Soviet demand for an expanded Soviet presence in the Western sectors, a question that for some months had been assuming increased importance. The West Germans and the French were ready to agree to the establishment of a Soviet consulate general in West Berlin, and the Germans contended that U.S. reluctance to make an early offer was seriously impeding the negotiations.

Visiting Washington a month earlier, in April 1971, Egon Bahr had told Henry Kissinger at a meeting at the White House at which State Department officials were present, that the Federal Republic, at first, felt it could accept any arrangement for an increased Soviet presence in West Berlin satisfactory to the Western powers except for a Soviet consulate general. However, while en route to the United States, his assistant had suggested that the establishment of a Soviet consulate general might not be so disadvantageous after all. Bahr was therefore reconsidering the matter. He noted that the three Western powers did not have consulates general in the Western sectors. Other countries, such as Switzerland and Greece, did. So, he reasoned, if the Soviet Union had a consulate general, it would be placing itself in the category of the other countries that had such offices rather than in the category of the three Western powers. This argument was poorly based in fact. Of the three Western powers, only the United States did not have a consulate general in West Berlin and it had had one there in the past. The real issue, however, was the role that a Soviet consul general might seek to play in West Berlin. There was serious concern about this within the U.S. government. There were also doubts in West Berlin. Subsequent to the London senior-level meeting, Governing Mayor Klaus Schütz told the three Western ambassadors that he disagreed on this question with his Social Democratic colleagues in Bonn. He feared the establishment of a Soviet consulate general in the Western sectors might be interpreted as a symbol of Four Power occupation of West Berlin. In his judgment, the only acceptable arrangement for a Soviet consulate general would be to have it subordinated directly to the Soviet embassy in Bonn. However, given the Soviet Union's views on the relationship of West Berlin to the Federation this would never be feasible. He would oppose an arrangement subordinating the consulate to the Soviet embassy in East Berlin, whereas a Soviet consulate independent of the Soviet embassies in Bonn and East Berlin might strengthen the Soviet case for identifying West Berlin as a separate political entity.

By mid-summer 1971 there was a consensus among the Western powers that the negotiations were reaching a climactic point and that agreement was a real possibility. Reviewing the situation in a memorandum to the White House at the beginning of August 1971, the State Department noted that the Western powers now saw the possibility of obtaining an agreement that would produce important improvements in the Berlin situation. However, there were still some unresolved questions of critical importance to the realization of Western objectives. The State Department concluded that an agreement based on the current Soviet positions could not be accepted. Further concessions would have to come from the Soviet side since, except for permitting the establishment of a Soviet consulate general in West Berlin, the Western side did not have additional concessions to make.

At this point this one remaining possible Western concession assumed critical importance. Abrasimov and Kvitsinsky stated categorically that unless the Soviet consulate general was accepted, they could not agree to allow the Federal Republic to represent West Berlin in the Soviet Union, and this, Bahr insisted, was a matter of great importance to the Bonn government. He felt it would be necessary to agree to the consulate general in order to obtain a satisfactory agreement. Ambassador Rush, for his part, assured Washington that if the United States concurred in the establishment of the consulate general a sound Berlin settlement could be obtained. The European Interdepartmental Group considered the matter again in this context and its conclusions were transmitted to the White House in a memorandum from the State Department. While pointing to a number of disadvantages inherent in the establishment of a Soviet consulate general in West Berlin, the group concluded and the Department of State recommended to the president, as has been indicated, that the consulate general should be agreed to by the United States provided all other major Western objectives were achieved. The president concurred but, on condition that all other requirements of the previous decision memorandum be retained, including the prohibition against including provision for the consulate general in the Quadripartite Agreement itself. The additional restrictions enumerated by the White House were: the consulate general would be accredited to the Western commandants; it would be directly subordinated to the Soviet foreign ministry and not to the Soviet embassy in East Berlin; its activities would be limited to consular functions and it could not under any circumstances become involved in political functions or any other functions derived from the rights and the responsibilities of the Four Powers for Berlin and Germany as a whole; its staff members had to be acceptable to the Western commandants, who would have to have prior notification; and it would have to abide by Allied laws and pertinent Berlin legislation.

On June 24, 1971, at a meeting with Berlin's governing Mayor, the French and British ambassadors pressed Ambassador Rush for a more forthcoming U.S. position on an expanded Soviet presence in the Western sectors. The French Ambassador said the time had come for the West to place its cards on this issue on the table. He asserted that this was clearly a matter of prime importance to the Soviets. In his view, the West ultimately would have to agree to the Soviet consulate general, and it made no sense from a negotiating standpoint for the West to hold back too long since that kind of tactic endangered the negotiating process. Ambassador Rush, who may already have signaled in his private meetings with Soviet Ambassador Falin that under certain conditions the consulate general was obtainable, insisted that major issues were still outstanding. Therefore, there was no need for the Western side to put all its cards on the table at one time, and certainly not before the Soviets had moved more definitively in the Western direction on other issues. The Department of State concurred and advised the ambassador that the department wanted the Soviets to realize the

United States, at least, was under no time pressure. To ensure effective control of the final contents and form of the Berlin agreement, the department added that any agreement reached at the August 10 and 11 ambassadorial meetings must be *ad referendum* to governments and could be neither initialed nor signed without explicit government approval. The department's admonition proved quixotic. It was not able to control the final stage of negotiations since the U.S. representative had access to a higher authority.

NOTES

1. *Die Welt,* March 27, 1970.
2. Conference press communiqué issued by the U.S. mission Berlin, March 26, 1970.
3. Arthur G. Kogan, "The Quadripartite Berlin Negotiations, 1970–1971," Research Project Number 1035, September 1977, Office of the Historian, Bureau of Public Affairs, Department of State, Washington, D.C. pp. 229–30.
4. Ibid., pp. 156–59.
5. Ibid.
6. From a transcript of discussion of parts of the manuscript of this book at a meeting at the Aspen Institute Berlin, January 24–26, 1983.
7. From Berlin Governing Mayor Klaus Schuetz' report of his discussion with President Nixon, in Washington, December 9, 1970.
8. Kogan, "The Quadripartite Berlin Negotiations, 1970–1971," pp. 292–93.
9. Statement to the press corps in Bonn by German government spokesperson, Rudigar von Wechmar, December 21, 1970.
10. Kogan, "The Quadripartite Berlin Negotiations, 1970–1971," pp. 269–77.
11. Ibid.
12. Ibid.
13. Interview with Ambassador Kenneth Rush by Erich Vogt, Bureau of German Television, New York, 1982.

9

Agreement Achieved

On August 6, 1971, four days before the opening of the final negotiating session in Berlin, the Washington senior review group, composed of senior representatives of the Department of State and Defense and of CIA, met at the White House under the chairmanship of Henry Kissinger. The subject of consideration was the proposed Soviet consulate general in West Berlin. Kissinger opened the meeting by noting that the point had now been reached that some people had foreseen when the West German *Ostpolitik* was initiated. The German government had signed its treaty with Moscow, which entailed a very substantial German quid on the assumption that the quo would be obtained from the Soviets elsewhere, namely in Berlin. However, at this juncture the German government was urging the United States to make additional concessions in Berlin so that it could ensure the ratification of the Moscow Treaty, for which it would be paying a rather high price, first by concessions in Moscow and now in Berlin. He added that only a people like the Germans, who had managed to bring about World War I while trying to avoid it, were capable of this kind of strategic thinking. As for the Berlin negotiations, Kissinger said he assumed everyone knew he thought the whole negotiations were an insanity.

None of the members of the senior review group were eager to agree at that point to the Soviet consulate general. Speaking for the Department of State, Assistant Secretary Hillenbrand repeated the position already stated in the messages sent to Bonn with White House clearance: the consulate general was acceptable if an otherwise satisfactory agreement depended on it and if it was not included in the Quadripartite Agreement itself. Deputy Secretary of Defense David Packard stated that the Defense Department considered the consulate general a very bad idea. Nonetheless, the Pentagon was prepared to go along with it provided certain conditions were met. Among these conditions were the use of the word "Berlin" in the preamble to make clear that the agreement dealt with more than just West Berlin; the satisfaction of all the essential requirements for access to Berlin; and finally, Soviet acceptance of Federal German passports for West Berliners.

At the end of the meeting Kissinger summarized what he took to be the consensus of the group—that the consulate general could be accepted in the event that the United States got satisfaction on all outstanding points on the Western side. Recognizing the importance of this issue, particularly its obvious impact on Washington's relations with German Chancellor Brandt and with the Soviets, Kissinger said the president must make the final decision and that a decision would be taken before the August 10 ambassadorial meeting in Berlin. It will be known only when the secret channel messages between Kissinger and Rush are released whether such a presidential decision had already been made and communicated.

The climactic marathon negotiating sessions began as scheduled in Berlin on the morning of August 10, 1971. It would appear from what is now known that the burden was on Rush and Dean on the U.S. side and Abrasimov and Kvitsinsky on the Soviet side to develop final wording with the French and British that would be in line with the understandings already developed in the Kissinger-Dobrynin-Rush-Falin-Bahr channel and to gain the State Department's concurrence in the process. The rules agreed to for the final negotiating sessions were that the ambassadors would work from the texts already developed by the advisers and neither side would make statements of positions on principles. The British ambassador, Jackling, who presided at the August 10 sessions, pointed out that the final solution on any point or section would depend on the overall balance of the entire agreement, with individual compromises remaining provisional until a completed agreement was produced. Jackling also reminded the others that any document agreed to by the four ambassadors could not bind governments until they had had the opportunity to assess the entire text. Only after governments had given their approval could the ambassadors sign or even initial the agreement. Finally, he proposed that the four ambassadors approve an agreed translation into German of the text when agreed, which would be transmitted to the German negotiators for their guidance in their subsequent negotiations.

Reporting back to Washington at the end of the August 10 session, Ambassador Rush stated that there had been considerable forward movement by the Soviets on the foreign representation issue and some movement on the Federal presence. The ambassadors had agreed tentatively on a text on the representation of the Western sectors abroad, although Abrasimov would not make any concession on the use of the Federal German passports by West Berliners travelling in the Soviet Union and seemed to make Soviet agreement on this section contingent upon Allied concessions to the Soviet Union on the establishment of the consulate general in the Western sectors. Rush noted that the ambassadors were less successful in developing an agreed text of a letter of clarification and interpretation concerning the ties between the Federal Republic of Germany and the

Western sectors. Rush put forward language to the effect that these sectors should continue not to be governed by the Federal Republic of Germany, which was ultimately incorporated into the final text. In responding to Abrasimov on the issue of the Soviet consulate general, Rush said the Western side was willing to back away from its earlier position. However, because of the seriousness of the issue it had to be considered in the framework of the entire agreement and logically it could only be taken up after the four main sections, on the Federal presence, representation abroad, access, and travel by West Berliners to the East, were ready. Abrasimov warned again that unless there was agreement on a consulate general, there would be no section on representation abroad in the agreement.

The second day's meeting was less productive than the first. But at the third session on August 12, Abrasimov proposed language related to the inspection of travelers and goods that, despite evident loopholes, signified progress. Returning to the theme of the Soviet consulate general, Abrasimov introduced what he identified as a new bargaining proposal. He said he might be prepared to reduce the level of this office to a consulate if the Western powers would drop their demands for Soviet acceptance of Federal German passports for West Berliners travelling to the Soviet Union. The meeting also produced agreed wording on a Final Quadripartite Protocol, which would satisfactorily bring the arrangements still to be worked out by the German negotiators within the compass of the Quadripartite Agreement. Abrasimov declared that 80 percent of the work of the drafting of the agreement had now been completed. The break between this and the next session was long enough to provide both sides with time to commemorate in their own ways on August 13 the tenth anniversary of the building of the Berlin wall. It also gave them an opportunity to assess the state of play. In the State Department's view the issue of access, which was at the top of the Western agenda, seemed still in an unsatisfactory state. It considered Abrasimov's latest formulation unacceptable because of its sweeping language and the principle it incorporated that the East Germans had the right to search and arrest autobahn travelers for violations of GDR laws. While prepared to recognize the East Germans' right to prevent illicit imports and exports on their own territory, the State Department felt that shipment of sealed cargoes between the Federal Republic and West Berlin offered no such possibility and neither did the through trains and buses. Therefore it saw no justification for granting the East Germans the right to inspect accompanying documents. As for unsealed cargoes, the State Department put forward the wording, "as a rule, inspection procedures will be limited to the inspection of accompanying documents except in exceptional circumstances when there was substantial cause for suspicion that the unsealed shipments contained materials intended for dissemination along the access routes." Washington objected to any East German right to exclude specific categories of persons. To grant this would conflict with the concept of "unimpeded access" and acknowledge East Germany's sovereignty over the access routes. The State Department reiterated Washington's objections to the use of the terms "transit traffic" and "in accordance with international practices." In connection with the Soviet consulate general, the department expressed the hope that once the consulate general had been brought into play as a bargaining chip, Soviet agreement on spot checks and other access questions would be among the counter-concessions obtained. The department insisted that if the quadripartite agreement was to serve its purpose, it had to improve the practical situation for the Berliners in a way that would be clearly evident, and that the agreement had to be sufficiently precise so that it would not lend itself to easy misinterpretation and circumvention by the Soviets or the East Germans.

On August 16, when the ambassadorial sessions resumed, the zigzagging pattern of Soviet negotiations continued. This meeting was divided into two parts separated by a two-hour break, which Ambassador Abrasimov insisted was absolutely essential since he needed to consult with his government (Foreign Minister Andrei Gromyko was by then in East Berlin for this purpose) as well as with the East Germans. In the morning, when access was under discussion, Abrasimov was unyielding in his insistence on the words "transit" and "in accordance with international practices." The British ambassador reminded the Soviet ambassador that an agreement had to satisfy two criteria, free movement of traffic on the access routes, and an acceptable definition of the word "abuse" to avoid the kind of chicanery that might interfere with the movement of people and goods between the Federal Republic and Berlin. Abrasimov warned the Western ambassadors that if they followed Ambassador Jackling's lead, they would take more than two steps backward. However, many of the points that seemed so far from resolution in the morning were essentially resolved in the afternoon following Abrasimov's consultations. In return for Allied willingness to accept the Soviet phrase "after consultation and agreement with the GDR," Abrasimov took the French ambassador's suggestion that the Soviet Union undertake to guarantee "unimpeded access" and accepted language on inspection procedures. With the expressed Soviet readiness that afternoon to guarantee unimpeded access and the Allies' willingness to guarantee that the Western sectors would continue not to be a constituent part of the Federal Republic, it was possible to move ahead to agreement on phraseology regarding the ties between the Western sectors and the Federal Republic worked out earlier between the Western powers and Egon Bahr and quite probably already reviewed by Bahr with the Soviet side. The language provided that

the ties between the Western Sectors of Berlin and the Federal Republic of Germany would be maintained and developed, taking into account that these Sectors continue not to be a constituent part of the Federal Republic of Germany and continue not to be governed by it.[1]

This language was important for the Western side since it acknowledged a continuing process rather than the establishment of a new and special situation. Moreover, it accepted the fact that the ties between the city and the Federal

Republic would not only be maintained, but would also be "developed." Wording earlier proposed by the Western side on the Federal government's presence in West Berlin was accepted. With these elements in place, the unresolved issues at the end of the August 16 session included a definition of the geographic area covered by the agreement and the Soviet-proposed phrase, "taking into account the existing situation"; provisions governing the use of the Federal German passports by West Berliners traveling to the Soviet Union and other countries of the Soviet bloc; a final refinement of the details on access; and the size and definition of the Soviet presence in West Berlin.

After the significant progress on August 16, Abrasimov, repeating an all too familiar pattern, tried to backtrack the following day. First, he withdrew some of his earlier concessions on access. He announced that the word "unimpeded" was not translatable into Russian, contending that the nearest Russian equivalent was "without difficulty," a linguistically unfounded assertion. He also tried to back away from the earlier agreement concerning sealed freight conveyances. His new text clearly was intended to open the possibility for spot checks by the East German authorities. Having accepted earlier a Western suggestion that the details of the ties issue be left out of the main part of the agreement and incorporated into a letter from the three Western ambassadors, Abrasimov now balked at any kind of Soviet acknowledgment of that letter. To provide such an acknowledgment, he explained, would imply Soviet acceptance of its contents and he was not prepared to go that far. Instead, he proposed that the Western ambassadors merely send him the letter by registered mail. In a subsequent exchange that day, Abrasimov also rejected a Western proposal to reopen the Teltow Canal. His condition for considering that subject at all, he said, would be an explicit Western readiness to turn over nominal control of all the canals in West Berlin to East Germany, an arrangement cancelled twenty years earlier. Having undone several textual understandings of importance to the Western side, Abrasimov then asked the Western ambassadors to begin to discuss the subject of importance to him—the so-called Soviet interests. Abrasimov warned that if he did not receive a definitive answer on this matter at the next session, that meeting would be a waste of time. Replying for the Western side, Ambassador Rush noted that several issues of importance to the Allies such as access and passports remained to be resolved. However, if the Western side obtained a good text on these subjects, he might be prepared to recommend to his government that it approve the establishment of a Soviet consulate general in West Berlin on a limited scale, with perhaps fifteen to twenty Soviet citizens, as well as several other manifestations of the Soviet Union's presence. The British and French ambassadors supported this approach. While Abrasimov thanked his colleagues for this "forthcomingness" he also expressed some wonderment that they still had not made their recommendations to their governments. He noted wryly, "they are only in a position to submit recommendations . . . even though most of the practical questions have already been discussed."[2]

Before the session ended Ambassador Jackling sought to overcome the Soviet resistance to accepting Federal German passports for West Berliners. While prepared to accept Abrasimov's assertion that under Soviet law a Soviet passport was evidence of nationality, Jackling explained that as a lawyer he believed that in international law states undertook to respect the practices of other countries. Under this practice the Soviet Union had to accept passports for use as they were intended by the issuing country. Abrasimov, ever ready to do battle, took Jackling to task for inferring that the Soviet people did not respect the laws of other countries. He asserted that the Soviet Union could not close its eyes to the fact that Western practice on the whole contradicted Jackling's ideas on the meaning of a passport. A passport meant that the bearer was a citizen of the issuing country. Before leaving the meeting room, Abrasimov reminded his colleagues that he had the right to reconsider language tentatively agreed. He charged that the United States had taken too much time thinking things over and announced with some finality that the present discussion had to be stopped so that the ambassadors could move to a constructive discussion of other questions.

August 18 turned out to be the day of decision. With Abrasimov in the chair, the proceedings moved briskly. At the outset, Abrasimov introduced a new version of the preamble and Part I. Again the debate focused on the omission of any mention of Berlin in the agreement, since the Soviet draft conspicuously dropped the Western reference to these "meetings on Berlin." Explaining the Soviet position, Abrasimov said that while the four ambassadors had spent months in reaching agreement, their discussions did not relate to all of Berlin. The talks had been limited to the Western sectors of the city. Now, "after all this time, the Western Ambassadors were still trying to reopen this point." "How long," he asked, "will it take to set the record straight?"[3] He objected, for essentially the same reasons, to the phrase stating that the quadripartite meetings had taken place in "the building formerly occupied by the Allied Control Council in the United States Sector of Berlin." As an alternative, he proposed "the Western Sectors of Berlin," patently in support of the Soviet thesis that the subject of the agreement was West Berlin. Unable to convince the three Western ambassadors of the logic of this phraseology, Abrasimov reminded them that the ambassadors had also met in the residence of the British and French ambassadors. Rush pointed out that there had also been meetings in the Soviet ambassador's residence in the Soviet sector of Berlin. Therefore, to be consistent, Rush suggested Abrasimov might be willing to accept the phrase "in the four sectors of Berlin." Abrasimov thereafter finally accepted the sentence, stating that the ambassadors had "held a series of meetings in the building formerly occupied by the Allied Control Council in the American Sector of Berlin." Abrasimov next took exception to the reference to "rights and responsibilities arising from the results of the Second World War." He asked how could there be a reference to World War II when Allied forces had entered Berlin two months after the war ended in Europe and, then, on the basis of quadripartite agreements rather than as a result of the outcome of the war? If the ambassadors really wanted to reopen the question of rights stemming from the war, Abrasimov warned that the negotiations could go on for another year. Abrasimov nonetheless finally accepted the British formulation, "acting on the basis of their quadripartite rights and responsibilities, and of the corresponding wartime and postwar agreements and decisions of the Four Powers, which are unaffected." On access, Abrasimov again insisted that the closest Russian equivalent to "unimpeded" was "without difficulty." In addition, he wanted a specific reference to the fact that the access routes were part of the German Democratic Republic. After a long and heated discussion, a tentative compromise was reached describing the access routes as running through the territory of the GDR. Abrasimov asked that agreement on this point remain tentative, for he would only be able to give the Western powers a definitive answer after lunch. He followed a similar course in connection with traffic between the Western sectors of the city and East Berlin and surrounding East German territory, having sought without success words that would identify East Berlin as part of the area of the German Democratic Republic.

After a prolonged luncheon break, the discussions on access resumed. Again a major issue was the disputed word 'unimpeded." At this point, Abrasimov admitted that he probably could find the appropriate Russian word if the Western side would agree to a phrase permitting the inspection of "accompanying documents," a request rejected earlier by the Western side. The Western ambassadors reminded Abrasimov that he had already gained Western agreement to the phrase "through the territory of the German Democratic Republic" in return for his acceptance of "unimpeded." Abrasimov finally yielded. A compromise solution on the inspection of seals and related documents on cargo traffic was also reached. Despite his earlier reservations, Abrasimov agreed at this session to acknowledge a letter from his three Western colleagues on the arrangements reached with the West German chancellor on ties between the FRG and the Western sectors.

The discussion then turned again to the question of utilization of Federal passports by West Berliners and Soviet interests in West Berlin. Abrasimov asked that the room be cleared of advisers. He explained that "it would be best to ask our colleagues to take a walk for a half hour, not because the Ambassadors did not trust them but because each of them had wives, and each wife had many women friends and one of them might say something to *Der Spiegel*."[4] He suggested the advisers do preparatory work on those issues that would be dealt with outside the regular agreement—the future of the National Democratic Party of Germany (NPD) and the demilitarization of West Berlin. With the room cleared, Abrasimov said his delegation had told him he had mentioned the issue of the Soviet consulate general in West Berlin thirty-two times. He was prepared to raise it a thirty-third time in the hope that he could finally solve the problem. If there was no reference to a Soviet consulate general in the main text of the agreement, there would be no agreement. If the understanding on the consulate general were dealt with outside the agreement itself, he said, the agreed language on the representation of the Western sectors abroad would also have to be handled by some arrangement outside the basic agreement. This involved a question of prestige for the Soviet Union. In passing he noted that Ambassador Jackling had supported him a long time ago (which was true, despite the British government's distinctly different views on this matter), as had his friend Ambassador Sauvagnargues. It was only Ambassador Rush who held out. Following a carefully prepared scenario, the French ambassador then proposed that the issues of representation of West Berlin abroad by the Federal German government and Soviet interests be linked in a single paragraph. Ambassador Rush then produced language which stated that "the representation abroad of the Western sectors of Berlin and the consular activities of the USSR in the Western sectors of Berlin can be exercised as set forth in Annex IV." After distributing the draft text of a letter to cover the consulate general and other Soviet interests, Rush explained that anything not covered by the letter could be negotiated in the period between the conclusion of the agreement and the signing of the Final Quadripartite Protocol. Before agreeing to these proposals, Abrasimov asked whether his understanding was correct—that in the communication from the three Western powers to the Soviet Union there would be an authorization for the Soviet consulate general and that a similar Soviet communication would constitute the Soviet reply. Receiving a positive answer, Abrasimov thanked the Western ambassadors for "this solution at last." There followed an extensive discussion of the details of Soviet representation in West Berlin during which Abrasimov sought to get as broad a license and eliminate as many restrictions as possible. He had considerable success, as is reflected in the wording of the agreement, but the Western ambassadors remained firm on their insistence that the consulate general would be accredited to the Allied commandants. In effect, once the Western powers accepted the Soviet consulate general without reverting to wording in other parts of the text that had been in dispute it was clear that a Four Power agreement had been achieved. This final session ended forty-five minutes past midnight. Before departing, the ambassadors indulged in a moment of mutual praise and some nostalgia. Ambassador Abrasimov said he wished

to emphasize that on this historical date we reached a new agreement on the Ambassadorial level on a very important problem affecting the center of Europe, a problem which touches deeply not only the bordering areas but also those which are very far from the area of our discussion. . . . There were, of course, moments when each side was trying to prove the rightness of its course. But I can say that all four tried to find the right decisions which will be beneficial for the people populating the American continent and our own. . . . We took decisions very important for the life of our people and for the preservation of peace.[5]

On behalf of his French and British colleagues, Ambassador Rush said he wanted to "say only that these negotiations had been extremely difficult. Points of view were far apart. The problems were complex. Therefore without the background of the long discussions agreement would never have been reached." He wanted to pay tribute to his Soviet colleague for his understanding and willingness in the negotiations to search for practical improvements. So much depended on this. . . . This agreement was an agreement to further world peace because it made a substantial contribution toward promoting an era of negotiation rather than an era of confrontation. A closer and stronger relationship between the Western countries and the Soviet Union had been established.

"This is a major advance," he said, and "we should realize the Soviets have made a major contribution in this direction."[6]

In Washington it had not been expected that the ambassadors would reach what amounted to final agreement on a text without further communication with capitals. During the final hours of the August 18 session, the Office of Central European Affairs in the State Department called the U.S. mission in Berlin to find out where the negotiations stood. The mission indicated they were advancing very rapidly. The department officer made clear that the Department of State expected Ambassador Rush to consult with Washington before agreeing to a text. The department, as has been indicated, considered the requirements for an agreement as defined by the president had not been fully met. The State Department was convinced that even though the text was *ad referendum* to governments, it would be impossible to change once the ambassadors had formally expressed their agreement. At this point Secretary of State William Rogers sent the personal message referred to in Chapter 7, informing Ambassador Rush that, having reviewed the draft agreement as of August 18, he had reservations about quite a number of aspects. The secretary of state noted that:

1. The agreement failed to refer specifically to Berlin and did not otherwise establish that the agreement was *not* limited to West Berlin.

2. The preamble, contrary to presidential guidelines, contained the phrase "taking into account the existing situation," thereby implying Western acknowledgment of the division of Berlin.

3. Despite explicit presidential guidelines to the contrary, in the agreed annex dealing with access there was a reference to "international practice," a term that could dilute the concept of "unimpeded access."

4. There was a reference in the text itself to Soviet consular activities in the Western sectors of Berlin and a paragraph in an annex authorizing the establishment of a Soviet consulate general, in violation of a presidential directive that required that the agreement proper should contain nothing on this issue.

5. The formulations on ties between the Federal Republic and Berlin seemed to offer room for interpretation inconsistent with earlier instructions.

For all these reasons, the secretary of state said he would like to have the opportunity to review these and other points with the ambassador urgently and he planned so to inform the British, French, and Germans.

It is reasonable to assume that prior to responding to the secretary of state's message, Ambassador Rush was in touch with Kissinger at the White House. He quickly sent Washington two pertinent documents. The first was a letter from Chancellor Willy Brandt to President Nixon, which stated:

> ... taking into account the realities of the Berlin situation, and putting wishful thinking aside, this draft represents a major achievement for the three Western Powers and for the Federal Republic. The draft safeguards the Western positions. In addition, improvements have been reached which many of us here had not considered feasible when the negotiations started. . . . This draft will find my full political support and I am sure that on Wednesday, the Cabinet will follow me in this judgement. . . . I am convinced that the draft will find your approval and you will regard it a limited but very important result of your policy.[7]

The second message was a summary of the discussion of the Bonn Group on August 21 reporting that the German foreign minister, Walter Scheel, had said he opposed "reopening discussions in areas where the Allies felt they may not have reached full satisfaction." Scheel reportedly felt that the draft "represented a delicate balance between the positions of the two sides" and "for the Allies to raise additional points at this time would only lead to the Soviets doing the same." Scheel also said that "from his experience in the German-Soviet negotiations . . . once the Soviets had agreed to the content of a draft, they would not go back on their word." He was convinced "that the Allies should sit with the agreement . . . and hold the Soviets to their commitment."[8]

Ambassador Rush then sent a personal message to the secretary arguing that it was fully understood that any agreement reached in the marathon sessions would be *ad referendum* to governments and could be neither initialed nor signed without government approval. He was therefore very surprised to receive the secretary's message, which arrived late in the evening of August 18, as negotiations were virtually complete. At that juncture, he said, it would have been extremely disruptive and no one here would have understood, had he suddenly refused to give his agreement to a text he had taken an active part in negotiating and formulating. The credibility of the U.S. government would be open to question. If the agreement he had concurred in *ad referendum* were disavowed, he would resign. This was a matter of importance not only to him, but to the United States as well. Having said this, the ambassador agreed to return immediately for consultations, the course of which has already been described.

Ambassador Rush was probably right in taking advantage of the moment to agree to a text that technically would be referred to the State Department, which would then find out (what Rush already knew) that the president's earlier directive was no longer binding. At the same time, the State Department had been right in assuming that once the four ambassadors agreed to the text, further changes would be impossible. None was sought by the Western side. Indeed, of the four, only the Soviet government, in the period between the conclusion of negotiations and signature, tried, in some instances with success, to obtain minor modifications of the agreement as reached.

NOTES

1. Arthur C. Kogan, "Berlin Quadripartite Agreement, 1970–1971," Research Project Number 1035, September 1977, Office of the Historian, Bureau of Public Affairs, Department of State, Washington, D.C. pp. 754–56.

2. Ibid., pp. 756–60.
3. Ibid., pp. 760–61.
4. Ibid.
5. Ibid.
6. Ibid.
7. Ibid., p. 780.
8. Ibid., pp. 782–84.

10

Language as a Substantive Problem

The Quadripartite Agreement on Berlin was negotiated essentially on the basis of English-language texts. In the advisers group the common language was German and much of the discussion was in that language, but the phraseology of the various sections of the agreement that was being considered was in English. French and English versions were maintained in parallel from the beginning and no disparities arose in preparing the final texts. No cross-checking against the Russian text was done, however, as negotiations progressed and no German text was prepared. After the agreement was completed, the Western representatives discovered that the Russian text differed substantively from the English and French texts on points that had been the subject of difficult and precise negotiations. Moreover, the Soviet side proved resistant to the insistence of the U.S. and British ambassadors that there be an agreed German translation of the text. Language in the strictest sense came to be seen, therefore, as an instrument being utilized by the Soviet Union and subsequently by the GDR to gain political points not achieved in the negotiations.

It will be recalled that when the final round of negotiations began on August 10, 1971, the British ambassador proposed that once agreement was reached on a completed text the four ambassadors approve a German translation and that it be transmitted to the German parties for their inner-German negotiations. At the final session, at which the four ambassadors were to ''wrap up loose ends'' after they had agreed on the final text, Ambassador Rush again raised the need for an approved German translation as essential for the Germans in their negotiations. He made the point that if there were any differences in interpretation it would be better to eliminate them now than later.

Ambassador Abrasimov summarily rejected the proposal and accused Rush of trying to intimidate him by suggesting that the lack of an agreed German translation might jeopardize the entire agreement. He argued that the agreement had been reached at the advisers' level in English and Russian and all that remained to be done was to produce a final French text. The ambassadors needed only to arrive at agreement on a detailed text in the three official languages and give these texts to the two German governments. It was up to the Germans to prepare their own translations. Abrasimov certainly knew that the text of the Four Power agreement had been developed by the four advisers in English, and that the advisers still had to deal with any translation differences between the English/French and Russian texts.

When the advisers subsequently met to iron out translation problems, they immediately encountered serious difficulties. The first was the phrase ''preferential treatment'' in describing travel between West Berlin and West Germany. The Russian translation was to the effect that ''transit traffic will be on the basis of favored treatment.'' Kvitsinsky explained that he had used ''favored'' rather than ''preferential'' in his Russian rendition of the phrase from the very beginning of the negotiations and had so reported the text to Moscow. Although the Russian language had a reasonable equivalent to the English word ''preferential,'' he said the Soviet side was unwilling to use it since this would mean West Berlin access traffic would have precedence over all other traffic using the designated routes including Soviet and East German military and civilian vehicles. This argument was not found convincing since Soviet and East German traffic had access to an unlimited number of routes, while the Berlin traffic was restricted to a few specifically designated highways. Of somewhat greater significance was the difference in the Russian version of the statement that

the ties between the Western Sectors and the Federal Republic of Germany will be maintained and developed, *taking into account that these Sectors continue not to be a constituent part of the Federal Republic of Germany and not governed by it* [emphasis added].

As explained earlier, this language was intended to make clear that the close political ties between West Berlin and West Germany would continue to develop and would not be weakened in any way by the new agreement with the Soviet Union. But in the Russian text the word ''relations'' (*otnosheniya*) was substituted for the word ''ties'' (*svyazy*). Politically the differences in meaning are substantial. While the word ''ties'' was meant to describe a close and special arrangement between the two political entities, the Russian word for ''relations'' suggests a relationship between two foreign states. And since the Soviet side had been insisting that West Berlin was a separate and independent political unit, the word used in the Russian text was hardly accidental. Additionally, while the agreed language in the agreement suggested a continuum by stating that the ''ties'' between West Berlin and the Federation would be ''maintained and developed,'' the Russian version dropped the suggestion of continuity and stated that West Berlin ''henceforth will not be governed by it [the Federal Republic].'' Similarly, the Soviet version of the agreement translated ''Permanent Liaison

Agency,'' the English title of the body that was to symbolize the continuing West German presence in West Berlin, as "the organ for relations.''

After considerable badgering, Kvitsinsky undertook to raise the language problems with Moscow. Subsequently, he alleged that he had talked by telephone with Gromyko three times about the textual problems. Gromyko had insisted that the Western powers were seeking a concession that went beyond the significance of the words. Kvitsinsky told his Western colleagues that the printing presses in Moscow had started to roll and there was no way to modify the existing Russian text. However, he gave assurances that the situation would create no practical problems for the Western powers since the Soviet Union would not question the English or French versions or request any change in them.

Three further attempts were made to obtain modifications in the Russian text and Soviet agreement to an agreed German text. In each instance, the Soviets refused and each refusal became firmer than the previous one. The three Western advisers finally told Kvitsinsky that until the differences had been resolved, the Western powers did not think that further action should be taken at the technical level to prepare final texts for signature. To emphasize this point, an experts' session that was scheduled to work on the final texts that day was cancelled.

At this point the Bonn government began to show concern about the situation. Foreign Minister Scheel, after consulting with Chancellor Brandt, instructed FRG representatives to state that the Federal Republic wanted a strong effort made to correct the Russian text but attached even greater value to obtaining an agreed German translation. There was an indication that Scheel was prepared to accept a delay in the signature of the agreement rather than face the possibility of divergent and conflicting German texts. By this point the French had concluded it was not worthwhile to pursue the textual differences further. Another tripartite demarche was therefore not possible. It was agreed among the Three Powers, however, that the U.S. minister in Berlin, David Klein, should raise the matter directly with Abrasimov on behalf of the United States and Britain, with the approval of the West German government. The minister was received at the Soviet embassy at 10:00 p.m. on August 31, but Abrasimov did not make himself available. Instead, the meeting was held with Kvitsinsky, whose response remained negative on both the Russian text and on an agreed German translation. The following morning, Kvitsinsky met with Jonathan Dean to deliver Abrasimov's formal and negative reply to the demarche of the previous evening. Dean then proposed a possible solution, suggesting that if there were a satisfactory German translation, the Russian text could be accepted as it stood provided that prior to the signature of the agreement, the Western side could announce Soviet assurances had been received that the Russian language text was the exact equivalent of the French and English versions. Kvitsinsky thought an exchange on the equivalence of the three official texts might be possible. However, he continued to resist a single German text insisting there was insufficient time to work one out. Dean then modified his own proposal, suggesting at a minimum an agreed German translation of certain particularly sensitive sections. Even this, in Kvitsinsky's view, was impossible. The French made clear they did not wish to insist upon an agreed German translation and felt that signature of the agreement should take place as scheduled on September 2 regardless of the status of the language question.

At this juncture, the sudden and real illness of Ambassador Rush intervened. On the afternoon of September 1, following his return from his sudden trip to Washington and California and after a heated argument with Ambassador Sauvagnargues on the question of proceeding without an agreed German text, Rush complained of light-headedness. He was ordered to bed by his physician for at least 24 hours. This automatically made it impossible to move ahead with the September 2 signing ceremony. The assumption in Berlin was that Rush's illness was diplomatic and calculated to put pressure on the Soviet side to modify its position on the translation issue. An immediate result was a request by Kvitsinsky to meet with Dean. Kvitsinsky assured Dean that Abrasimov would be willing to give oral assurances at the signing ceremonies that the English, French, and Russian texts of the agreement were identical in meaning and substance, albeit without any reference to the fact that English had been the language of agreement from the outset. Kvitsinsky warned Dean that the Soviets would refuse to accept any additional preconditions for the signature of the agreement, such as a uniform approved German translation. Nevertheless, Kvitsinsky told Dean that the Soviet side now was willing to try to arrange a meeting between the East and West Germans to produce such a document. These negotiations got under way at 8:00 p.m. on September 1 and continued until 2:30 a.m. on September 2. While some agreement was reached during that tense session, some points remained unresolved. Dean then called Kvitsinsky at 5:00 a.m. that same morning to warn him that the United States would not sign until there was an agreed German text. The German negotiators resumed their meeting shortly thereafter. Kvitsinsky and Dean themselves worked out several compromise proposals, which they passed on to the German negotiators. This process reduced the points of difference to three: "ties," "constituent part," and "as provided by international practice," all related to the differences in the English/French and Russian texts. Having reached a stalemate the negotiating sessions were suspended until the morning of September 3. The East Germans indicated they needed further instructions from their authorities, giving some expectation of further progress the following morning. At 10:30 on the morning of September 3, Dean again called Kvitsinsky to tell him that Ambassador Rush's condition had improved and that Rush would be able to sign the agreement, but the signing could not take place until the three essential differences in the German translations had been resolved. An hour later Dean was advised by the Federal German authorities that agreement had been reached on all points. As far as anyone was aware, no conditions were attached. With the problem seemingly resolved, the signing ceremonies took place at noon that same day.

At a private meeting that preceded the public ceremonies, Ambassador Sauvagnargues stated that concerning the authenticity of the French, English, and Russian texts of the Quadripartite Agreement, my colleagues and I proceed from the premise that all parts of the Russian language text of the Quadripartite Agreement are identical in meaning and in substance with the French and English texts. I would appreciate receiving confirmation from Ambassador Abrasimov.

The Soviet reply was something less than anticipated. Abrasimov stated that he had been informed by his colleagues that "the text in the English and French languages conformed in form and substance to the Russian language text," thus leaving open the question as to which text was governing. The divergences between the Russian and English/French texts remained.

As it turned out, the noon ceremony put the language issue to rest only temporarily. Immediately after the signing on September 3, the East Germans released to the press their official version of the text. The German word *Verbindungen* (relations) reappeared instead of *Bindungen* for "ties" and "not a constituent part" was translated as they had earlier insisted, *"kein Bestandteil der Bundesrepublik"*—a translation of the Russian wording. There also were textual distortions having to do with the description of West German offices in West Berlin, as well as the words used to spell out West Berliners' right to obtain visas and passports issued by the Federal Republic in order to travel to the Soviet Union and other countries in Eastern Europe. The East Germans adopted the Soviets' description of the agreement using the phrase "Four-Sided Agreement" rather than "Quadripartite Agreement." Moreover, the East German press suggested that the prohibition on political activities of the Soviet consulate general in the agreement related only to political problems arising from the Quadripartite Agreement itself. The Federal government considered it best to try to resolve the problem as a routine matter without dramatizing it. The task was given to a middle echelon officer, Hans Otto Bräutigam, who had worked closely with Bahr in the inner-German negotiations. Bräutigam sent a telegram to his East German counterpart, Seidel, pointing out that the text of the agreement carried in the East German press was inconsistent with that agreed by the two sides before the signing ceremonies. Bräutigam suggested that perhaps the East German authorities had not had sufficient time to get the agreed version to the press and that the necessary rectifications could now be taken care of in a clarification to the East German media. Seidel responded that he had no responsibility for media matters but charged that a report carried by the West German wire service DPA left blanks for two contested points and thereby drew attention to the fact that they had been under discussion. This was a breach of confidence and the consequences would have to be borne by the West German side. The next West German message to the East German side took note of the fact that the text of the agreed German translation of the Quadripartite Agreement had not been put into question. The West German side was therefore proceeding on the assumption that the agreed text, particularly the two disputed points, would be made public in an appropriate way. The West Germans, meanwhile,

Signing of the Quadripartite Agreement of September 3, 1971 (*from left*: Jean Sauvagnargues, France; Sir Roger Jackling, Britain; Pyotr Abrasimov, Soviet Union; Kenneth Rush, United States). Photo courtesy of the German Information Center, New York.

assured the three Western Allies that agreement on the translation points had been reached on the morning of September 3. The German words had been read into the record of both sides, with five delegates present for each.

To support the West German effort, the U.S. embassy counselor, Dean, again called Kvitsinsky who was still in East Berlin. Dean reminded Kvitsinsky that Ambassador Rush had notified Ambassador Abrasimov of his willingness to proceed with the signing of the agreement on the basis of assurances received from the West German authorities that the two German sides had reached agreement on the translation, including the two important points of "ties" and "constituent part," now thrown into question. Dean said that the United States was not prepared to acquiesce in such a breach of confidence and did not feel that the German implementing discussions could get under way unless the matter had been publicly clarified beforehand. Kvitsinsky said he was unable to do anything about the matter, since Abrasimov was no longer in East Berlin. State Secretary Egon Bahr then sent a telegram to his opposite number, Kohl, reviewing the problem and expressing his hope that the necessary clarification by the German Democratic Republic would be forthcoming in an appropriate form so that the negotiations could begin and be carried on to a rapid and mutually satisfactory conclusion. There was a personal understanding between Egon Bahr and Ambassador Rush that the clarification being sought did not have to take the form of a corrected text published in the East German press. Both were prepared to accept private East German confirmation of the agreement reached on September 3. However, Kohl's response was no more helpful than Seidel's. While Seidel had expressed surprise at the West German *démarche*, Kohl said he was "shocked" by the West German request and did not know whether to go to Bonn for the scheduled inner-German negotiations. To forestall a breakdown in the German talks, Bahr told Kohl he expected the matter to be clarified either before Kohl left East Berlin for Bonn, or at the latest at the outset of the talks in Bonn. Kohl appeared in Bonn on schedule, but the problem remained unresolved.

The West Germans then again asked the Americans to intervene with the Soviet embassy in East Berlin. Dean, instructed by Ambassador Rush to make the *démarche*, not only did so with the Soviet minister in the Soviet embassy in East Berlin; he also had the opportunity to pursue the matter with Moscow's ambassador to Bonn, Valentin Falin, who was traveling to Berlin on the same plane as Dean. In his conversations with both Soviet officers Dean made the point that these issues were not really internal German matters, since the U.S. ambassador had signed the Quadripartite Agreement on September 3 only in the understanding that the two German sides had reached full agreement on a translation. He also noted that the issue, if unresolved, could have a profound effect on East Germany's future relations with the Western powers.

Falin told Dean that in his view the West German translation "was not accurate," particularly as regards the word *Bindungen,* which in his judgment was not a precise translation of the Russian, French, or English word "ties." In his judgement *Bindungen* meant "close ties." Moreover, he added, there was the issue of political prestige affecting both governments, and that had to be taken into account. In Dean's subsequent conversation in the Soviet embassy, Soviet representatives insisted that the decisive point was that the four ambassadors had exchanged statements prior to the signing of the Quadripartite Agreement that the English, French, and Russian texts were equally authentic. The East German translation of the points at issue in their view was more accurate than Bonn's (which was not entirely invalid, if the translation was from the Soviet text).

There was clearly no give on the Eastern side. On September 14, following Dean's unsuccessful efforts with Soviet representatives, the East German negotiator, Kohl, insisted there had been no written agreement on September 3 on a German text and neither side had been officially authorized by its government to negotiate such an agreement. The consequent problem for Bonn was how to get on with the task of working out the detailed implementing parts of the Quadripartite Agreement in the absence of agreement on the authentic translation of the text. The U.S. embassy in Bonn continued to assert that if sufficient pressure were maintained, the East Germans would eventually give in on the translation points under dispute. That, however, was not to happen. On October 2, in a further effort to get the German negotiations under way, Bahr agreed to a minute—notable for its circumlocution—which read as follows:

Kohl declared that according to its final provisions, the text of the Four Power Agreement was binding in the English, French, and Russian languages. There was agreement that the result of the common effort to find a German translation reached in September 1971, did not constitute a governmental agreement between the Federal Republic of Germany and the German Democratic Republic and the result had not been approved by the Ambassadors of France, Great Britain, the United States, and the Soviet Union. Kohl had taken note of the fact that I would make use of the substance of these remarks in public statements.

On this basis the inner-German negotiations began. But the language problem continued to plague the discussions, as will be seen in the next chapter. The East Germans never altered their German text to comply with the agreement reached in the hectic September negotiations with the West Germans. The official text as published by the GDR uses *Verbindung* rather than *Bindungen* for "ties" and "not a constituent part" remains "kein Bestandteil der Bundesrepublik." Twelve years later, in 1983, Bahr, in a reflective mood, said the West Germans probably needed just a few more hours in order to resolve the translation problem properly. That seems highly doubtful. The pattern had been set with Soviet insistence on a Russian text that was at odds with the English and French texts. The East Germans were presumably convinced that they, too, could stand firm and expect to win.

In the years since 1971 the differences in language over which such a hard but short battle was fought have had no perceptible effect. The linguistic distinctions involved, while potentially significant in their implications, are too subtle and complex to provide a publicly convincing argument in favor of the Soviet and East German positions on the status of West Berlin. Despite their threats, the three Western Allies, and certainly the Federal Republic, were not prepared to compromise the major achievement that the Quadripartite Agreement constituted because of a few differences in translation, something the Soviets had demonstrated before the East Germans had their turn. Yet for the prudent negotiator some useful lessons emerge. Had Ambassador Rush always had his own Russian-language interpreter with him in discussions of the agreement with his Soviet counterpart the differences in the Russian phraseology could well have become evident earlier and differences resolved *before* the point of final agreement—and diminished Western leverage—had been reached. Inevitably, a negotiator who is not fluent in the other party's language puts himself at a disadvantage if he relies entirely on the other party's interpreter, who can have no interest in pinpointing or highlighting differences in what is said in Russian (or any other language) and what the American assumes is meant because of the context and previous conversations.

Another lesson is the importance of language as such in multilateral agreements. The experience of the Four Power negotiations demonstrates that the wise negotiator will ensure that when a difficult point is resolved it is resolved in all the official languages in which the text will be signed. Like the Americans, British, French, and West Germans in the case of the Berlin agreement, other negotiators, too, would find it difficult to hold out on a point of translation *after* all else has been agreed.

In the Berlin translation battle there may have been, also, a nonlinguistic factor. The Soviet side, knowing that Ambassador Rush had bypassed the State Department, may have assumed that in insisting on identical Russian and German language texts, he was simply satisfying State Department instructions for the record, but would come around, as he had on other points, on the basis of the higher and more flexible authority represented by the secret channel.

11

The Inner-German Agreements

The Quadripartite Agreement of September 3, 1971 established the political basis for improving access to West Berlin and the conditions of life for its inhabitants, but the text of the agreement was limited largely to principles and specific guidelines. The implementing details were to be worked out through negotiations by the two German states and between the West Berlin *Senat* and the East German government. The implementation of the Four Power agreement was made conditional upon the successful conclusion of these so-called inner-German agreements and their incorporation in the quadripartite framework.

The German agreements have four parts, consisting of:

—the agreement of September 30, 1971, between the FRG and the GDR covering improvements in telecommunication facilities between the Western sectors and East Berlin and other areas
—the Transit Agreement of December 17, 1971, between the FRG and the GDR
—the agreement on Visits of December 20, 1971, between the GDR and the Berlin *Senat*
—the agreement on Territorial Exchanges of December 20, 1971, between the GDR and the Berlin *Senat*.

Along with the agreement on the exchange of territories, there also was a supplemental understanding "on the inclusion of the area at the former Potsdam train station" reached by the Berlin *Senat* and the East German government on July 21, 1971.

Additionally, a Traffic Treaty (May 26, 1972) and a Basic Treaty of Relations (December 21, 1972) were concluded between the Federal Republic of Germany and the German Democratic Republic, which, while of great importance in regulating the relations between the two German states, were not part of the Berlin agreement, and therefore are not dealt with here.

THE BEGINNING OF THE GERMAN NEGOTIATIONS

The discussions between the two German states on the normalization of their mutual relations did not wait on the conclusion of the Four Power agreement. They got under way following Chancellor Willy Brandt's initial Government Policy Declaration, in which he said that the government in Bonn accepted the sovereignty of the East German state but did not consider East Germany a foreign country. His precise formulation was: "Even if two states exist in Germany, they are not foreign countries for each other; their relations with one another can be only of a special kind."[1]

That pronouncement produced a qualitative change in the relationship between the two German states. It represented a major shift in policy from that pursued by previous Federal German governments and opened new possibilities for the resolution of practical problems involving West and East Germany. The government in East Berlin took immediate cognizance of the Brandt pronouncement and early in November 1969 forwarded to Bonn the draft of a possible traffic treaty and, in December, the draft of a treaty for the establishment of "equal [gleichberechtigte] relations" between the two German states. In the Federal government's reply to East Berlin on January 21, 1970, Chancellor Brandt did not deal with the East German treaty drafts directly. Instead, he proposed the negotiation of a treaty on the renunciation of force, which also would give the two states an opportunity to exchange views on a variety of problems facing both of them, including the matter of "equal relations." Acknowledgment of the sovereignty of the GDR was a major step, and the Federal government clearly did not wish to challenge the conservative opposition further by establishing semi-diplomatic relations immediately. Instead, Brandt preferred to talk initially about possible practical cooperation with the GDR, which represented a continuation and major expansion of his earlier concept of small pragmatic steps. The East German reaction was favorable and a dialogue was begun.

In a letter of February 11, 1970, Willi Stoph, the chairman of the GDR Council of Ministers, invited the West German chancellor to come to East Berlin for talks with Stoph and the East German foreign minister, Otto Winzer. However, the proposed meeting site was politically impossible for the chancellor. A visit to East Berlin that avoided West Berlin was totally unacceptable for any West German chancellor and especially for Brandt, who had been the governing mayor of West Berlin. Both sides finally agreed to have two meetings in the "provinces," outside their capitals—in Erfurt in East Germany and Kassel in West Germany.

The speed with which the meetings took place was breathtaking even by German standards. For decades all direct communication between these two entities had been avoided. All contacts, however trivial, were burdened by political and legal reservations. Suddenly everything went extremely fast, seemingly without any difficulty. On March 19, 1970, the first meeting between

Brandt and Stoph took place in Erfurt, just one week before the opening of the Four Power negotiations in Berlin. The timing probably was not coincidental. Expectations raised by the Erfurt meeting were high. This was especially true for the East German population, many of whom forced their way to the meeting site and publicly displayed their sympathy and affection for the chancellor of the Federal Republic. The chant, "Willy, Willy" echoed through the street of Erfurt, from where Brandt could be seen in a window of the hotel where he was meeting with Stoph. While Brandt was unable to meet with the crowd, he raised his hands in an effort to quiet them, which the East German police themselves were unable to do. The scene in Erfurt made doubly clear that German-German dialogue had to be handled skillfully. Raising false hopes about unification could only endanger the process of gradual reconciliation. The views expressed by both sides were, it turned out, very far apart. Stoph repeatedly stressed the GDR's insistence upon the "establishment of full diplomatic [*völkerrechtlicher*] relations on the basis of full equality". Brandt, in turn, insisted that while the forces for separation could not be ignored, it was necessary to "give priority to those issues where agreement was possible."

What the Chancellor meant was spelled out in his "Twenty Points,"[2] which he gave Stoph at their second meeting in Kassel on May 21, 1970. These contained the Federal government's proposals on "Principles and Elements of a Treaty for the Establishment of Equal Relations between the Federal Republic of Germany and the German Democratic Republic". The catalogue of issues to be addressed in a treaty on the normalization of relations had as its basic assumption the unity of the German nation. It considered both German states equal (*gleichberechtigt*), and called for the renunciation of both the threat and the application of force. However, it did not touch the Four Powers' responsibility for Berlin and Germany as a whole. Additionally, the catalogue contained proposals for cooperation in various fields, for an exchange of missions, and the membership of both states in international organizations. For the GDR this was not satisfactory. Stoph, therefore, proposed a break in these exchanges "to permit time for reflection." However, he was careful to make clear his readiness to continue the talks "as soon as the Federal Republic would demonstrate a more realistic attitude on the issue of diplomatic [*völkerrechtliche*] recognition of the German Democratic Republic."

The following day it became clear that East Berlin rather than Bonn would have to be "more realistic." For on May 22, 1970, Egon Bahr, the state secretary in the chancellor's office, and Andrei Gromyko, the Soviet foreign minister, settled on the so-called Bahr Paper.[3] This came at the end of an extensive exchange of views between Bahr and Gromyko that lasted from January until May 1970. Originally the Bahr paper was intended to serve as the basis of an agreed report of the two delegations to their governments. However, after the contents of these confidential notes became public as a result of leaks in Bonn in the early summer of 1970, they acquired a political significance as such. They were quickly seen as defining commitments made by the Federal Republic and the Soviet Union not easily subject to change. In the Bahr paper neither diplomatic recognition of the GDR by the Federal Republic nor diplomatic treaties (*völkerrechtliche Verträge*) between the Federal Republic and the GDR were mentioned. The Soviet Union clearly had made a major shift from its earlier position in these matters. Strenuous efforts by Walter Ulbricht, the first secretary of the East German Communist (Socialist Unity) party, to deter the Soviets during a visit to Moscow, the last week of the talks between Bahr and Gromyko and five days before the meeting between Brandt and Stoph in Kassel, were of no avail.

The modified position, as expressed in the Bahr paper, forced the GDR leadership to reconsider its negotiating stance since it was in no position to torpedo the negotiations between the Soviet Union and the FRG. To avoid the risk of losing all influence on the course of events, and to emphasize the East German claim to participation on Berlin matters, the East German minister president, Willi Stoph, on October 29, 1970, sent two emissaries to Bonn, offering a new proposal on matters of mutual interest, "whose resolution would serve to bring about a relaxation of tension in the heart of Europe". The point at issue clearly was Berlin. The GDR hoped—even without prior diplomatic recognition by the Federal Republic—to initiate negotiations between the two German states that would be parallel to, but independent of, the Four Power talks. The East German concept was to reduce the Federal German presence in Berlin in exchange for improvements in the transit/traffic arrangements to and from Berlin for citizens of the Federal Republic. The GDR intended to negotiate access arrangements for West Berlin residents directly with the West Berlin Senat.

For the Federal government this offer raised delicate questions. On the one hand, Bonn was not free to negotiate with the GDR on a subject already being dealt with in the negotiations of the Four Powers and for which only the Four Powers possessed the necessary political competence. On the other hand, it was equally clear in Bonn that after agreement between the Four Powers had been reached, supplementary arrangements between the Federal Republic and the GDR would be necessary and the sooner the better. Therefore, the GDR's proposals could not be rejected out of hand.

The Federal government decided in the circumstances to further expand the catalogue of issues to be considered by the two German states, including "questions of mutual interest for both German states." The emphasis on Berlin in the GDR proposal was ignored. On November 27, 1970, State Secretary Egon Bahr and Michael Kohl of the GDR met for the first time in the Council of Ministers offices in East Berlin. Thereafter they met regularly, usually every second week and when necessary weekly, alternating between Bonn and East Berlin. They reviewed the entire spectrum of inner-German relations. A major concern, however, was the issue of traffic between the two German states. Only after the Quadripartite Agreement had been completed in September 1971 did Berlin again become a principal issue.

DIFFERENCES IN INTERPRETATION OF THE FOUR POWER AGREEMENT

In a letter dated September 3, 1971, the three Western ambassadors transmitted to the Federal government officially the text of the Four Power agreement, reaffirming their rights and responsibilities for Berlin as a whole and calling attention to the inner-German agreements that were foreseen for incorporation within the Quadripartite Agreement. It was noted that the Federal Republic was to undertake negotiations with the GDR "on behalf of the Berlin *Senat*" on the traffic "between West Berlin and the Federal Republic." In another note of September 3, 1971, the Berlin *Senat* was asked by the Allied *Kommandatura* to begin negotiations with the GDR on the matter of access of West Berlin citizens to East Berlin and to the GDR, as well as on other communication problems and territorial exchanges.

In effect this meant that the German negotiations for developing implementing details of the Quadripartite Agreement had to be conducted on two levels: between the Federal Republic and the GDR and between West Berlin and the GDR. Egon Bahr continued to represent the Bonn government in the negotiations he had begun with the GDR in November 1970. His opposite number on the Eastern side was, as before, State Secretary Kohl. For the Berlin *Senat,* Ulrich Mueller, the chief of chancery, negotiated with Guenter Kohrt, state secretary in the GDR foreign ministry. At the suggestion of the GDR, Mueller and Kohrt had been in touch since March 6, 1971, to resume the Berlin pass negotiations.

All these agreements were concluded before Christmas. However, the relatively short negotiation period camouflaged, to some extent, the difficulties the negotiators encountered. Two areas were especially complicated, as was evident during the first round of negotiations between Bahr and Kohl: (1) Despite all efforts described in the previous chapter, the GDR German translation of the Quadripartite Agreement continued to differ from that agreed upon immediately before the signing of the text by five experts of the two German states—two officials and three interpreters on each side; and (2) the GDR now insisted that the transit negotiations between Bahr and Kohl should deal only with the traffic of citizens of the Federal Republic of Germany while the transit of citizens of West Berlin should be dealt with separately at the Berlin level by Mueller and Kohrt.

In the Quadripartite Agreement the Four Powers had stated only that the detailed arrangements with regard to civilian travel would be "agreed upon between the competent German authorities." But who were the competent authorities? The three Western powers, in their letter of transmission of September 3, had asked the Federal government to negotiate with the GDR "also on behalf of the *Senat*." Additionally the Soviet Union in Annex IV of the Quadripartite Agreement had declared that an extension of international (*voelkerrechtliche*) agreements and arrangements, which the Federal Republic concluded, could be extended to the Western sectors of Berlin. The Federal government inferred from this that it not only was entitled, but indeed had the obligation to negotiate with the GDR the agreements covering the traffic to and from West Berlin—an interpretation that the Soviet Union first disputed but ultimately seemed tacitly to accept in the quadripartite negotiations.

The German Democratic Republic, nevertheless, tried to impose its own interpretation on the negotiating framework. It considered the West German involvement in defining transit arrangements for the inhabitants of West Berlin a significant and unacceptable expansion of the Federal presence in Berlin and a reduction in the autonomous character of West Berlin. This, again, raised questions about status, which lay within the competence of the Four Powers. In fact many important aspects of the agreement were subject to dispute and this became increasingly obvious as the two German states tried to work out the specific details.

By mid-September Chancellor Brandt felt compelled to suspend the negotiations, since the GDR showed total inflexibility during the first round of talks. This interruption in the negotiations probably was facilitated by the fact that Brandt had been invited at this time, in September, to meet with Leonid Brezhnev in Oreanda, where the Soviet leader had "a spacious and comfortable estate on the Black Sea"—as Brandt recalls in his memoirs, *People and Politics*.[4] Not far away, in the neighboring town of Yalta, Stalin, Roosevelt, and Churchill had met to decide the fate of a conquered Germany. Brezhnev, who clearly had a sense of history, was obviously quite aware of this. When the Bundeswehr plane that had brought the small German delegation to the southern part of the Soviet Union on September 16, 1971, landed at the airport of Simferopol, he asked the photographers not to miss the historic event. Was this a new beginning? Welcoming the Germans, the Soviet leader reminded the audience that Germans and Soviets "had bad relations long enough"; now there was no need to spoil these relations any longer. Brandt considered this an "optimistic variant of a formulation used earlier by Egon Bahr concerning the GDR when he noted that for too long we had had no relations at all, now we at least had bad ones."[5]

The Oreanda visit afforded an opportunity to discuss at the highest level the difficulties that had arisen in the negotiations between the two German sides, and Brandt meant to use this opportunity to try to persuade Brezhnev to put pressure on East Berlin. The general secretary, for his part, was apparently mainly interested in the ratification by the German Bundestag of the Moscow Treaty on the non-use of force. Brezhnev noted that failure would produce a political "setback that could affect us all for decades."[6] Brandt told the Soviet general secretary that the fate of his government was closely linked to the ratification of the Eastern treaties and that he was convinced that the treaties would be ratified in the spring of 1972, albeit by a very small majority in the Bundestag.

Brezhnev returned to the subject of ratification of the Moscow Treaty a number of times during his discussions with Brandt and stated that the Berlin Agreement could go into effect only after the ratification of the Moscow Treaty, thus establishing a reverse linkage to that of the Western side that the Moscow Treaty could not be ratified until there was a satisfactory Berlin Agreement.[7] Foreign Minister Gromyko repeated the reverse linkage established by Brezhnev to Foreign Minister Scheel during this meeting at the United Nations in New York in early October 1971. Gromyko was quite specific in stipulating that even if both German states reached agreement, the Berlin Agreement could go into effect only after the Bundestag ratified the Moscow Treaty. When Brandt explained the problems that had arisen in the inner-German negotiations to Brezhnev, the Soviet leader responded carefully. He thanked the chancellor for this information. He pointed out, however, that the Soviet side could not and would not interfere in the question of the German translation of the agreement. He, Brezhnev, had never asked anything from the GDR, and would not ask anything of the East Germans in this connection either.

It was reported in the Western press that Brandt had received private assurances from Brezhnev that he would press the GDR to take a constructive position in the inner-German negotiations. Naturally this would only be evident after a certain time lapse so that the GDR could save face.[8] This was borne out by events.

When State Secretaries Bahr and Kohl met for the third round of negotiations on September 22, following Brandt's return from Oreanda, everything seemed unchanged. The talks ended after half an hour without any progress in resolving the disputed interpretations of the treaty language. Progress was made only at the end of the month, but not between Bahr and Kohl. Rather, this occurred in negotiations that had hardly attracted any attention—the negotiations between delegations of the postal ministries of the two German states.

THE POSTAL PROTOCOL

The postal negotiations were aimed at improving the mail and telephone service between the Federal Republic and the GDR. The protocol that was signed on September 30, 1971 set an important precedent because West Berlin was included in arrangements that had been worked out by the two German ministries. The Federal Republic undertook to pay the GDR a lump sum of DM250 million for services provided by the GDR postal system, and the requirements of the West Berlin *Senat* were to be computed similarly. Most importantly, however, it was stated in paragraphs 6 and 7 of the protocol that by December 15, 1971 (i.e., within a relatively short time frame) sixty additional telephone lines would be installed between West and East Berlin to improve communication between the two parts of the city, that the telegraphic service would be automated, and that improved telex connections would be established. This was evidently in implementation of Section II, paragraph C of the Quadripartite Agreement, which says: "Communications between the Western Sectors of Berlin and the territory that borders on these Sectors . . . will be improved," and of paragraph 4 of Annex

II, which reads, "telephone, telegraph, transport and other connections of the Western sectors with the outside will be improved."

These paragraphs of the postal protocol constituted the first success in the improvement of human conditions foreseen in the Quadripartite Agreement and became an integral part of it under the final protocol of the agreement.

The inclusion of West Berlin in the postal protocol between the two German states was significant, especially since the three Western ambassadors in their letter to the chancellor of September 3, 1971 had asked the Federal government to negotiate with the GDR only on transit, without mentioning improved communications for the Western sectors. The East German concession, which probably resulted from Soviet pressure as well as from the financial inducements provided by the Federal Republic, could be interpreted as a signal for a general breakthrough in the inner-German negotiations. For the first time the GDR had agreed to an arrangement negotiated by the Federal government on behalf of West Berlin. In a press conference on the day after the signing of the postal protocol, on October 1, 1971, Egon Bahr expressed optimism. While pointing out that problems arising from differing translations of the Four Power agreement had only been "circumvented for the time being," and not solved, he suggested that if the GDR continued to deal with the problem of ties as they had in the postal settlement, serious negotiations were possible.[9]

Bahr's professed optimism notwithstanding, the talks continued to drag on with great difficulty, and by the end of October little progress had been made. In the transit negotiations Bahr and Kohl continued to differ sharply on the issue of a possible misuse of transit routes. The GDR allegedly feared that East German stability could be undermined by accepting too liberal a procedure for the three transit routes. The East Germans considered each car and truck crossing the demarcation line without undergoing a rigid search a potential escape vehicle for East Germans seeking to flee to the West. The sealing of trucks by GDR authorities and rigid regulations covering possible misuse of the autobahn were considered absolutely necessary to reduce the risk of a new wave of defections.

The negotiations involving the Berlin *Senat* were no less difficult. However, in this instance, the problem had nothing to do with people escaping; rather, the problem lay in the reverse possibility of too many West Berliners flooding East Berlin and the GDR. A quota system was suggested by GDR representatives as a way to limit the number of West Berlin citizens visiting East Berlin and East Germany. The Federal German government and the Berlin *Senat* rejected this suggestion. Unrestricted access to West Berlin from the Federal Republic and increased travel by West Berlin residents into East Berlin and the GDR, they said, were the goals of West German policy and indeed a major element in the rationale for the Quadripartite Agreement. If the GDR persisted, the central element of the Berlin Agreement would be negated. Therefore, the Federal government and the Berlin *Senat* had no choice but to remain firm, even if that resulted in stalemated negotiations.

This development apparently caused some uneasiness on the Soviet side, which was ever more interested in the rapid conclusion of the Berlin complex of negotiations to avoid endangering the ratification of the Moscow Treaty. The Kremlin seemed to understand the political difficulties facing the Social-Liberal coalition in Bonn. Every new obstacle erected by the GDR and every delay in the inner-German negotiations could strengthen those opposed to the treaties, and make ratification more difficult, if not impossible. After the conclusion of a six-day state visit to France, Brezhnev stopped in East Berlin en route to Moscow and discussed the problems of the inner-German negotiations with the East German leadership, including the former party chief, Walter Ulbricht. In these talks Brezhnev evidently left no doubt about the Soviet desire for the GDR leadership to conclude the talks with the Federal German government and the West Berlin *Senat* as quickly as possible.

Following the Brezhnev visit the new East German party leader, Erich Honecker, declared that the negotiations could be brought to a conclusion soon if all sides demonstrated good will. It was, he said, in the interest of the GDR to bring the dialogue between the two German states and between the GDR and West Berlin to a positive conclusion by the end of November. Honecker undertook to consider any constructive proposal submitted by the Brandt government.[10] The talks then proceeded apace. By mid-November Bahr and Kohl had resolved most of their differences on the transit agreement. However, on the Western side there were increasing complaints about Bahr's handling of the negotiations. The critics were led by the then Interior Minister Hans-Dietrich Genscher, Foreign Minister Scheel, and Undersecretary of State Paul Frank, and included the head of the political department in the Foreign Office, Berndt von Staden. They felt Bahr was making too many concessions in order to conclude the negotiations as quickly as possible. The issue of possible arrests of former refugees from the GDR on the transit routes was particularly troublesome to them. This issue affected a very large number of people, possibly millions. Bahr successfully worked out a clause protecting those who had escaped from East Germany prior to the time the Quadripartite Agreement went into effect. However, there was no protection for those alleged to have committed "serious crimes" before or during their escape. This was unacceptable in Bonn, and Foreign Minister Scheel insisted upon a definition of "serious crimes" that would clearly exclude political offenses, and would limit the application of misuse to those who had "really committed serious violations of the law."

Scheel's intervention was successful. Bahr and Kohl ultimately agreed upon a formula that gave the GDR the right to reject (*Zurückweisen*) those people who had committed crimes against life, against the physical safety (*körperliche Unversehrtheit*) of people, and against property (*Vermögen*). This meant that the GDR could not arrest such persons, but could only turn them back at the border. Chancellor Brandt said he had not assumed that "such a positive and reasonable agreement" could be reached. This GDR concession deprived the regime of the possibility of apprehending criminals (by their definition) on its own territory, including those accused of illegally escaping from the GDR (*Republikflucht*). Undersecretary of State Kohl therefore was not prepared at the time to confirm it publicly.[11]

While Bahr and Kohl were still negotiating, Foreign Minister Scheel went to Moscow on November 24 to try to persuade the Soviets to remove the "reverse linkage." He proposed a declaration by the Four Powers that the Berlin Agreement was "complete" and would "not be changed anymore." This, he argued, would permit Chancellor Brandt to accomplish the long and difficult ratification process of the Eastern treaties even before the Four Powers had signed the final protocol on Berlin. The Soviets promised to consider Scheel's proposal, but avoided any commitment on the Berlin Agreement so long as the bilateral treaty between the Soviet Union and the Federal Republic remained unratified. The Soviet leadership was not unaware of Scheel's role in the inner-German negotiations and they no doubt remembered only too well that Scheel had been the first formally to state the linkage between ratification of the Moscow Treaty and completion of a satisfactory Berlin Agreement.[12] When General Secretary Brezhnev visited Bonn several years later, in May 1973, he announced loudly on his arrival, "Ah, there is Herr Scheel, who complicates and hinders the *Ostpolitik!*"[13]

Since Bahr and Kohl had resolved the outstanding issues of the transit arrangements on December 3, 1971, the initialing of the agreements could have taken place the next day. But Bahr had to wait until the negotiations at the Berlin level between Mueller and Kohrt had been concluded. They waited in vain. The East Germans and the *Senat* were stalled on the visit arrangements. Determined to limit visiting possibilities for West Berliners, the East German side proposed that visits to East Germany and/or East Berlin should be for no more than thirty days a year; that visas be issued only at five GDR offices in West Berlin, which would be opened solely for that purpose; and that those offices would be open only during regular business hours (i.e., not at night or on Sundays or holidays). They also wanted to restrict visitors from West Berlin to the use of public transportation; private vehicles would be prohibited. Apart from the thirty-day limit on visits, in which the Western side finally acquiesced, the *Senat* considered these conditions unacceptable. Given this apparent impasse, the negotiations in Berlin were recessed on December 4 to give both sides sufficient time to reexamine their positions.

In Bonn new difficulties had arisen. The Berlin FDP found booby traps in the agreed provisions regarding misuse of the access routes and, conscious that impending NATO ministerial consideration of a European security conference offered additional leverage, asked that Bahr renegotiate this part of the agreement to close the gaps. Bahr publicly complained about the "disturbing behavior" of the Free Democrats but nevertheless sat down again with Kohl. By adding eight additional words, the term "serious crimes," which would justify barring a traveler from the access routes, was clarified.

However, initialing was still impossible because the GDR and the *Senat* remained at odds on their agreement.

When the talks resumed in Berlin on December 7, the Eastern side was no longer represented by Guenter Kohrt, who had suddenly "fallen ill." The new East German negotiator was Peter Florin. It became clear at the outset that Florin had instructions to conclude the negotiations with the Berlin *Senat* as quickly as possible. The remaining outstanding problems were resolved in a night session that came to a successful end at 4 A.M. on the morning of December 8. The GDR made major concessions on all the outstanding points. Visas would be issued without excessive examination on a case-by-case basis; the visa issuing offices would be open not only during the customary business hours, but also for several hours during the weekend and on holidays; and West Berliners would be allowed to visit East Berlin and the GDR in private vehicles if they were disabled or had small children, or if they needed to travel a lengthy distance within the GDR.

Agreement was reached not only on the visiting regulations, which had been controversial for so long, but also on an exchange and purchase of territory to tidy up the East-West Berlin border. Several border areas and enclaves were exchanged. The Steinstücken exclave, which had been a persistent cause of difficulties, was joined to West Berlin. The GDR was given seventeen hectares of land belonging to West Berlin. West Berlin, in turn, obtained territory around the former Potsdam railway station. Since West Berlin obtained more from this land exchange than the East Germans, the latter were compensated financially. West Berlin private plot owners whose lands were transferred to the GDR were paid for their properties by the West Berlin *Senat*.

The simultaneous initialing of the agreements between the Federal Republic and the GDR and between the GDR and the Berlin *Senat* took place on December 11, 1971. Consultations with the Four Powers followed. In a letter of December 16, 1971, the Western powers informed the Federal government that the German transit agreement was "in accordance with the Quadripartite Agreement of September 3, 1971." Additionally, the *Senat* of Berlin was "authorized" by the Allied commandants (also by a letter dated December 16) to sign the agreements with the GDR. Both actions demonstrated the subordinate status of the Germans *vis-à-vis* the Allies in Berlin matters, but the new political reality was that both German governments had played crucial roles in arriving at a Berlin settlement. On December 17 the inner-German agreements, supplementing the Quadripartite Agreement, were signed in Bonn and East Berlin with great pomp—a historic moment in postwar German history.

The Four Power agreement, however, did not go into effect immediately. The Soviet Union was waiting for the ratification of the Moscow Treaty by the German Bundestag in accordance with the reverse linkage it had established. Consequently, only on June 3, 1972 did the inner-German arrangements go into effect, when on this same day the Four Powers signed the

Signing of the Inner-German Agreements incorporated in the Quadripartite Agreement (*from left*: Egon Bahr, representative of the Federal Republic of Germany; Michael Kohl, representative of the German Democratic Republic). Photo courtesy of the German Information Center, New York.

final protocol of the Berlin Agreement, and the FRG's treaties with Moscow and Warsaw on the non-use of force went into effect through an exchange of ratification documents. In the end, the two linkages had brought the result desired by the FRG, the three Western Allies, the Soviets and, by no means least, the residents of West Berlin.

NOTES

1. *Zehn Jahre Deutschlandpolitik. Die Entwicklung der Beziehungen zwischen der Bundesrepublik Deutschland und der DDR 1969–1979. Bericht und Dokumentation* (Bonn: Bundesministerium für Innerdeutsche Beziehungen, 1980), p. 119.

2. Text in Heinrich von Seigler (ed.), *Dokumentation zur Deutschlandfrage in Verbindung mit der Ostpolitik. Hauptband VI: Chronik der Ereignisse von der Regierungeserklarung Brandts im Oktober 1969 bis Ende 1970* (Bonn, Vienna, and Zurich: Siegler Verlag, 1972).

3. Text in *The Treaty of August 12, 1970 between the Federal Republic of Germany and the Union of Soviet Socialist Republics* (Bonn: Federal Press and Information Office, 1970), pp. 15–18.

4. Brandt, *People and Politics*, p. 348.

5. Ibid., p. 346.

6. Ibid., p. 349.

7. In an internal note prepared in the West German Foreign Office in February 1971, the attitude of the Federal government was summarized as follows:

There is no formal linkage between any of the treaties to be concluded and a Berlin settlement. Indeed there cannot be, since the Federal Republic has no legal competence for Berlin under international law. According to German law, Berlin is a *Land* of the Federal Republic. But this law was suspended by the Allies. However, the Federal Government has always made clear that, in addition to the Moscow Treaty, there also must be a Berlin settlement. In the talks between Undersecretary of State Bahr and Foreign Minister Gromyko, and in the Moscow talks between Foreign Minister Scheel and Mr. Gromyko our wishes with regard to Berlin have been expressed unequivocally time and again. Moreover, there exists a factual linkage between the Eastern treaties and a Berlin settlement. Detente cannot be established in Central Europe if the issue which has been demonstrated to be most critical can be used at any time to create new tensions.

8. See the *Washington Post,* September 23, 1971.

9. Quoted in *Der Spiegel,* October 5, 1971.

10. Quoted in *Neues Deutschland,* November 5, 1971.

11. This provision is not included in the transit agreement of December 17, 1971. It is only noted in the accompanying documentation and was announced by Minister Egon Franke in the Federal government's statement to the Bundestag of October 15, 1971.

12. In a television interview on July 8, 1970, Scheel had declared that a "renunciation

of force treaty with the Soviet Union'' would not go into effect until a ''satisfactory Berlin Agreement'' had been reached.

13. See Arnulf Baring (in cooperation with Manfred Goertemaker), *Machtwechsel. Die Ära Brandt-Scheel* (Stuttgart: Deutsche Verlags-Anstalt, 1982), p. 326.

Berlin in the United Nations

In his first policy statement to the Bundestag as chancellor on October 28, 1969, Willy Brandt included an offer to achieve cooperation between the FRG and the GDR through a treaty to be negotiated between the two states. East Berlin replied in December by forwarding a draft model treaty. This draft provided for membership in the United Nations of the GDR and the FRG, an idea that the GDR had pursued more than three years earlier when Walter Ulbricht, then Chairman of the GDR Council of Ministers, submitted a formal application for membership in the international organization.[1] While previous West German governments had strongly opposed GDR participation in UN bodies, Brandt saw such membership as a logical and inevitable step in the process of normalizing relations between the two states in Germany. Accordingly, the twenty points that he proposed to East German Premier Stoph in Kassel on May 21, 1970 summarized the FRG's ideas on "principles and contractual elements for the establishment of relations based on equal rights."[2] Point 20 proposed that the question of membership in the United Nations be settled in a treaty. UN membership for the two German states was also mentioned in the informal paper agreed to by State Secretary Egon Bahr and Foreign Minister Gromyko in Moscow during the same month.[3] When the Basic Treaty between the FRG and the GDR was signed in November 1972 it included as annexes an exchange of letters indicating the intention of each government to achieve UN membership and to inform the other of the date on which application would be made.[4] Thus UN membership was essentially part of the process of normalization of relations between the two German states. Inevitably, however, this raised the question of the status of Berlin and constituted a test of the provisions incorporated in the Four Power agreement relative to the representation of the Western sectors in international relations. The ambassadors of the four occupying powers reassembled in the

Control Council building in Berlin to agree on the text of a formal statement without which UN membership could not have become a reality. In this sense, the Four Power agreement on UN membership was part (the last point, so to speak) of the Berlin Agreement negotiating process. While Kenneth Rush had been replaced as U.S. ambassador by Martin J. Killenbrand, Henry Kissinger was still in the White House and reactivated his private negotiating channel with Soviet Ambassador Dobrynin, to the considerable confusion of the regular negotiation process and without notable effect on the outcome.

The basic problem inherent in UN membership for the two German states from the perspective of the Western Allies was the possible implication that in accepting the GDR's entry they would be acknowledging its full sovereignty while certain restrictions on such sovereignty relative to access to Berlin, the status of all of Berlin, and the ultimate settlement of Germany's borders continued in effect and needed to be maintained. It was concluded that this problem could be dealt with by a clarifying Four Power statement. The Soviet Union, which presumably shared with the Western Allies the desire to preserve an ultimate responsibility for the status of Germany as a whole and which, in addition, was anxious to see the GDR in the United Nations, agreed.

In late September 1972 Foreign Minister Gromyko visited Washington, as was his annual custom, during the regular session of the General Assembly of the United Nations. Secretary Rogers was in New York for the opening days of the assembly, and during a meeting with FRG Foreign Minister Scheel discussed the necessity of a Four Power declaration on their rights and responsibilities in Germany in connection with the expected applications of the two German states for UN membership. A draft of such a declaration had already been developed in the Bonn Group. The conversations with Foreign Minister Gromyko in the White House went considerably further. He and Henry Kissinger actually worked out the following text for a Four Power statement:

The governments of the Soviet Union, Great Britain, the United States and France . . . have agreed to support the application for UN membership when submitted by the FRG and GDR and to affirm in this connection that such membership shall in no way affect or change the question of the Four Power rights and responsibilities, or the agreements, decisions, and practices which relate to them.

Having achieved tentative agreement on this text, Kissinger did something he had never done in his private channel dealings during the negotiations on the Four Power agreement: he sought clearance from the Department of State. He telephoned the text to Walter Stoessel, who had become assistant secretary of state for European affairs on Hillenbrand's departure for Bonn. It was noted in the State Department that the text contained the rather ambiguous wording, ''the question of the Four Power rights and responsibilities,'' which had been used in the declarations exchanged by Gromyko and West German Foreign Minister Scheel on August 6, 1970, as part of the treaty of August 12, 1970 between the

Soviet Union and the FRG.[5] The Western powers had accepted that wording somewhat reluctantly and, in their responses to a note from the Federal government quoting the exchange, had taken cognizance of it but, for their part, had declared that the rights and responsibilities of the Four Powers, rather than the "question of the rights," were not affected. It was nonetheless concluded that the wording worked out between Kissinger and Gromyko dealing with UN membership, while less than ideal, was adequate since it included the phrase "or the agreements, decisions, and practices which relate to them [the Four Power rights and responsibilities]," and this phrase was not modified by "the question of." Stoessel expressed this view to Kissinger, who was in a great hurry to reach final agreement on the text with Ambassador Dobrynin, Gromyko having departed. Stoessel proposed that the text be shown to Secretary Rogers, but Kissinger demurred on the ground that this raised various questions of responsibility that could only cause problems. The secretary of state therefore remained ignorant of the text agreed with the Soviet Union by Henry Kissinger. Stoessel did inform the secretary in general terms that during his conversations in the White House, Gromyko had indicated receptivity to the idea of a Four Power declaration on their rights and responsibilities in connection with admission to the United Nations of the two German states. Rogers said that he himself had raised the subject with Gromyko during the SALT signature ceremonies and Gromyko had told him he thought something could be worked out.

Ambassador Hillenbrand then had the difficult task of introducing the text into the quadripartite negotiations in Berlin as if it were a new U.S. proposal when it was the Americans who had expressed the strongest reservations about similar phraseology when used in the Gromyko-Scheel exchange. The British and French quickly suspected U.S.-Soviet collusion and the French refused to go along with the text. In the end the French persevered and the final text, to which the Soviets agreed, reads:

The Governments of the French Republic, the Union of Soviet Socialist Republics, the United Kingdom of Great Britain and Northern Ireland and the United States of America, having been represented by their Ambassadors, who held a series of meetings in the building formerly occupied by the Allied Control Council, are in agreement that they will support the applications of the Federal Republic of Germany and the German Democratic Republic, and affirm in this connection that this membership shall in no way affect the rights and responsibilities of the Four Powers and the corresponding related Quadripartite agreements, decisions, and practices.[6]

The compromise that Henry Kissinger had been eager to reach with the Soviets was proven by French firmness to have been unnecessary.

The Four Power declaration made no mention of Berlin. As in the case of the Four Power agreement itself, the city where agreement on the declaration was reached was not identified—only the building was. Yet Berlin was much involved, for named or not it was intended that East Berlin would be covered through the UN membership of the GDR and the Western sectors through the membership of the FRG. The way that this was accomplished tested successfully the provision of the Four Power agreement (Annex IV), according to which the Federal Republic may represent the Western sectors in international organizations in so far as questions of security and status are not concerned. It did nothing, however, to strengthen the contention of the Western powers that East Berlin is part of the special area of Berlin and not an integral part of the GDR.

The Four Power declaration was accepted with considerable reservations by the CDU opposition in the Bundestag, especially on the question of Berlin. Dr. Karl Carstens, who was later to become the president of the Federal Republic, spoke as rapporteur for the CDU on the subject in the Bundestag on May 3, 1973. "If one takes a closer look at this Declaration", he said, "one finds to one's surprise that this Declaration says not one word as to which object the rights and responsibilities of the Four Powers refer . . . it does not even once contain the words 'in Berlin.' " Professor Carstens said that some members of the opposition were prepared to support the manner in which Berlin would be dealt with in connection with the Federal Republic's accession to the United Nations, especially in light of the following statement made by a representative of the Federal government before the Bundestag Foreign Affairs Committee:

A question raised by members of the Committee whether the inclusion of Berlin free of all doubt—with the well-known reservation, status and security—is the unconditional prerequisite for the accession of the Federal Republic of Germany to the United Nations Organization was answered in the affirmative by the Federal Government. On the other hand, some Opposition Members regarded this assurance as not entirely satisfying. They demanded that it should be made absolutely clear that the Soviet Union, in conformity with the . . . 1971 Quadripartite Agreement, will raise no objections against the planned extension of the accession of the Federal Republic of Germany to *Land* Berlin.[7]

In a speech to the German Bundestag on February 16, 1973, the parliamentary secretary in the Ministry for Foreign Affairs, Karl Moersch, explained how the Western sectors of Berlin would be dealt with in connection with representation in the United Nations in the following terms:

Now, how do matters stand with Berlin? Here, doubt has been raised as to whether the Federal Republic of Germany is in a position legally and in fact to represent Berlin in the United Nations and its agencies. The position is as follows:

On accession to the United Nations the Federal Government will incorporate Berlin (West) within the framework established by the Quadripartite Agreement. I make express reference to the Quadripartite Agreement. This is in accordance with our constant practice and is done in the interest of the city's viability and particularly to ensure its participation in the activities of the United Nations, which are of ever-increasing importance in the fields of international economic and social co-operation.

However, in this connection the Federal Government has to be aware, and it is aware, that naturally the Charter of the United Nations handles, or at least touches upon, subjects with regard to which an extension of an international agreement to Berlin (West) by the Federal Republic of Germany is, in conformity with the provisions of the Quadripartite Agreement, impossible. It is a matter, account taken of these given limitations, of achieving for Berlin what can be achieved. In correspondence with this is the Berlin clause embodied in Article 2 of the Law on Accession, with its reservation in favour of the rights and responsibilities of the Allied Authorities, including those affecting matters of security and status. In the relationship with the United Nations, the Federal Government will, when making application, make an appropriate declaration to the UN Secretary-General. The Three Powers for their part will make an official statement relating to the reservation of security and status both in Berlin and *vis-à-vis* the United Nations. We believe that in this process, in the course of which there will be consultation, on every single detail, with the Three Powers, account will be taken of all aspects of this delicate question: the ties between Berlin and the Federation, the status of the Three Powers, our principal Allies in the city, and the text and purport of the Quadripartite Agreement.[8]

The difference of view within the CDU/CSU was reflected in the final vote in the Bundestag on the Law of Accession to the Charter of the United Nations, the results of which were 364 (including 99 CDU/CSU deputies) in favor and 121 deputies (all CDU/CSU) opposed. The Berlin deputies, whose votes were not included, split according to party lines with thirteen SPD and FDP in favor and nine from the CDU opposed.

Since, as indicated by Moersch, the Law on United Nations Accession contained a Berlin clause, it was, after passage in Bonn, referred to Berlin to be "taken over" by the West Berlin legislature. As part of this procedure the text was sent to the Allied *Kommandatura* for review. On April 13, 1973, in BKC/L(73)l, the *Kommandatura* replied:

In accordance with the arrangements referred to in Annex IV A of the Quadripartite Agreement of September 3, 1971, and in particular with the exception of matters concerning security and status:
(a) The Allied Kommandatura has no objection to the acceptance by the Federal Republic of Germany of the rights and obligations contained in the United Nations Charter with respect also to the Western Sectors of Berlin;
(b) The Allied Kommandatura approves the representation of the interests of the Western Sectors of Berlin in the United Nations and its subsidiary organs by the Federal Republic.

Then, at the time of its application for membership in the United Nations, the FRG submitted the following separate letter to the secretary general of the United Nations:

Bonn, June 13, 1973

Mr. Secretary-General,
    In connection with the application of the Federal Republic of Germany made today for membership in the United Nations, I have the honour to state that, respecting the validity of the Charter of the United Nations for Berlin (West), the Federal Republic of

Germany will, from the day on which she is admitted as a Member of the United Nations, assume except in questions of security and status, for Berlin (West) also the rights and obligations arising out of the Charter of the United Nations and will represent the interests of Berlin (West) in the United Nations and its subsidiary agencies.

I have the honour to request the circulation of the Note as an official document of the United Nations.

Walter Scheel
Federal Minister for Foreign Affairs of the Federal Republic of Germany[9]

Lest there be the slightest misinterpretation of what this might imply concerning the relationship between West Berlin and the Federal Republic, the Soviet permanent representative to the United Nations sent the following letter to the UN secretary general a week later:

In connection with the letter dated 13 June 1973 (A/9071-S/10950) of Mr. W. Scheel, Minister for Foreign Affairs of the Federal Republic of Germany, concerning the representation of the interests of West Berlin in the United Nations and its organs, I have the honour to communicate the following.

The Western Sectors of Berlin are not a constituent part of the Federal Republic of Germany and cannot be governed by it. It was established in the Quadripartite Agreement of 3 September 1971 that the Federal Republic of Germany would maintain and develop its ties with those Sectors subject to recognition of this fact.

According to the Quadripartite Agreement, the Governments of the United States, the United Kingdom and France maintain their rights and responsibilities relating to the representation abroad of the interests of the Western Sectors of Berlin and their permanent residents, including rights and responsibilities concerning matters of security and status, both in international organizations and in relations with other countries.

Provided the matters concerning security and status remain unaffected, the Federal Republic of Germany may represent the interests of the Western Sectors of Berlin in certain specific spheres enumerated in Annex IV of the Quadripartite Agreement, including the representation of the interests of the Western Sectors of Berlin in international organizations (Annex IV A2(c)). The basis for such representation is the Quadripartite Agreement of 3 September 1971 regulating its permissible nature and scope.

I should be grateful if you would have this letter circulated as an official document of the Security Council and of the General Assembly.

(signed) Y. Malik
Permanent Representative of the USSR to the United Nations[10]

The applications of the Federal Republic and the German Democratic Republic were considered by the Security Council on June 21, 1973, after the Declaration of the Four Powers of November 9, 1972 had been circulated as an official document of the Council. The Security Council agreed unanimously to recommend to the General Assembly that the German Democratic Republic and the Federal Republic of Germany be admitted to membership, which the General Assembly accomplished by acclamation on the following day. Neither the Security Council nor the General Assembly made any reference to Berlin.

The reservation contained in the Four Power agreement that the Federal Republic could represent the Western sectors of Berlin except in matters concerning security and status means in the case of the United Nations, at least in the assumption of the Western powers, that the Federal Republic cannot represent West Berlin in a matter before the Security Council since by definition the Council is concerned with security. Thus, should a need arise, as in 1948–49, to bring a Berlin development before the Security Council, one or more of the three Western powers would have to do it, and the Federal Republic would not be qualified to speak on behalf of Berlin (West), although it could presumably express its own views on the matter to the Council as an interested party. No instance that would test this understanding has arisen. The Federal Republic has served as a member of the Security Council and has felt no need to specify that in doing so it did not represent West Berlin.

Such difficulties as have arisen in the United Nations with regard to Berlin have been rather trivial but have caused the Soviet Union and the three Western powers to restate officially their conflicting legal positions on Berlin in essentially the same language as was used before the Berlin Agreement was signed. A recurrent issue predating the entry of the two German states into the United Nations was the manner in which Berlin is listed in the *United Nations Demographic Year Book*. The Western powers always took exception to the listing of the statistics for East Berlin as part of the German Democratic Republic. When they again objected after the Berlin Agreement was concluded and the Four Power declaration was issued, the Soviet Union sent the following *note verbale* to the secretary general:

The Soviet Union rejects, as having no legal or *de facto* basis, the assertions in the letter of the representatives of France, the United Kingdom and the United States that the status of the capital of the German Democratic Republic and the status of the Western Sectors of Berlin are identical. As is known, the Quadripartite agreements and decisions regarding the joint administration by the Four Powers of Berlin which was the capital of the former Soviet occupation zone, were violated by the three Powers, while the Western Sectors of Berlin were cut off from their natural environment. The present situation in this area is characterized by the fact that for the past 25 years East Berlin has been the capital of the German Democratic Republic and an inseparable and integral part thereof, in which are situated the central State institutions of the Republic. The Western Sectors of Berlin on the other hand are still under the occupation of the United States, the United Kingdom and France and do not form an integral part of the Federal Republic of Germany.

With regard to the references by the representatives of France, the United Kingdom and the United States to the Quadripartite Declaration of 9 November 1972 (document S/10955), the Soviet Union would like to emphasize that the attempts to represent the capital of the Democratic Republic of Germany as being one of the sectors having quadripartite status are completely groundless. They can in no way be passed off as quadripartite practice, as referred to in the said Declaration.[11]

This prompted the following response from the Western Powers:

The Permanent Representatives of France, the United Kingdom and the United States of America, with reference to the above-mentioned communication, reaffirm the terms of their letter of 19 September 1974 (A/9761). In so far as new points are raised by the latest communication of the Permanent Representative of the USSR, they wish to state the following:

1. The quadripartite status of greater Berlin stems from the original rights and responsibilities of the Four Powers. Quadripartite wartime and postwar agreements and decisions based on these rights and responsibilities stipulated that greater Berlin was to be a special area under the joint authority of the Four Powers entirely distinct from the Soviet zone of occupation in Germany.

2. Any change in the status of greater Berlin as reflected in these agreements and decisions would require the agreement of all Four Powers. No such agreement altering the status of Berlin or providing for a special status for any of its sectors has ever been concluded. No unilateral steps taken by the Soviet Union in violation of the Quadripartite agreements and decisions relating to greater Berlin, nor the fact that the seat of government of the German Democratic Republic is currently located in the Eastern Sector of the city, can imply that the quadripartite rights and responsibilities relating to the Eastern Sector are in any way affected. In fact, the Four Powers continue to exercise their quadripartite rights and responsibilities in all four sectors of the city.

3. The Quadripartite Agreement, signed in Berlin on 3 September 1971, was explicitly concluded on the basis that the quadripartite rights and responsibilities and the corresponding wartime and post-war agreements and decisions of the Four Powers are not affected. Moreover, the Four Powers affirmed in the Quadripartite Declaration made in Berlin on 9 November 1972 and circulated on 18 June 1973 as a document of the United Nations (S/10955), that membership of the Federal Republic of Germany and the German Democratic Republic in the United Nations shall in no way affect the rights and responsibilities of the Four Powers and the corresponding related Quadripartite agreements, decisions and practices. The three Powers will continue, as in the past, to fulfill their obligations flowing from the Quadripartite agreements and decisions relating to Berlin.[12]

It will be noted that this position is very close to that stated by the Western powers to the Soviet Union at the time of the blockade. After this exchange a solution was found to the *Yearbook* problem according to which Berlin is listed first among the cities of the GDR (as capital) and last among the cities of the FRG with the following footnote: "Designation and data for Berlin appearing on this page were supplied by the competent authorities pursuant to the relevant agreements of the Four Powers." The populations listed under the two Berlin headings are respectively those of East Berlin and West Berlin.

When the Federal Republic in 1976 appointed the director of the Federal Office for the Supervision of Cartels and Trusts, which is located in West Berlin, as a member of its delegation to the UN Commission on Transnational Corporations, the Soviet Union along with most of its Warsaw Pact allies—led by the GDR—expressed strenuous objections. These were rebutted by the three Western powers and the representative continued to serve, with annual official objections and rebuttals for the record. The following is the text of the first Soviet letter on the subject in 1975:

The Permanent Mission of the USSR to the United Nations is obliged to draw attention to the fact that the provisional list of representatives of States to the first session of the United Nations Commission on Transnational Corporations indicates that the official representative of the Federal Republic of Germany will be Professor E. Guenther, the President of the Federal Office for the Supervision of Cartels and Trusts in the Federal Republic of Germany, an office which has its headquarters in West Berlin.

This action by the Federal Republic of Germany is clearly contrary to the Quadripartite Agreement of 3 September 1971 on West Berlin, according to which West Berlin is not a constituent part of the Federal Republic of Germany and is not governed by it. Accordingly, the activities in West Berlin of the Federal Office for the Supervision of Cartels and Trusts, representing an attempt to establish the jurisdiction of the Federal Republic of Germany over West Berlin, are contrary to the Quadripartite Agreement and incompatible with its provisions.

The nomination of a person from West Berlin as the accredited representative of the Federal Republic of Germany to the United Nations Commission on Transnational Corporations does not facilitate the efforts of the United Nations to reduce international tension and expand international co-operation. The attempts of the Federal Republic of Germany to involve the United Nations in such violations of international agreements are not consonant with international detente and do not advance the goal of maintaining a normal situation around West Berlin. They can only create misunderstandings and complications. For these reasons, the Permanent Mission of the USSR to the United Nations and the representative of the USSR to the United Nations Commission on Transnational Corporations cannot recognize the legality of the nomination of Professor Guenther as the representative of the Federal Republic of Germany to that Commission.[13]

The three Western powers responded as follows:

We have the honour to refer to the letter to you from the Permanent Representative of the Union of Soviet Socialist Republics to the United Nations of 24 March 1975 (A/10062) concerning the representation of the Federal Republic of Germany at the first session of the United Nations Commission on Transnational Corporations.

The contention of the Permanent Representative of the Union of Soviet Socialist Republics that the designation of Dr. Eberhard Guenther as a representative of the Federal Republic of Germany at the first session of the United Nations Commission on Transnational Corporations is contrary to the Quadripartite Agreement of 3 September 1971 is without foundation. That Agreement, which was signed in Berlin by the Governments of France, the United Kingdom of Great Britain and Northern Ireland, the United States of America and the Union of Soviet Socialist Republics, contains no provision from which such a contention could be drawn.

The location of the Federal Office for the Supervision of Cartels and Trusts in the Western Sectors of Berlin was approved in 1957 by the British, French and United States authorities acting on the basis of their supreme authority. They are satisfied that the Federal Office for the Supervision of Cartels and Trusts does not perform in the Western Sectors of Berlin acts in exercise of direct state authority over the Western Sectors of

Berlin. Neither the location nor the activities of that Office in the Western Sectors of Berlin therefore contravene any of the provisions of the Quadripartite Agreement.

The letter from the Permanent Representative of the Union of Soviet Socialist Republics which is referred to above contains an incomplete and consequently misleading reference to the Quadripartite Agreement. The relevant passage of that Agreement to which the Soviet representative referred provides that the ties between the Western Sectors of Berlin and the Federal Republic of Germany will be maintained and developed, taking into account that these Sectors continue not to be a constituent part of the Federal Republic of Germany and not to be governed by it.

Regarding other communications on this subject which have been sent to the Secretary-General, we wish to point out that States which are not parties to the Quadripartite Agreement are not competent to comment authoritatively on its provisions.[14]

When similar protests were circulated in subsequent years, the Western powers simply responded by referring to their earlier positions, and the official from the Cartel Office in Berlin continued to represent the Federal Republic.

The only importance of those exchanges was to highlight once again the fact that the Four Power agreement of 1971 did not eliminate the differences between the Soviet Union and the Western powers on the legal status of Berlin and that the meaning of the Four Power agreement with regard to the Federal presence in Berlin was, and will remain, subject to different interpretations.

The Four Power declaration in support of UN membership of the two German states effectively preserved "the rights and responsibilities of the Four Powers and the corresponding Quadripartite agreements, decisions and practices," presumably in Berlin as well as in Germany as a whole, since while Berlin is not mentioned, neither is it specifically excluded. However, given the fact that there really is no agreement between East and West on the status of Berlin, the actions of the two sides in the United Nations with regard to Berlin would seem to have more importance than the declaration. The exchanges on the *Demographic Yearbook* and the representation of the Federal Republic by an official of a Federal Office located in West Berlin amounted to a minor victory for the Western side since in practice the "man from Berlin" was not withdrawn and Berlin is now listed under both the FRG and GDR headings. In the UN entry procedure, however, the opposite was true. The GDR and the Soviet Union took no special action to bring about the applicability of the UN Charter in East Berlin, nor was any reservation expressed or accepted concerning limitations on the competency of the GDR to represent East Berlin in matters of status and security. The Western powers remained silent on this at the time of UN entry, although their position on the special status of *all* of Berlin was made clear in their subsequent letter of 14 April 1975, which has been quoted. Still, it would be fair to say that both the Soviet Union and the GDR have proceeded in the United Nations as if East Berlin were an integral part of the GDR, and the Western powers have not sought to alter this.

It must be added as a rather melancholy footnote that despite the specific provision in the Quadripartite Agreement for the holding of international meetings in West Berlin, the Soviet Union has continued to oppose the holding of UN conferences there. UN offices have cooperated with the German Institute for Development, which is located in West Berlin, and UN representatives have participated in conferences sponsored by it both in Berlin and elsewhere. This has usually prompted a Soviet objection, especially if a senior UN official was involved. Two secretaries-general have visited West Berlin and East Berlin. (The Western powers took umbrage over the presence of units of the East German army in Berlin on the latter occasion.) So a *modus vivendi* has developed for dealing with Berlin in the United Nations that reflects the strengths and the weaknesses of the Berlin Agreement. Benefits for the Western sectors have been minimal, but without the provision for the representation of the Western sectors by the Federal Republic, UN membership for the two German states would not have been possible. The Federal Republic would not have been able to aspire to the leading position in the world organization that it has now achieved, followed always by the GDR, which, like the FRG, has served as a member of the Security Council and provided a president of the General Assembly—the same Peter Florin who represented the GDR in the final successful stage of negotiations with the Berlin *Senat* on visits and travel to East Berlin and the GDR.

NOTES

1. UN Document S/7192, 28 February 1966.
2. Quoted in Willy Brandt, *People and Politics* (Boston: Little, Brown, 1978), p. 383.
3. Text of Bahr paper is contained in *The Treaty of August 12, 1970* (Bonn: Federal Republic of Germany Press and Information Office, 1970), pp. 15–18.
4. For texts see *Die Bundesrepublik Deutschland Mitglied der Vereinten Nationen* (Bonn: Federal Republic of Germany Press and Information 1973), p. 190.
5. *Documents on Germany, 1940–1970* (Washington, D.C.: U.S. Govt. Printing Office, 1971), p. 861.
6. *Die Bundesrepublik Deutschland Mitglied der Vereinten Nationen*, p. 191.
7. Ibid., pp. 204–8.
8. Ibid., pp. 194–98.
9. UN Document A/9071-S/10950.
10. UN Document A/9082-S/10958.
11. UN Document A/9855, 14 November 1974.
12. UN Document A/10078, 23 April 1975.
13. Letter to the Secretary general dated 24 March 1975, UN Document A/10062, 25 March 1975.
14. Letter dated 26 June 1975 addressed to the secretary general, UN Document A/10127, 27 June 1975.

Did Everyone Win?

The Quadripartite Agreement of September 3, 1971 did not constitute a "solution" of the Berlin problem as it has been delineated in these pages—the problem of a city divided and geographically isolated by conquering forces and by conflicting political systems. Since 1945 the Western sectors of Berlin have been part of the West but surrounded by the East. The status of the city remains abnormal, indeed, unique. It is still a potential source of tension and a point of confrontation between East and West in Europe. But renewed pressure by the Soviet Union or the German Democratic Republic on access, on the Allied position in the city, or on the essential ties between the Western sectors and the Federal Republic—that is, any moves against the provisions of the Quadripartite Agreement—would now be a clear indication of a hostile turn in Soviet policy, with immediate implications as to Moscow's broader intent in Europe and elsewhere. A great deal more than the well-being of West Berlin's residents now depends on the maintenance of the improved *modus vivendi* for Berlin that the Quadripartite Agreement defined. Thus, the role of Berlin has altered from that of *Frontstadt* to that of a keystone in the peaceful (if heavily armed) relationship that has developed between East and West in Europe. Does this mark a victory for Western policy, despite the fact that Berlin remains a divided city in a divided country? For the Soviet Union and the GDR, despite the fact that West Berlin remains an extension of Western political, economic, social and military presence within the area of dominant Soviet influence and deep within East German territory? For the West Berliners, despite their continuing separation from the free German society of which they are a part? Or is it a victory for all?

The present situation is not one that, by any stretch of the imagination, policy planners of one or more of the Four Powers could have defined in 1944 or 1945 as a desirable objective. As has been shown, the United States, and the British

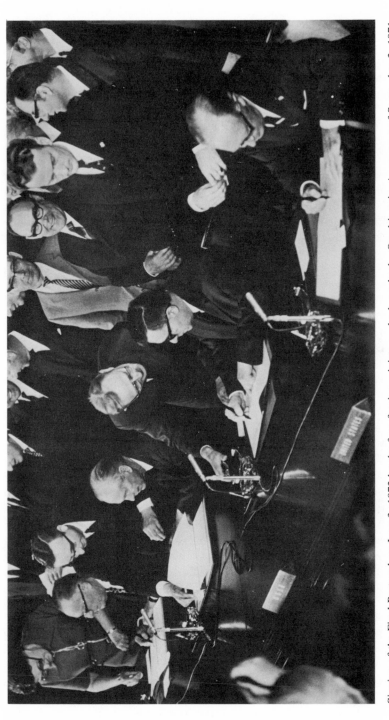

Signing of the Final Protocol on June 3, 1972 by the four foreign ministers who brought the Quadripartite Agreement of September 3, 1971 into effect (from left: Robert Schumann, France; Sir Alec Douglas-Home, Britain; Andrei Gromyko, Soviet Union; William Rogers, United States). Photo courtesy of the German Information Center, New York.

and French as well, entered Berlin at the end of the war in Europe without any discrete objectives for the city. In the United States the occupation of war-torn Germany was viewed as temporary. The planning done in the State Department was focused on Germany—whether one state or several—not on an unimaginable situation of a Western enclave of more than 2 million people surrounded by hostile forces. There were neither long-range plans nor a long-term commitment for the security of Berlin nor was there a realistic understanding of what a protracted and shared occupation of the city with the Soviet Union would entail. Such evidence as exists would suggest that the Soviet Union also lacked a comprehensive plan for postwar Germany or for Berlin. Stalin clearly had a broad strategic objective to enhance the security of the Soviet Union and strengthen its political and military position in Europe by securing lasting Soviet domination of the areas its armies had conquered—Poland, the Balkans, the Baltic, and a substantial part of Germany. In one basic sense the policies of the Soviets and the three Western governments in Germany were similar. All were aimed at retaining within their respective spheres of influence at least the zones of Germany that they occupied and ensuring that the potential strength of *all* of Germany did not accrue to the other side. Berlin, however, was part of no zone and the prospects for the three Western Allies to maintain their position in the city and integrate ''their'' sectors into a new democratic German society appeared singularly unpromising. Nevertheless, essentially *ad hoc* decisions were taken, particularly at the time of the Berlin blockade, to do just this. That the Western Allies have successfully done so, despite negative geographic and at least regional military circumstances, reflects their recognition of the geopolitical importance of Berlin in maintaining the security and independence of Western Europe as a whole, and of West Germany in particular.

There have been two occasions when, in theory at least, the Western powers might reasonably have sought to alter in a fundamental way the status of Berlin. The first was the Berlin blockade. It will probably never be possible to answer definitively whether at that time a different Western policy might have led to the restoration of a united (possibly neutralized) German state with Berlin as its capital. Berlin was still seen then by all the parties as an integral part of the ''German problem,'' and the end of the blockade was tied to a new paper commitment by the Four Powers to seek German unity. However, the principle of holding on to what one controlled proved determinative. The Western powers were not prepared to sacrifice the integration of a democratic West German state into the Western community in exchange for a unified, neutral Germany in the center of Europe.

The Four Power negotiations that began in 1969 offered another theoretical opportunity to seek a basic change in the situation of Berlin. But the Western powers made a clear decision at the beginning that this was not their goal. It would appear that the Soviet Union had done the same. Both sides had come to the conclusion that it was desirable for their particular and differing purposes to remove or decrease the persistent causes of friction between them in Berlin. For this, improvements in the existing situation were needed but not a fundamental change. This, then, is the perspective from which the results of the Quadripartite Agreement must be judged and the question posed by the title of this chapter answered.

WESTERN ACHIEVEMENTS

The most visible positive result of the Quadripartite Agreement, and one energetically sought by the Western powers, has been the facilitation of access to Berlin over the surface routes and of travel to East Berlin and the GDR by residents of Berlin's Western sectors. Travel statistics tell the story. In 1971, the last year before the agreement came into effect, the surface access routes between West Berlin and the Federal Republic were used for 8,822,000 individual trips (7,556,000 by car or bus and 1,266,000 by train). By 1987 these figures had tripled. In that year 22,980,000 trips to and from Berlin by car or bus on the autobahns were registered and 3,320,000 by train, making a total of 26,300,000 trips. During these years air traffic dropped from 6,120,000 to 5,280,000 passengers.

Given the large numbers of people using the access routes, the occasions on which the East Germans have utilized the provisions of the Quadripartite Agreement to limit access travel have been relatively few. In 1986, according to the statistics of the West Berlin government, 578 people were turned back, 85 were arrested, and there were 216 instances of searches. The arrests were attributed to "misuse" of the transit routes and involved traffic accidents, drunk driving, disregard for customs laws, or attempts to utilize the access routes to aid East Germans to escape to the West. The sheer number of travelers indicates that confidence in the security of the access routes has greatly increased. There have, however, been several instances of clearly politically motivated East German interference with access.

When the German Bundestag voted in 1974, to establish a Federal Office for the Protection of the Environment in West Berlin, both the Soviet Union and the GDR expressed strong objections, claiming that this extension of the Federal presence in Berlin was contrary to the Four Power agreement. Subsequently, the head of a main department of the office was turned back by East German guards as he sought to travel to Berlin by autobahn. The Western powers protested both in East Berlin and in Moscow, and the harassment of the travel of staff members of the Environment Protection Office eventually ceased. Later, however, members of the youth organization of the West German CDU (*Junge Union*) were on two occasions—in 1976 and again in 1978—also denied passage on the autobahn. In response to protests from the Western powers, GDR authorities claimed that their action was justified because the *Junge Union* members intended to "misuse" the autobahn by distributing posters and handbills along the route.

The most blatant instance of politically motivated East German access harassment took place on the occasion of a visit by President Jimmy Carter to Berlin in 1978. He was accompanied by West German Chancellor Helmut Schmidt. The East Germans claimed that this constituted an official government act by the chancellor in Berlin and was contrary to the Quadripartite Agreement. To make clear their objections, East German guards proceeded to slow down the processing of all non-Allied traffic on the autobahn. When the Western powers again protested, the Soviet Union in its reply spoke of "unintentional developments," while the GDR claimed that the delays had resulted from a "shortage of personnel" and a high rate of "illness." There were no delays in 1987 when President Reagan was accompanied by Chancellor Kohl on a visit to Berlin.

After 1978 the number of persons arrested for assisting East Germans to escape diminished. In the period 1973–78 as many as 120 arrests were made on this ground annually. In 1979 this figure fell to 28 and in 1987 to 11. This undoubtedly resulted in part from the smaller number of persons fleeing East Germany. It would also seem to reflect, however, a more relaxed attitude on the part of the East German authorities and, possibly, some recognition of the high sensitivity for the FRG and the Berlin *Senat* of "escape assistance" arrests. In any event, the decline in this type of arrests shows clearly that the East German authorities have been able, acting within the provisions of the Quadripartite Agreement, to discourage a massive wave of escape attempts through this route—and that the number of arrests could be increased if the GDR should deem this advisable.

The system of annual lump-sum payments by the Federal Republic to cover utilization of the surface access routes foreseen in the Quadripartite Agreement has functioned smoothly at considerable expense to the Bonn government and substantial financial benefit to the GDR. Between 1971 and 1975 the Federal government paid DM234.9 million annually to cover fees for access travelers. Reflecting the increase in traffic, this figure rose to DM525 million annually for the period 1980–89. The FRG and GDR have agreed that the annual figure will be DM860 million from 1990 until 1999. Until recently none of these funds were used by the GDR to maintain the access routes, which by 1971 had deteriorated badly. (Now the GDR has agreed to allocate DM30 million of the lump-sum payments to autobahn improvements.) By the time of the new access arrangements, the heavily used Helmstedt-Berlin autobahn was in particularly bad shape, needing complete reconstruction. The FRG agreed to pay 65 percent of the cost, some DM263 million. In addition, the two German governments agreed in 1978 to build a new autobahn from Hamburg to Berlin for which the FRG undertook to pay DM1.2 billion. Somewhat later a further inner-German agreement was reached to construct an autobahn extension at a cost of DM268 million to the Federal Republic. For various improvements in the rail and water access routes the FRG has paid DM410 million. These measures have complemented the improved procedural arrangements to make surface travel to Berlin not only more secure and convenient, but also more pleasant than before 1972.

Freight transport to and from the Western sectors of Berlin has been "unimpeded" as agreed by the Four Powers, with full use made of the provision for sealed cargo.

The increase in travel from West Berlin to East Berlin and the GDR as a result of the Quadripartite Agreement has been equally impressive. Between the time of the construction of the wall in 1961 and 1972, such travel was impossible except under the very limited holiday pass arrangement described earlier. With the Quadripartite Agreement the situation changed dramatically. Between June 1972 and June 1987 38.5 million visits by West Berliners to East Berlin or the GDR were registered. The largest number, 3.7 million, occurred in the first year, reflecting the pent-up desire to see relatives and friends after a long separation. This was apparently more than the GDR had bargained for, and than it felt could safely be absorbed without an adverse effect on political stability. Consequently, within a year (in 1973) the East German government sought to limit the flow by raising the amount of money that each visitor had to exchange from DM10 to DM20, thus doubling the cost of a visit.

The number of visits dropped sharply. Under heavy pressure from the FRG, the GDR, late in 1974, reduced the mandatory exchange amount to DM13 and the number of visits again passed the 3 million mark. Then, in 1980, the GDR introduced new regulations, this time raising the mandatory amount that had to be exchanged and spent to DM25. This posed a serious hardship for the elderly and those of limited income and resulted again in a sharp drop in visitors. The GDR subsequently reduced the mandatory exchange amount for pensioners to DM15, but the number of visitors has remained well below the original peak. Between 1972 and June 1987, 13,866 complaints of harassment or mistreatment were registered by visitors on their return to West Berlin. This amounts to 0.4 percent of the 34.6 million visits. On the whole West Berliners have reported that they have been courteously processed and well received.

Some of the decline in the number of visits may be attributable to the restored availability of telephone contact. It will be recalled that early in the Four Power negotiations, Soviet Ambassador Abrasimov announced that as a gesture of good will, telephone links between East and West Berlin, which had been cut in 1952, were being reopened, and, in fact, thirty-one lines were installed in 1971. Forty-six additional lines were opened in 1972 and 218 more in 1982. Whereas no telephone calls had been possible between West and East Berlin between 1952 and 1971, and calls between West Berlin and the GDR had been extremely complicated and expensive, 8,000 calls were made daily from West Berlin to East Berlin or the GDR in 1973. Since then the number has grown steadily and now more than 30,000 calls are made daily between East and West Berlin and 4,500 between West Berlin and the GDR. While East Berlin residents gained no possibility to visit West Berlin under the Four Power agreement, they have profited from the restored and expanded telephone connections since they *can* now telephone to West Berlin. With the other less far-reaching improvements realized—the reopening of the Teltow Canal in West Berlin, the territorial adjustments that eliminated the separation of exclaves from the rest of West Berlin, the establishment of additional crossing points between West and East Berlin— the Four Power agreement has clearly resulted in a very substantial improvement in the conditions of life in West Berlin. The most persistent causes of tension and insecurity have been eliminated. A principal objective of the three Western Allies in the negotiations was thus achieved.

The results in terms of objectives of particular concern to the Federal Republic have been more ambiguous. Although the Soviet Union acknowledged the legitimacy of ties between West Berlin and the Federal Republic and agreed that they should be developed, the word "ties" was deliberately mistranslated in the Russian and East German texts as something closer to "relations". In the years since 1972 the Soviet Union and the GDR have continued to object to any new official links between the FRG and West Berlin and they have maintained some of the objections to existing ties that they had expressed before the Quadripartite Agreement was concluded. Just a few days after the signing of the agreement, the Soviet embassy in East Berlin delivered a sharp diplomatic note to the Western Allies protesting a reception given by the Federal German president, Gustav Heinemann, at his official residence in Berlin, Schloss Bellevue. The reception was a long-standing annual event held to honor leading West Berlin residents for their contributions to the well-being of the city.

Ironically, one of the first actions of the newly appointed Soviet consul general on arriving in West Berlin was to declare that he would not pay the customary courtesy call on the governing mayor unless the Federal German flag, hanging in the main hall of the *Rathaus,* was removed. The West Berlin government refused to remove the flag and after several sharp public exchanges, the consul general nonetheless found it possible to call on the mayor.

Soviet authorities have since protested against other manifestations of the Federal presence in Berlin. One that was particularly notable has already been mentioned, namely the establishment in Berlin of the Federal Office for Environmental Protection (*Bundesampt für Umweltschutz*). In establishing this office, the Federal Republic clearly intended to take advantage of the provision of the Quadripartite Agreement that authorized the further development of ties between West Berlin and the Federal Republic. The Environmental Protection Office seemed in Bonn to be particularly suitable for this purpose since it had a universally accepted constructive purpose and had no conceivable security implications. It appeared an unlikely initiative to prompt a Soviet objection. This proved to be a very mistaken assumption. The establishment of the office produced a sharp controversy with the Soviet Union, the GDR, *and* with the Western Allies. The Western powers were unhappy since they had had no opportunity to have their views considered and knew they would have to defend the FRG's action with the Soviet Union. They complained publicly of inadequate consultation. The evident Western discomfiture probably encouraged the Eastern side to react by denying passage on the autobahn to the Federal official who was on his way to Berlin to open the office. Protests and counter-protests followed in Moscow and Berlin. The West Germans tried a conciliatory cosmetic gesture, resorting to language, in this case to resolve, rather than create, a political problem. The Federal government changed the name of the *Bundesampt für*

Umweltschutz to *Umweltbundesampt,* thus decreasing the prominence of the "federal" or *Bund* identification of the office. Eventually Soviet and East German objections died away, but the very limited Soviet interpretation of the further development of ties between West Berlin and the FRG had been demonstrated. The FRG has not ventured another initiative of this sort. All in all the Soviet Union has maintained essentially the same attitude toward the political ties between the FRG and West Berlin as it had before the Quadripartite Agreement was signed.

The bargain that the Berlin Agreement constitutes also includes a Soviet commitment to end "discriminatory restrictions" against the economy of West Berlin and against its residents in their contacts with the countries of Eastern Europe; to permit the Federal Republic to perform consular services for permanent residents of West Berlin visiting in the Soviet Union and other countires of Eastern Europe; to allow international agreements and other arrangements entered into by the Federal Republic to be extended to Berlin; to concur in the representation of the interests of the Western sectors of Berlin in international organizations and conferences by the Federal Republic; to accept the participation of permanent residents of West Berlin in international exchanges and meetings in which the residents of the Federal Republic participate; and no longer to question the legitimacy of organizing international meetings and conferences in West Berlin provided that invitations to such events are issued either by the Berlin *Senat* or by the *Senat* jointly with the Federal Republic. All of these fell within the FRG objective of obtaining Soviet concurrence in representation of West Berlin abroad by the Federal Republic, something to which the Bonn government attributed major importance. The Soviet government has never fully honored this part of the agreement, and as in the case of the ties between West Berlin and Bonn, the situation is not very different from what it was before the agreement came into effect.

West Berliners, for example, still cannot use Federal German passports for travel to the Soviet Union and other Warsaw Pact countries. The governments there still insist that for them, West Berlin identity cards are the only acceptable travel documents. Protests from the FRG and the Berlin *Senat* have been to no avail. West Berlin officials have found it difficult to visit Moscow since the conclusion of the agreement because of the Soviet Union's refusal to permit the West German embassy there to make the normal protocol arrangements, as representing West Berlin. Rather than appear to endorse the Soviet position on the status of West Berlin as a separate political entity, West Berlin political leaders have, in effect, declared official visits to the Soviet Union and other countries of Eastern Europe politically off limits. The Soviet Union and the GDR have also consistently objected to the presence and activities of the German Institute for Development in West Berlin and, as indicated in the previous chapter, have strongly objected to the participation of UN officials in meetings sponsored by the institute, even when the meetings were not held in Berlin. Representatives from Warsaw Pact countries have declined to take part in its activities. An important milestone was marked in September 1988, however, when the World Bank and the International Monetary Fund, both specialized agencies of the United Nations, held their annual meeting in West Berlin. Since the Soviet Union is not a member it could not prevent the meeting from taking place there. Those of its allies that are members, Poland and Hungary, did attend and at the ministerial level. West Berlin and West German officials attributed much significance to this large, highly publicized multilateral meeting as a notable breakthrough.

Perhaps most exasperating for the West German government have been the protracted difficulties in concluding cultural exchanges with the Soviet Union and its allies because of their unwillingness to accept the participation of West Berliners in projected programs. A treaty on economic cooperation between the European Community and the European Council for Mutual Economic Assistance (CEMA) was long delayed, in part because of the refusal of the Council to accept specific reference to West Berlin as included in the treaty's coverage. Signature finally took place in 1988 when a circumlocution was adopted that defined coverage as including the adherents to the Treaty of Rome (establishing the European Community), of which West Berlin was one. West Berlin was not mentioned in the new treaty's text.

The present president of the Federal Republic, Richard von Weizäcker, argued, when he was still governing mayor of Berlin, that such problems stemmed in part from the failure of the Western powers to exploit fully the opportunities afforded by the agreement. Recalling that the Soviet side frequently called for "full implementation," he suggested greater Western initiative. For example, the headquarters of international organizations could be brought to West Berlin.[1] Shortly after the initialing of the agreement Willy Brandt did, in fact, suggest an initiative, albeit one he had had in mind before. He proposed to the U.S. and British ambassadors that the Western powers take advantage of the interim before the signing of the Final Protocol, when a sense of euphoria prevailed, to authorize the direct election of Berlin's representatives in the Bundestag and to rescind the prohibition against their voting on substantive parliamentary action, including legislation. Such a change, he contended, would give significant political meaning to the provision in the Quadripartite Agreement for the further development of ties between West Berlin and the FRG. The U.S. and British ambassadors were sympathetic to Brandt's suggestion and Ambassador Rush informed staff members that he had obtained President Nixon's approval to support such a move. (He did not mention the State Department.) The British ambassador also indicated that he had obtained authority from his prime minister to do the same. It was never clear whether the issue had been raised with the French or what their attitude was. As it turned out, the entire proposal was academic since the Brandt government itself backed away from it, possibly because of fear of muddying the waters when the inner-German negotiations were under way. No explanation was given.

SOVIET AND EAST GERMAN ACHIEVEMENTS

The additional Soviet facilities in West Berlin foreseen in the Quadripartite Agreement, including the consulate general, were promptly opened with the cooperation of the Western powers and the Berlin *Senat*. The Federal Assembly (*Bundesversammlung*), the Federal Council (*Bundesrat*), and the Federal parliament (*Bundestag*), including committees and parliamentary groups, all of which had met on an *ad hoc* basis in Berlin (the *Bundesversammlung* had only met in Berlin) have not held official meetings in the city since the agreement was signed. In addition, as desired by the Soviet Union, the activities of the National Party of Germany (NPD) were effectively eliminated by a ban on public meetings. (The French were ready to ban the party altogether, but because of British and U.S. concern for the principle of political freedom, the party was not banned outright.)

To respond to the Soviet demand for the prohibition of the manufacture of military goods in West Berlin and maintenance of its demilitarized status, the Western powers undertook to inform a Berlin manufacturer interested in obtaining authorization to produce a given product that Allied permission would be granted only with the explicit understanding that the specific item of manufacture met Allied regulations on demilitarization, "which continue in effect." This was promptly accomplished when at the end of August 1971 a large electrical firm in the U.S. sector requested a license under Allied Control Council Law no. 43 to export telegraphic equipment to a Swiss company. (The Western powers maintain that East Berlin also remains subject to demilitarization under Control Council legislation and routinely protest East German military parades and other military manifestations there. The protests have been without any evident effect other than maintaining for the record a position of principle.)

The absence of official meetings in the Western sectors of West German governmental and party groups has reaffirmed the separate status of West Berlin. In the strictly Berlin framework, this, presumably, was a major Soviet gain from the agreement. Yet in its spirit, its economy, its political system, and in its culture, West Berlin is de facto integrated into the Federal Republic. The Quadripartite Agreement has not changed this. The presence in Berlin of a Soviet consulate general, which was so controversial in the negotiations, has not until now brought with it any greater Soviet influence on the administration or political orientation of West Berlin. The consul general has not complied strictly with the prohibition against political activities contained in the agreement, but in this infringement he has been encouraged by the West Berlin government, which has found that a visible Soviet presence in Berlin's public life enhances the prestige of the city, as long as no effort is made to exercise any form of Soviet control. The Soviet Union has no doubt gained some commercial and possibly intelligence advantage from its expanded business and information representation in the Western sectors, but, on the whole, the gains of the Soviet Union strictly in the context of Berlin have been modest. The major Soviet achievements lie rather in the broader field of Soviet objectives in Europe.

The first of these was legitimization of the GDR as a recognized member of the international community and de facto acceptance of its borders, a matter of high security and political importance to the Soviet Union since the GDR's western border is also the border of the Soviet area of domination in Europe. In the Soviet perception denial of the legitimacy of the GDR amounted to a denial of the permanence of the western border of the postwar Soviet empire. In the texts of the various documents that make up the Four Power agreement there are frequent references to the GDR. It figures as negotiating partner and co-signatory of the inner-German agreements that are incorporated into the Four Power agreement. The agreement contains no reference to East Berlin or the Eastern sector, which would imply a separate status from the GDR. Thus the agreement tacitly acknowledges GDR control in East Berlin even while avoiding *de jure* recognition of East German sovereignty there. Moreover, the inner-German agreements concerning visits and travel of West Berlin residents refer only to visits and travel to the territory of the GDR, even though visits and travel to East Berlin are included. Similarly, in the exchanges of territory, the areas gained by the communist side are said henceforth to belong to the GDR. Finally, as has been previously noted, the phrase in the preamble, "taking into account the existing situation in the relevant area," can be interpreted as de facto recognition by all the signatories of the agreement of the incorporation of East Berlin into the sovereign territory of the GDR, although this interpretation is countered by the statement, also in the preamble, that "wartime and postwar agreements and decisions are not affected." In practice the residual status of Berlin as an area under Four Power control is still recognized only in the absence of East German control over entry to, and egress from, East Berlin of official personnel of the three Western powers, including military patrols.

While not provided for in the Quadripartite Agreement itself, it was clearly understood by all the parties that with the successful completion of negotiations the three Western powers, along with the rest of NATO, would accord diplomatic recognition to the GDR and establish embassies in East Berlin. Moreover, the three Western powers would join with the Soviet Union in supporting UN membership for the two German states. These actions took place expeditiously.

The establishment of a more beneficent *modus vivendi* in Berlin through the Quadripartite Agreement removed, or at least greatly reduced, a persistent impediment to an improved relationship between the Soviet Union and the Federal Republic, which was central to Soviet aspirations for increased Soviet, and decreased American, influence in Western Europe. Conclusion of the agreement, moreover, was the *sine qua non* for ratification by the Federal Republic of treaties with the Soviet Union and Poland on the non-use of force that constituted acceptance not only of the western border of the GDR but also of the geographic status quo in central Europe. The wide attention given to the more positively articulated foreign policy of the Soviet Union under Mikhail Gorbachev has tended to obscure the fact that the Berlin Agreement, which was and remains a vital element in the detente that has characterized the situation in Europe in the 1980s, was entered into in the Brezhnev era, under the guidance of the man frequently branded as a hard-liner, Andrei Gromyko.

THE COMMON GAIN

The goals of the Western powers and the Soviet Union in pursuing an agreement on Berlin were clearly different. In U.S. policy papers the word "pragmatic" frequently appeared, the goal being pragmatic and immediate improvements in the conditions of life for West Berlin and its residents. The Federal Republic saw as a principal objective solidification of the relationship between West Berlin and Bonn. The Soviet Union no doubt saw the elimination of Berlin as a source of friction and tension with the Western powers as essential for its longer-range objective of enhanced influence in Western Europe. While disparate, these objectives were not contradictory. Some within the U.S. government (and in Bonn and London) felt that the course of events of which the Berlin Agreement was part (recognition of the GDR, normalization of relations between the Federal Republic and the Soviet Union, acceptance of the postwar boundaries in eastern and central Europe) would lead ultimately to a decrease in U.S. influence and the neutralization of Western Europe. Enough time has elapsed now since the Berlin Agreement was signed and Bonn's Eastern treaties ratified to indicate that such fears were groundless. If there has been, and continues to be, a decline in U.S. influence in Western Europe, the causes lie not in a normalization of relations between East and West in Europe, but rather in the increased self-confidence and economic strength of Western European countries, the relative declining economic strength of the United States and differences with regard to some U.S. policies outside the European area on which, in the American view, European support has been inadequate.

The reality is that Berlin, though still divided, is a city at peace. The circumstances of life are stable. Since the Berlin Agreement was signed, the city has been free of military confrontations. There has been no serious interference with West Berlin's vital links with the Federal Republic. Problems arise from time to time, but the consequent protests that are exchanged have lost their fire. Some West Berliners worried as the political climate cooled, fearing that West Berlin would become a backwater, forgotten by the Western world of which it is part. It is evident, in observing life in West Berlin today, however, that its inhabitants have grown accustomed to the relatively normal environment of a large and sophisticated urban area without a hinterland.

President Kennedy once referred to Berlin as a millstone around his neck since the recurrent crises and persistent tension there were always an impediment to achieving a more constructive relationship with the Soviet Union. The Berlin Agreement lifted this particular millstone (though there were others elsewhere in the world), leaving the Western powers and the Soviet Union freer to pursue new possibilities for peaceful stabilization of East-West relations in Europe. This has been especially important for the Federal Republic, which had a strong and legitimate interest in achieving a relationship with the Soviet Union and its East European allies comparable to that enjoyed by other Western European countries. It sought an understanding on Berlin in this interest (as well as in the interest of the Berliners), calculating, too, that elimination of recurrent crises over Berlin, and the normalization of relations with the GDR, would ultimately bring the two parts of Germany, and of Berlin, closer together. This has proved to be true. Despite its improved international status, the East German regime remains insecure in the face of the enormous political and economic attraction of the free West German society. It continues to restrict, albeit with decreasing rigidity, its citizens' contacts with the temptations of West German associations. Moreover, East Berlin remains ultimately under Soviet control and must take account of Soviet interests in the conduct of its relations with the FRG. This has not prevented, however, a notable continuity of cooperation in inner-German relations since the mid–1970s. This relationship has been largely immune from the effect of tensions in East-West relations resulting from developments elsewhere in the world, such as the Soviet invasion of Afghanistan. When martial law was imposed in Poland and the free trade union Solidarity outlawed, both the West German chancellor, Helmut Schmidt, and the East German Communist party leader, Eric Honecker, publicly regretted the action but continued their bilateral relations undisturbed.

The answer, then, to the question posed by the title of this chapter is clearly yes. The three Western powers, the Federal Republic, the Soviet Union, and West Berlin's residents gained significantly from the conclusion and implementation of the Quadripartite Agreement of September 3, 1971. In a broader sense the agreement, as an essential part of the development of a less antagonistic and more open relationship between East and West in Europe, that is now taking place, stands as a victory for all who benefit from a more secure peace on that continent. In one way or another, that encompasses most countries of the world. But is the Berlin Agreement and the resultant *modus vivendi* that now exists with regard to the city the end of the story that began when the British devised their plan for the occupation of defeated Germany, which placed Berlin in the middle of the Soviet Zone? What comes next?

The reunification of Berlin would be feasible only under two circumstances: (1) the reunification of Germany; or (2) the incorporation of all of Berlin into the GDR. Neither seems remotely possible. The Berlin Agreement, by recognizing, in effect, the legitimacy of the GDR and of its borders, made even stronger the division of Germany. Valentin Falin, while Soviet ambassador to Bonn, once said that some day Berlin will fall into our lap like a ripe apple that falls from a tree. Given the Western political capital that is invested in Berlin and the extent of the integration of the Western sectors into the Federal Republic, this seems as unlikely as the reunification of Germany. The present situation of Berlin, while totally satisfactory to none of the parties concerned, is tolerable to all. The interests of no country are seriously threatened. Any catalyst for change will come from the Germans, since they are the ones most directly concerned. There is among the leadership in West Berlin a certain impatience with continuing Allied control. This was evident, for example, when the Allied commandants prevented the governing mayor from crossing into East Berlin and participating in East German ceremonies on the occasion of the 750th anniversary of the founding of the city. In Bonn, too, there is occasional unhappiness, not over continuing Allied control, but over the way in which it is exercised. The three Allies will probably need to stay in Berlin indefinitely. Their presence should become increasingly discreet, however, as German authorities move to arrange their inner-Berlin and inner-German relationships with increasing confidence. Over time, as these relationships develop and the East Germans feel less threatened, it is possible to contemplate greater freedom of movement from East to West through the wall, and even eventually the elimination of that awkward monument to communism's failure. Greater political integration of West Berlin into the Federal Republic is conceivable under such circumstances, although there will always be limits—limits that the Western Allies will, themselves, insist upon as long as they retain ultimate responsibility for the security of West Berlin. Further improvement in the Berlin *modus vivendi* is likely to stem in the future as in the past from the concept that Willy Brandt introduced of *Wandel durch Annährung*. A gradual lessening of the barriers between East and West Berlin through the will of Germans on both sides of the Wall, a slow recognition in Moscow and East Berlin now becoming evident under Gorbachev that closer political ties (closer *Bindungen*) between the Western sectors and Bonn, are in accord with the reality of a stable European order—these are the elements of change that can bring further improvement to the Berlin situation. Western policies should be directed toward this end. A major benefit of the Berlin Agreement is that it has facilitated movement in this direction. A framework exists, constructed by the Four Powers, with the active participation of the two German governments, for cooperation in dealing with Berlin's problems. Berlin, under these circumstances, can be more easily accommodated within a German nation whose parts are likely to remain discrete but increasingly integrated. The Germans henceforth seem destined to be the principal actors in a play in which a consciousness of common identity and common interests replaces confrontation and mutual distrust.

NOTE

1. From transcript of meeting at Aspen Institute Berlin, 24–26 January 1983.

Appendix: The Quadripartite Agreement of September 3, 1971

The Governments of the United States of America, the French Republic, the Union of Soviet Socialist Republics, and the United Kingdom of Great Britain and Northern Ireland, represented by their Ambassadors, who held a series of meetings in the building formerly occupied by the Allied Control Council in the American Sector of Berlin,

Acting on the basis of their quadripartite rights and responsibilites, and of the corresponding wartime and postwar agreements and decisions of the Four Powers, which are not affected,

Taking into account the existing situation in the relevant area,

Guided by the desire to contribute to practical improvements of the situation,

Without prejudice to their legal positions,

Have agreed on the following:

PART I

General Provisions

1. The four Governments will strive to promote the elimination of tension and the prevention of complications in the relevant area.

2. The four Governments, taking into account their obligations under the Charter of the United Nations, agree that there shall be no use or threat of force in the area and that disputes shall be settled solely by peaceful means.

3. The four Governments will mutually respect their individual and joint rights and responsibilities, which remain unchanged.

4. The four Governments agree that, irrespective of the differences in legal views, the situation which has developed in the area, and as it is defined in this Agreement as well as in the other agreements referred to in this Agreement, shall not be changed unilaterally.

PART II

Provisions Relating to the Western Sectors of Berlin

A. The Government of the Union of Soviet Socialist Republics declares that transit traffic by road, rail and waterways through the territory of the German Democratic Republic of civilian persons and goods between the Western Sectors of Berlin and the Federal Republic of Germany will be unimpeded; that such traffic will be facilitated so as to take place in the most simple and expeditious manner; and that it will receive preferential treatment.

Detailed arrangements concerning this civilian traffic, as set forth in Annex I, will be agreed by the competent German authorities.

B. The Governments of the French Republic, the United Kingdom and the United States of America declare that the ties between the Western Sectors of Berlin and the Federal Republic of Germany will be maintained and developed, taking into account that these Sectors continue not to be a constituent part of the Federal Republic of Germany and not to be governed by it.

Detailed arrangements concerning the relationship between the Western Sectors of Berlin and the Federal Republic of Germany are set forth in Annex II.

C. The Government of the Union of Soviet Socialist Republics declares that communications between the Western Sectors of Berlin and areas bordering on these Sectors and those areas of the German Democratic Republic which do not border on these Sectors will be improved. Permanent residents of the Western Sectors of Berlin will be able to travel to and visit such areas for compassionate, family, religious, cultural or commercial reasons, or as tourists, under conditions comparable to those applying to other persons entering these areas.

The problems of the small enclaves, including Steinstücken, and of other small areas may be solved by exchange of territory.

Detailed arrangements concerning travel, communications and the exchange of territory, as set forth in Annex III, will be agreed by the competent German authorities.

D. Representation abroad of the interests of the Western Sectors of Berlin and consular activities of the Union of Soviet Socialist Republics in the Western Sectors of Berlin can be exercised as set forth in Annex IV.

PART III

Final Provisions

This Quadripartite Agreement will enter into force on the date specified in a Final Quadripartite Protocol to be concluded when the measures envisaged in Part II of this Quadripartite Agreement and in its Annexes have been agreed.

DONE at the building formerly occupied by the Allied Control Council in the American Sector of Berlin, this 3rd day of September, 1971, in four originals, each in the English, French and Russian languages, all texts being equally authentic.

For the Government of the French Republic:

Jean Sauvagnargues

For the Government of the Union of Soviet
Socialist Republics:

Piotr Abrasimov

For the Government of the United Kingdom
of Great Britain and Northern Ireland:

R. W. Jackling

For the Government of the United States
of America:

Kenneth Rush

ANNEX I

**Communication from the Government of the Union of
Soviet Socialist Republics to the Governments of the
French Republic, the United Kingdom and the United
States of America**

The Government of the Union of Soviet Socialist Republics, with reference to Part II A of the Quadripartite Agreement of this date and after consultation and agreement with the Government of the German Democratic Republic, has the honour to inform the Governments of the French Republic, the United Kingdom and the United States of America that:

1. Transit traffic by road, rail and waterways through the territory of the German Democratic Republic of civilian persons and goods between the Western Sectors of Berlin and the Federal Republic of Germany will be facilitated and unimpeded. It will receive the most simple, expeditious and preferential treatment provided by international practice.

2. Accordingly,

   (a) Conveyances sealed before departure may be used for the transport of civilian goods by road, rail and waterways between the Western Sectors of Berlin and the Federal Republic of Germany. Inspection procedures will be limited to the inspection of seals and accompanying documents.

   (b) With regard to conveyances which cannot be sealed, such as open trucks, inspection procedures will be limited to the inspection of accompanying documents. In special cases where there is sufficient reason to suspect that unsealed conveyances contain either material intended for dissemination along the designated routes or persons or material put on board along these routes, the content of unsealed conveyances may be inspected. Procedures for dealing with such cases will be agreed by the competent German authorities.

   (c) Through trains and buses may be used for travel between the Western Sectors of Berlin and the Federal Republic of Germany. Inspection procedures will not include any formalities other than identification of persons.

   (d) Persons identified as through travellers using individual vehicles between the Western Sectors of Berlin and the Federal Republic of Germany on routes designated for through traffic will be able to proceed to their destinations without paying individual tolls and fees for the use of the transit routes. Procedures applied for such travellers shall not involve delay.

   The travellers, their vehicles and personal baggage will not be subject to search, detention or exclusion from use of the designated routes, except in special cases, as may be agreed by the competent German authorities, where there is sufficient reason to suspect that misuse of the transit routes is intended for purposes not related to direct travel to and from the Western Sectors of Berlin and contrary to generally applicable regulations concerning public order.

(e) Appropriate compensation for fees and tolls and for other costs related to traffic on the communication routes between the Western Sectors of Berlin and the Federal Republic of Germany, including the maintenance of adequate routes, facilities and installations used for such traffic, may be made in the form of an annual lump sum paid to the German Democratic Republic by the Federal Republic of Germany.

3. Arrangements implementing and supplementing the provisions of Paragraphs 1 and 2 above will be agreed by the competent German authorities.

ANNEX II

Communication from the Governments of the French Republic, the United Kingdom and the United States of America to the Government of the Union of Soviet Socialist Republics

The Governments of the French Republic, the United Kingdom and the United States of America, with reference to Part II B of the Quadripartite Agreement of this date and after consultation with the Government of the Federal Republic of Germany, have the honour to inform the Government of the Union of Soviet Socialist Republics that:

1. They declare, in the exercise of their rights and responsibilities, that the ties between the Western Sectors

of Berlin and the Federal Republic of Germany will be maintained and developed, taking into account that these Sectors continue not to be a constituent part of the Federal Republic of Germany and not to be governed by it. The provisions of the Basic Law of the Federal Republic of Germany and of the Constitution operative in the Western Sectors of Berlin which contradict the above have been suspended and continue not to be in effect.

2. The Federal President, the Federal Government, the Bundesversammlung, the Bundesrat and the Bundestag, including their Committees and Fraktionen, as well as other state bodies of the Federal Republic of Germany will not perform in the Western Sectors of Berlin constitutional or official acts which contradict the provisions of Paragraph 1.

3. The Government of the Federal Republic of Germany will be represented in the Western Sectors of Berlin to the authorities of the three Governments and to the Senat by a permanent liaison agency.

ANNEX III

Communication from the Government of the Union of Soviet Socialist Republics to the Governments of the French Republic, the United Kingdom and the United States of America

The Government of the Union of Soviet Socialist Republics, with reference to Part II C of the Quadripartite Agreement of this date and after consultation and agreement with the Government of the German Democratic Republic, has the honour to inform the Governments of the French Republic, the United Kingdom and the United States of America that:

1. Communications between the Western Sectors of Berlin and areas bordering on these Sectors and those areas of the German Democratic Republic which do not border on these Sectors will be improved.

2. Permanent residents of the Western Sectors of Berlin will be able to travel to and visit such areas for compassionate, family, religious, cultural or commercial reasons, or as tourists, under conditions comparable to those applying to other persons entering these areas. In order to facilitate visits and travel, as described above, by permanent residents of the Western Sectors of Berlin, additional crossing points will be opened.

3. The problems of the small enclaves, including Steinstücken, and of other small areas may be solved by exchange of territory.

4. Telephonic, telegraphic, transport and other external communications of the Western Sectors of Berlin will be expanded.

5. Arrangements implementing and supplementing the provisions of Paragraphs 1 to 4 above will be agreed by the competent German authorities.

ANNEX IV

A. Communication from the Governments of the French Republic, the United Kingdom and the United States of America to the Government of the Union of Soviet Socialist Republics

The Governments of the French Republic, the United Kingdom and the United States of America, with reference to Part II D of the Quadripartite Agreement of this date and after consultation with the Government of the Federal

Republic of Germany, have the honour to inform the Government of the Union of Soviet Socialist Republics that:

1. The Governments of the French Republic, the United Kingdom and the United States of America maintain their rights and responsibilities relating to the representation abroad of the interests of the Western Sectors of Berlin and their permanent residents, including those rights and responsibilities concerning matters of security and status, both in international organizations and in relations with other countries.

2. Without prejudice to the above and provided that matters of security and status are not affected, they have agreed that:

   (a) The Federal Republic of Germany may perform consular services for permanent residents of the Western Sectors of Berlin.

   (b) In accordance with established procedures, international agreements and arrangements entered into by the Federal Republic of Germany may be extended to the Western Sectors of Berlin provided that the extension of such agreements and arrangements is specified in each case.

   (c) The Federal Republic of Germany may represent the interests of the Western Sectors of Berlin in international organizations and international conferences.

   (d) Permanent residents of the Western Sectors of Berlin may participate jointly with participants from the Federal Republic of Germany in international exchanges and exhibitions. Meetings of international organizations and international conferences as well as exhibitions with international participation may be held in the Western Sectors

of Berlin. Invitations will be issued by the Senat
or jointly by the Federal Republic of Germany
and the Senat.

3. The three Governments authorize the establishment of
   a Consulate General of the USSR in the Western Sectors
   of Berlin accredited to the appropriate authorities of
   the three Governments in accordance with the usual
   procedures applied in those Sectors, for the purpose of
   performing consular services, subject to provisions set
   forth in a separate document of this date.

B. Communication from the Government of the Union of Soviet Socialist Republics to the Governments of the French Republic, the United Kingdom and the United States of America

The Government of the Union of Soviet Socialist Republics, with reference to Part II D of the Quadripartite
Agreement of this date and to the communication of the
Governments of the French Republic, the United Kingdom
and the United States of America with regard to the
representation abroad of the interests of the Western
Sectors of Berlin and their permanent residents, has the
honour to inform the Governments of the French Republic,
the United Kingdom and the United States of America
that:

1. The Government of the Union of Soviet Socialist Republics takes note of the fact that the three Governments maintain their rights and responsibilities relating
   to the representation abroad of the interests of the
   Western Sectors of Berlin and their permanent residents,
   including those rights and responsibilities concerning
   matters of security and status, both in international
   organizations and in relations with other countries.

2. Provided that matters of security and status are not affected, for its part it will raise no objection to:

(a) The performance by the Federal Republic of Germany of consular services for permanent residents of the Western Sectors of Berlin.

(b) In accordance with established procedures, the extension to the Western Sectors of Berlin of international agreements and arrangements entered into by the Federal Republic of Germany provided that the extension of such agreements and arrangements is specified in each case.

(c) The representation of the interests of the Western Sectors of Berlin by the Federal Republic of Germany in international organizations and international conferences.

(d) The participation jointly with participants from the Federal Republic of Germany of permanent residents of the Western Sectors of Berlin in international exchanges and exhibitions, or the holding in those Sectors of meetings of international organizations and international conferences as well as exhibitions with international participation, taking into account that invitations will be issued by the Senat or jointly by the Federal Republic of Germany and the Senat.

3. The Government of the Union of Soviet Socialist Republics takes note of the fact that the three Governments have given their consent to the establishment of a Consulate General of the USSR in the Western Sectors of Berlin. It will be accredited to the appropriate authorities of the three Governments, for purposes and subject to provisions described in their communication and as set forth in a separate document of this date.

Note of the Three Ambassadors
to the Soviet Ambassador

The Ambassadors of the French Republic, the United Kingdom of Great Britain and Northern Ireland and the United States of America have the honour, with reference to the statements contained in Annex II of the Quadripartite Agreement to be signed on this date concerning the relationship between the Federal Republic of Germany and the Western Sectors of Berlin, to inform the Ambassador of the Union of Soviet Socialist Republics of their intention to send to the Chancellor of the Federal Republic of Germany immediately following signature of the Quadripartite Agreement a letter containing clarifications and interpretations which represent the understanding of their Governments of the statements contained in Annex II of the Quadripartite Agreement. A copy of the letter to be sent to the Chancellor of the Federal Republic of Germany is attached to this Note.

(Formal close)

Soviet Reply Note

The Ambassador of the Union of Soviet Socialist Republics has the honour to acknowledge receipt of the Note of the Ambassadors of the French Republic, the United Kingdom of Great Britain and Northern Ireland and the United States of America, dated September 3, 1971, and takes note of the communication of the three Ambassadors.

(Formal close)

Letter of the Three Ambassadors
to Chancellor Willy Brandt

Concerning Interpretation of Annex II

His Excellency
The Chancellor of the
Federal Republic of Germany

Your Excellency:

With reference to the Quadripartite Agreement signed on September 3, 1971, our Governments wish by this letter to inform the Government of the Federal Republic of Germany of the following clarifications and interpretations of the statements contained in Annex II, which was the subject of consultation with the Government of the Federal Republic of Germany during the quadripartite negotiations.

These clarifications and interpretations represent the understanding of our Governments of this part of the Quadriparite Agreement, as follows:

(a) The Phrase in Paragraph 2 of Annex II of the Quadripartite Agreement which reads: ". . . will not perform in the Western Sectors of Berlin constitutional or official acts which contradict the provisions of Paragraph 1" shall be interpreted to mean acts in exercise of direct state authority over the Western Sectors of Berlin.

(b) Meetings of the Bundesversammlung will not take place and plenary sessions of the Bundesrat and the Bundestag will continue not to take place in the Western Sectors of Berlin. Single committees of the Bundesrat and the Bundestag may meet in the Western Sectors of Berlin in connection with maintaining and developing the ties between those Sectors and the Federal Republic of Germany. In the case of Fraktionen, meetings will not be held simultaneously.

(c) The liaison agency of the Federal Government in the Western Sectors of Berlin includes departments charged with liaison functions in their respective fields.

(d) Established procedures concerning the applicability to the Western Sectors of Berlin of legislation of the Federal Republic of Germany shall remain unchanged.

(e) The term "state bodies" in Paragraph 2 of Annex II shall be interpreted to mean: the Federal President, the Federal Chancellor, the Federal Cabinet, the Federal Ministers and Ministries, and the branch offices of those Ministries, the Bundesrat and the Bundestag and all Federal courts.

(Formal close)

For the Government of the French Republic:

Jean Sauvagnargues

For the Government of the United Kingdom of Great Britain and Northern Ireland:

R. W. Jackling

For the Government of the United States of America:

Kenneth Rush

Agreed Minute I

It is understood that permanent residents of the Western Sectors of Berlin shall, in order to receive at appropriate Soviet offices visas for entry into the Union of Soviet Socialist Republics, present:

(a) A passport stamped "issued in accordance with the Quadripartite Agreement of September 3, 1971".

(b) An identity card or other appropriately drawn up document confirming that the person requesting the visa is a permanent resident of the Western Sectors of Berlin and containing the bearer's full address and a personal photograph.

During his stay in the Union of Soviet Socialist Republics, a permanent resident of the Western Sectors of Berlin who has received a visa in this way may carry both documents or either of them as he chooses. The visa issued by a Soviet office will serve as the basis for entry into the Union of Soviet Socialist Republics, and the passport or identity card will serve as the basis for consular services in accordance with the Quadripartite Agreement during the stay of that person in the territory of the Union of Soviet Socialist Republics.

The above-mentioned stamp will appear in all passports used by permanent residents of the Western Sectors of Berlin for journeys to such countries as may require it.

Agreed Minute II

Provision is hereby made for the establishment of a Consulate General of the USSR in the Western Sectors of Berlin. It is understood that the details concerning this Consulate General will include the following:

The Consulate General will be accredited to the appropriate authorities of the three Governments in accordance with the usual procedures applying in those Sectors.

Applicable Allied and German legislation and regulations will apply to the Consulate General. The activities of the Consulate General will be of a consular character and will not include political functions or any matters related to quadripartite rights or responsibilities.

The three Governments are willing to authorize an increase in Soviet commercial activities in the Western Sectors of Berlin as described below. It is understood that pertinent Allied and German legislation and regulations will apply to these activities. This authorization will be extended indefinitely, subject to compliance with the provisions outlined herein. Adequate provision for consultation will be made. This increase will include establishment of an "Office of Soviet Foreign Trade Associations in the Western Sectors of Berlin", with commercial status authorized to buy and sell on behalf of foreign trade associations of the Union of Soviet Socialist Republics. Soyuzpushnina, Prodintorg and Novoexport may each establish a bonded warehouse in the Western Sectors of Berlin to provide storage and display for their goods. The activities of the Intourist office in the British Sector of Berlin may be expanded to include the sale of tickets and vouchers for travel and tours in the Union of Soviet Socialist Republics and other countries. An office of Aeroflot may be established for the sale of passenger tickets and air freight services.

The assignment of personnel to the Consulate General and to permitted Soviet commercial organizations will be subject to agreement with the appropriate authorities of the three Governments. The number of such personnel will not exceed twenty Soviet nationals in the Consulate General; twenty in the office of the Soviet Foreign Trade Associations; one each in the bonded warehouses; six in the Intourist office; and five in the Aeroflot office. The personnel of the Soviet Consulate General and of permitted Soviet commercial organizations and their dependents may reside in the Western Sectors of Berlin upon individual authorization.

The property of the Union of Soviet Socialist Republics at Lietzenburgerstrasse 11 and at Am Sandwerder 1 may be used for purposes to be agreed between appropriate representatives of the three Governments and of the Government of the Union of Soviet Socialist Republics.

Details of implementation of the measures above and a time schedule for carrying them out will be agreed between the four Ambassadors in the period between the signature of the Quadripartite Agreement and the signature of the Final Quadripartite Protocol envisaged in that Agreement.

Letter of the Three Western Ambassadors
to Chancellor Willy Brandt

His Excellency
The Chancellor
of the Federal Republic of Germany,
Bonn

Your Excellency:

We have the honour by means of this letter to convey to
the Government of the Federal Republic of Germany the
text of the Quadripartite Agreement signed this day in
Berlin. The Quadripartite Agreement was concluded by
the Four Powers in the exercise of their rights and responsibilities with respect to Berlin.

We note that, pursuant to the terms of the Agreement
and of the Final Quadripartite Protocol which ultimately
will bring it into force, the text of which has been agreed,
these rights and responsibilities are not affected and remain
unchanged. Our Governments will continue, as heretofore,
to exercise supreme authority in the Western Sectors of
Berlin, within the framework of the Four Power responsibility which we share for Berlin as a whole.

In accordance with Part II (A) of the Quadripartite Agreement, arrangements implementing and supplementing the
provisions relating to civilian traffic will be agreed by the
competent German authorities. Part III of the Quadripartite
Agreement provides that the Agreement will enter into
force on a date to be specified in a Final Quadripartite
Protocol which will be concluded when the arrangements
envisaged between the competent German authorities have
been agreed. It is the request of our Governments that the

envisaged negotiations now take place between authorities of the Federal Republic of Germany, also acting on behalf of the Senat, and authorities of the German Democratic Republic.

Part II (B) and (D) and Annexes II and IV of the Quadripartite Agreement relate to the relationship between the Western Sectors of Berlin and the Federal Republic. In this connection, the following are recalled inter alia:

—the communications of the three Western Military Governors to the Parliamentary Council of 2 March, 22 April and 12 May, 1949,

—the letter of the three High Commissioners to the Federal Chancellor concerning the exercise of the reserved Allied rights relating to Berlin of 26 May 1952 in the version of the letter X of 23 October 1954,

—the Aide Memoire of the three Governments of 18 April 1967 concerning the decision of the Federal Constitutional Court of 20 January 1966 in the Niekisch case.

Our Governments take this occasion to state, in exercise of the rights and responsibilities relating to Berlin, which they retained in Article 2 of the Convention on Relations between the Three Powers and the Federal Republic of Germany of 26 May 1952 as amended October 23, 1954, that Part II (B) and (D) and Annexes II and IV of the Quadripartite Agreement concerning the relationship between the Federal Republic of Germany and the Western Sectors of Berlin accord with the position in the above-mentioned documents, which remains unchanged.

With regard to the existing ties between the Federal Republic and the Western Sectors of Berlin, it is the firm intention of our Governments that, as stated in Part II (B) (1) of the Quadripartite Agreement, these ties will be maintained and developed in accordance with the letter from the three High Commissioners to the Federal Chancellor on the exercise of the reserved rights relating to Berlin of 26 May 1952, in the version of letter X of October 23, 1954, and with pertinent decisions of the Allied Kommandatura of Berlin.

(Formal close)

Letter of the Federal Chancellor in Reply to the Three Western Ambassadors

Your Excellency:

I have the honour to confirm receipt of the letter of the Ambassadors of France, the United Kingdom and the United States of America of September 3 together with which the text of the Quadripartite Agreement signed on September 3, 1971, in Berlin was communicated to the Government of the Federal Republic of Germany.

I also have the honour to confirm receipt of the letter of the Three Ambassadors of the same date containing clarifications and interpretations which reflect what their Governments understand by the declarations contained in Annex II to the Quadripartite Agreement with regard to the relationship between the Federal Republic of Germany and the Western Sectors of Berlin.

The Government of the Federal Republic of Germany intends taking steps immediately in order to arrive at agreements on concrete arrangements relating to civilian traffic as envisaged in Part II A of the Quadripartite Agreement.

The Government of the Federal Republic of Germany has taken note of the contents of Your Excellency's letter which were communicated to it in exercising the rights and responsibilities which were retained in pursuance of Article 2 of the Convention on Relations between the Federal Republic of Germany and the Three Powers of May 26, 1952, as amended on October 23, 1954, and which will continue to be respected by the Government of the Federal Republic of Germany.

The Government of the Federal Republic of Germany shares the view and the determination that the ties between the Federal Republic of Germany and Berlin shall be maintained and developed.

(Formal close)

Final Quadripartite Protocol

The Governments of the Union of Soviet Socialist Republics, the United Kingdom of Great Britain and Northern Ireland, the United States of America and the French Republic,

Having in mind Part III of the Quadripartite Agreement of September 3, 1971, and taking note with satisfaction of the fact that the agreements and arrangements mentioned below have been concluded,

Have agreed on the following:

1. The four Governments, by virtue of this Protocol, bring into force the Quadripartite Agreement, which, like this Protocol, does not affect quadripartite agreements or decisions previously concluded or reached.

2. The four Governments proceed on the basis that the following agreements and arrangements concluded between the competent German authorities (list of agreements and arrangements) shall enter into force simultaneously with the Quadripartite Agreement.

3. The Quadripartite Agreement and the consequent agreements and arrangements of the competent German authorities referred to in this Protocol settle important issues examined in the course of the negotiations and shall remain in force together.

4. In the event of a difficulty in the application of the Quadripartite Agreement or any of the above-mentioned agreements or arrangements which any of the four Governments consider serious, or in the event of non-implementation of any part thereof, that Government will have the right to draw the attention of the other three Governments to the provisions of the Quadripartite Agreement and this Protocol and to conduct the requisite quadripartite consultations in order to ensure

the observance of the commitments undertaken and to bring the situation into conformity with the Quadripartite Agreement and this Protocol.

5. This Protocol enters into force on the date of signature

Done at the building formerly occupied by the Allied Control Council in the American Sector of Berlin this third day of June 1972, in four originals each in the English, French and Russian languages, all texts being equally authentic.

For the Government of the French Republic

Maurice Schumann

For the Government of the Union of Soviet
Socialist Republics

A. Gromyko

For the Government of the United Kingdom
of Great Britain and Northern Ireland

Douglas-Home

For the Government of the United States
of America

William Rogers

Select Bibliography

BOOKS

Baring, Arnulf. *Machtwechsel. Die Aera Brandt-Scheel*. Stuttgart: Deutsche Verlagsanstalt, 1982.

Bender, Peter. *Offensive Entspannung*. Berlin and Cologne: Verlag Kiepenheuer und Witsch, 1964.

Brandt, Willy. *The Ordeal of Coexistence*. Cambridge, MA: Harvard University Press, 1963.

————. *People and Politics*. Boston, MA: Little, Brown and Company, 1976.

Clay, Lucius D. *Decision in Germany*. Garden City, NY: Doubleday, 1950.

Friedensburg, Ferdinand. *Es Ging um Deutschlands Einheit*. Berlin: Haude & Spenersche Verlagsbuchhandlung, 1971.

Hull, Cordell. *Memoirs*. New York: Macmillan, 1948.

Kissinger, Henry. *The White House Years*. Boston, MA: Little, Brown and Company, 1979.

Leonhard, Wolfgang. *Die Revolution entlässt ihre Kinder*. Cologne and Berlin: Kiepenheuer und Witsch Verlag, 1974.

Mahnke, Dieter. *Berlin im geteilten Deutschland*. Munich and Vienna: Oldenbourg Verlag, 1973.

Siegler, Heinrich von (ed). *Dokumentation zur Deutschlandfrage in Verbindung mit der Ostpolitik*. Bonn, Vienna, Zurich: Siegler Verlag, 1972.

Truman, Harry S. *Memoirs*. Garden City, NY: Doubleday, 1955.

Windsor, Philip. *City on Leave: A History of Berlin 1945–1962*. New York: Praeger, 1963.

Ziemke, Earl F. *The US Army in the Occupation of Germany, 1944–1948*. Washington, D.C.: Center of Military History, 1975.

Zivier, Ernest R. *Der Rechstatus des Landes Berlin. Eine Untersuchung nach dem Viermächteabkommen vom 3 September 1971*. Berlin: Berlin Verlag, 1977.

GOVERNMENT PUBLICATIONS

The Berlin Crisis: A Report on the Moscow Discussions 1948. Washington, D.C.: Department of State, 1949.

Berlin, Quellen und Dokumente. Berlin: Spitzing Verlag, 1964.

Die Bundesrepublik Deutschland, Mitglied der Vereinten Nationen. Bonn: Federal Republic of Germany Press and Information Office, 1973.

Documents on Germany, 1944–1970. Washington, D.C.: Senate Committee on Foreign Relations, 1971.

Dokumente zur Berlin Frage, 1944–1946. Munich and Vienna: Oldenbourg Verlag, 1967.

Germany 1947–1949: The Story in Documents. Washington, D.C.: Department of State, 1950.

Zehn Jahre Deutschlandpolitik. Die Entwicklung der Beziehungen zwischen der Bundesrepublik Deutschland und der DDR, 1969–1979. Bonn: Federal Ministry for Inner German Relations, 1980.

Index

ABOUT THE AUTHORS

JAMES S. SUTTERLIN served in the U.S. Foreign Service for 28 years. He first was posted in Berlin in 1946 where he experienced the blockade. He was assigned to Berlin again in the 1950s. From 1965 until 1968, during the time of the West German Grand Coalition government, Sutterlin was political counselor at the U.S. Embassy in Bonn. From 1969 to 1973 he was director of the Office of Central European Affairs in the Department of State, and had major responsibility in developing U.S. policy for the Four Power negotiations on Berlin.

In 1974 Sutterlin became a senior aide and speech writer for the secretary-general of the United Nations. He presently teaches international affairs at Long Island University and is a visiting fellow at Yale University where he is undertaking an oral history of the United Nations.

DAVID KLEIN served in the United States Foreign Service for almost 30 years. Appointed to the U.S. Embassy in Moscow he witnessed the demise of Stalin and the rise of Khrushchev. Transferred to Berlin in 1955 and to Bonn in 1957, he was involved in the conduct of U.S.-Soviet relations as they affected Germany. Returning to Washington in 1960, he was assigned to the National Security Council and was an original member of the Berlin task force. After a second tour in Moscow (1966–68), Klein served as U.S. Minister in Berlin during the Four Power negotiations on the Berlin agreement.

Upon retirement from the Foreign Service Klein became executive director of the American Council on Germany. He now is an assistant to the president for international programs at Fairleigh Dickinson University in New Jersey and teaches at the University of California in San Diego.